KINGS OF QUEENS

Also by Erik Sherman

MOOKIE: LIFE, BASEBALL AND THE '86 METS
(with Mookie Wilson)

A PIRATE FOR LIFE: STEVE BLASS
(with Steve Blass)

OUT AT HOME: THE TRUE STORY OF GLENN BURKE,
BASEBALL'S FIRST OPENLY GAY PLAYER
(with Glenn Burke)

KINGS

of
Queens

LIFE BEYOND BASEBALL
WITH THE
'86 Mets

ERIK SHERMAN

BERKLEY BOOKS, NEW YORK

BERKLEY

An imprint of Penguin Random House LLC
375 Hudson Street, New York, New York 10014

This book is an original publication of Penguin Random House LLC.

For more information, visit penguin.com.

Library of Congress Cataloging-in-Publication Data

Names: Sherman, Erik.
Title: Kings of Queens : life beyond baseball with '86 Mets / Erik Sherman.
Description: New York, NY : Berkley, 2016.
Identifiers: LCCN 2015039205 | ISBN 9780425281970 (hardback)
Subjects: LCSH: New York Mets (Baseball team) | BISAC: SPORTS & RECREATION /
Baseball / History. | BIOGRAPHY & AUTOBIOGRAPHY / Sports. |
SPORTS & RECREATION / Baseball / General.
Classification: LCC GV875.N45 S53 2016 | DDC 796.357/6409747243—dc23 LC record
available at http://lccn.loc.gov/2015039205

First edition: March 2016

PRINTED IN THE UNITED STATES OF AMERICA

10 9 8 7 6 5 4 3 2 1

Jacket photos (clockwise from left): Gary Carter photograph by Louis Requena. MLB Photos via Getty
Images. Dwight Gooden photograph by Focus On Sport / Getty Images. Mookie Wilson photograph by
Focus On Sport / Getty Images. Doug Sisk photograph by Jacqueline Duvoisin / Sports Illustrated / Getty
Images. Kevin MItchell photograph by Focus on Sport / Getty Images. Danny Heep photograph by
AP Photo / Forrest Aderson. Wally Backman photograph by T. G. Higgins / Getty Images.
Bobby Ojeda photograph by Richard Mackson / Sports Illustrated / Getty Images. Rafael Santana
photograph by Focus on Sport / Getty Images. Daryl Strawberry photograph by T. G. Higgins / Getty
Images. Ed Hearn photograph by B Bennett / Getty Images. Lenny Dykstra photograph by Focus on Sport /
Getty Images. Howard Johnson photograph by T. G. Higgins / Getty Images. Keith Hernandez
photograph by Focus on Sport / Getty Images.
Jacket design by Sandra Chiu.
Text design by Kristin del Rosario.

Penguin
Random
House

MAY 0 5 2016

Dedicated to
Habiba, Alex, and Sabrina,

and the memory of
Frank Cashen, Gary Carter,

and the man who fueled
my love of baseball and journalism,
my father, Frank Sherman

It breaks your heart. It is designed to break your heart. The game begins in the spring, when everything else begins again, and it blossoms in the summer, filling the afternoons and evenings. And then as soon as the chill rain comes, it stops, and leaves you to face the fall alone.

—A. BARTLETT GIAMATTI,
FORMER COMMISSIONER OF BASEBALL
AND ONETIME PRESIDENT OF YALE
FROM "THE GREEN FIELDS OF THE MIND"

CONTENTS

KINGS OF QUEENS

FOREWORD

When Frank Cashen hired me to manage the Mets in 1984, I told him, "I like to work for smart people and you're smart because you wanted to hire me as the manager."

It might have sounded slightly brash, but I think the strength in any organization is knowing the talent in the system. Well, I knew the Mets' young talent, how to take care of it, how to nurture it, and how to tell our players at that time what they did good and not emphasize what they did bad.

And I knew how to put the pieces together.

After having very successful seasons in '84 and '85 but coming up a little short, I made a bold prediction in front of the entire team at spring training in 1986 that we weren't just going to win the championship, but we were going to *dominate*. It wasn't the usual managerial rhetoric. Through either the minor-league system or astute trades, we had eliminated all of our weaknesses that had been exploited by the other clubs, like not having a strong enough bullpen, or a potent enough right side of the bench, and playing with a young starting pitching staff that was still learning how to pitch. So once we addressed those areas, as a manager I knew where we were at, knew my talent, knew how to manage that talent, and knew what talent I was up against. It wasn't rocket science. So that statement I made about dominating was a no-brainer for me.

And *dominate* we did.

I have to think that after the first month of the season, Cardinals manager Whitey Herzog must have been thinking, *We ain't catching the Mets.*

But what made 1986 so much fun was all the different personalities on our team. There was something on it for every fan in the world. We had characters galore and I didn't try to stifle them.

Be who you are.

Express your talent.

I really encouraged those things.

One of the all-time characters was Keith Hernandez, a very gifted, great hitter. But there's a guy that when he didn't feel like he was going very good would actually wink at me to put the hit-and-run on, basically dictating a strategic move. We made Hernandez the team captain and then a few years after trading for Gary Carter, I made them co-captains. They were two great, entirely different players, but both led by their performance and their enjoyment of the game. I was very fortunate to have two great leaders like that on the ball club.

I also had a young, bright, strong-willed pitcher, Ron Darling, who had great stuff, a great arm, but threw all over the place. He wanted to throw to the corners, but his ball moved so damned much. I had to tell Carter to just sit in the middle of the plate so when Ron pitched the ball it moved to the corners naturally. Darling would become a truly great pitcher.

Then there was Lenny Dykstra, the skinny kid that wanted to be a home-run hitter. He wanted to pump iron during spring training, but I had him run a lot instead. Lenny was such a competitor—a gambler really. We used to golf together, and Lenny was probably about an eight handicap, but he thought he was like a scratch. Anyway, I'd be beating Lenny like a redheaded stepchild and he'd say, "Five hundred bucks on this hole," or some outrageous amount. But he didn't want a shot. He wanted to beat me even. And, of course, I'd kick his ass and he'd shell out the money. But that's just who he was. He was going to take the action and it didn't matter the number—the higher the better. The more excitement the better. Just put it all on the line and let's see how good we are.

Another gamer similar to that was Wally Backman. The organization wanted me to play Brian Giles at second instead of Wally because he had tons of ability—better arm, better hitter, better everything. But Backman was always the consummate competitor. He was the kind of down-and-dirty guy that would battle you all the way and do whatever it took to shut the table and win a ball game. When I first got him, he wasn't a good fielder, but I told him, "Just take some ground balls and soften up. I have confidence in you."

And he rewarded me by working his butt off and becoming a great second baseman.

The whole team was built around that kind of makeup. And some pretty damn good talent, too.

The only regrets I had, really, were with Darryl Strawberry and Doc Gooden, two of the most naturally gifted ballplayers I've ever seen and both great guys.

With Darryl, I tried to be a father image for him, because he didn't really have one. He came from LA and had the pressures of being the number one pick in the nation. Off the field, we donated our time together to charities in Queens, but I knew there were always things he was going to have to deal with—which he didn't always handle so great.

Doc, on the other hand, I didn't think he would ever have a problem. He came from a great family, a great coach, was always the first guy at the ballpark, and an unbelievable talent. I had him when he was seventeen at Kingsport and watched him quickly develop into a dominating pitcher. But the only thing with Doc was he didn't know how to say no to some of his homeboys. He may have meant to say no, but he didn't know how to express it. So he got in trouble later on.

As their manager, I had little influence over what happened to them away from the ballpark, especially with the temptations in New York and all the people heaping praise on these guys. They think they're impervious. You can talk to them until you're blue in the face, but it's their decision on what they're going to do with their lives. You have to try to impress on them that they've got God-given talent and need to take care of it—be an adult. And most of the time, everybody gets that, but sometimes guys stray off the path. If there was a magic formula or pill that you could hypnotize someone with to keep him straight, we'd all do it.

People talk about chemistry and how you get it on a ball club. Many say it comes from winning. I call that BS because chemistry really comes on a team where everybody knows his role. And our ball club knew when and how they were going to be used, were mentally prepared, and were all pulling together.

Those are just some of the key things you have to have on any team. It takes twenty-five guys plus your coaches to all be on the same page to be successful. Plain and simple.

As many people know, I was never big on giving my players a long list of rules to follow. I did have the basic ones everybody has—don't be late, play hard, always hustle.

But I did have some funny rules, too.

I would say, "You guys don't have to run hard to first base, but I may invoke the Darryl Strawberry Rule. If you hit a ground ball to shortstop and you're not running hard and he bobbles it, it's five hundred bucks. And if you hit a fly ball to the outfield and you're not running and he drops the ball and you're not on second, it's another five hundred bucks!"

So I got them to do what I wanted without actually making demands.

Those were just simple rules that we all lived by anyway. We put pressure on the other guy, and if he made a mistake, we took advantage of it. But I didn't have a lot of rules and those guys knew it. They were grown men and ruled themselves.

A lot has been written about how that team loved to party and stay out late. But, you know, baseball is kind of a late-night sport. We played late in the evening and guys might have a beer or so in the clubhouse because they're so wired after a game. Then they might go out and have another beer somewhere else. But I'll tell you, to a man, all of them—*with the exception of Strawberry in Chicago sometimes*—got their rest and took care of themselves.

I walked through the clubhouse. I knew how each guy was feeling. And they came ready to play. *Every day.* There was always a lot of energy; they were relaxed and ready to hit the field. For a manager, that's a perfect storm.

They can say we were a bunch of *rounders*, but no, we really weren't. In fact, some of the players' wives might have fit that description more than we did.

On that infamous flight back from Houston after we won the National League championship, I blame the wives who were involved even more than the players. Actually, it wasn't as trashed as has been reported, but the guys knew better than to throw a beer on the floor. But a lot of the wives didn't know the rules.

Anyway, I was ready to ante up the five thousand dollars to cover the damage.

I told the guys before the World Series, "I don't think it was that bad. You're not going to be responsible for this. I'll take care of it. I'll pay it." That's all I said.

My thinking was I didn't want to charge the players for their wives trashing the plane. It would have looked bad if I charged them for something their wives had done. I thought, *You win the pennant, you're going to the World Series, and now you get fined; so then you're never going to want your wives to come on the plane again. And that means we're never going to the World Series again.*

So this was another no-brainer for me.

As it turned out, the Mets didn't make me pay. After all, that Game Six clincher in Houston was the biggest game of our season and we had a right to blow off some steam and celebrate. Down 3–0 against Bob Knepper in the ninth, we needed to win that game because we didn't want to face Mike Scott. So we come back, of course, and tie it up to send the game into extra innings. I can't say it surprised me, because when you win 108 regular season games, you're pretty confident in your ability to win ball games late.

What was funny was I was sitting next to Mel Stottlemyre after we went up a run in the fourteenth and said, "Mel, it doesn't get any better than this. How can you *not* enjoy this? This is the best it gets, man!"

But he's nervous as all get out. And about that time, Billy Hatcher hits the home run for the Astros to tie it up again.

Thankfully, we went on to score three runs in the sixteenth inning to win the ball game and didn't have to face Scott and his scuffed balls.

We again showed our resilience in the World Series after dropping the first two games. Much has been made about my giving the guys the day off before Game Three in Boston. Well, I thought they were a little stressed out—not so much physically, but more mentally from all the hype from the press and all the other stuff going on. I couldn't do that today. If I canceled a workout before a World Series game, I might get banned from baseball and fined a ton of money. But I had the ability to do it then, and that's what I felt we needed going into Game Three, so I canceled the practice.

And it worked.

We took it to the Red Sox the next night and won that thrilling World Series a week later.

Sure, we had great talent. But those two series showed how much *character* the Mets had. They showed the camaraderie we shared. But most of all, they displayed our intense competitive spirit.

So when you hear about the problems that some of the stars from that team have encountered since then, it kind of crushes you. It kind of hurts. I follow their lives because I care for and respect each and every one of them.

I care about Doc's and Darryl's recovery from drug addiction. I care about how some of Wally's off-the-field issues have kept him from managing in the majors. And it's heartrending to see how guys like Lenny made a lot more money than I did but didn't know how to handle it.

I've been blessed. People think that I'm upset because I was fired five times. No way. You know why? Because I got to coach the Netherlands baseball team at the Olympics in Athens and then

Team USA at the Beijing Games. I got to coach in the European championships and managed all over Europe and Asia. Those are life experiences that you can't replace.

So when I look at other players, I just pray that they'll have the same kinds of opportunities and experiences that I've had. Thus, when I see guys struggle, I feel for them because I haven't had any of that kind of despair.

For me, I know there are some sad tales in this book because I know about them and who they affected. But a lot of people may not. And I think from a human interest side of it—in a before-and-after theme—there will be a lot of interest, because in our society we build characters up to a certain level that we look up to and we don't want to see them fail.

Thankfully, there are mostly happy conclusions and varying degrees of redemption for most of the guys whose stories are chronicled in this book—despite the sadness along the way. And I'm thrilled that some of the others have done very well for themselves in spite of their personal challenges and hurdles they have had to overcome.

I still love seeing the guys when I get the chance because it just brings back such fond memories. And when I find myself thinking about the team, I end up smiling and laughing. I know it's a mixed bag, but I prefer to think of the many positives, not the negatives.

I'm so proud of what we accomplished in that magical 1986 season and the brotherhood that we still have for one another all these years later. Enjoy reading a very personal portrayal of one of baseball history's greatest and most charismatic teams.

Davey Johnson
Winter Park, Florida

INTRODUCTION

May 3, 2014

"I wonder what Sid's doing."

It was those five words uttered from the mouth of Mookie Wilson's wife, Rosa, that served as the inspiration for the book you now hold in your hands.

We were sitting beside Mookie as he signed countless books at the Words Bookshop in Maplewood, New Jersey, for a line of people that literally stretched out of the store and a block down the street. Passing the time, Rosa asked me what my next book project might be. I told her I was considering doing one on Roberto Clemente, seeing as how I had a strong rapport with many of his old Pirates' teammates, but I lamented how seemingly every angle of the legendary player's life had already been researched and reported ad nauseam in the many books written about him.

Rosa offered that she would love to know what Sid Fernandez

and, for that matter, some of the other '86 Mets were up to these days and thought that would make an interesting book. I agreed, and additionally, it was quickly becoming apparent to me that, based on the rock star–like book-signing turnouts for Mookie—as big a symbol of the spirit of the '86 Mets as there was—that nearly thirty years later, New York–area fans still had an insatiable hunger for that long bygone era of Mets baseball.

But *another* book on the '86 Mets?

That would certainly be nothing new. So many have given it a try—even some of the players themselves.

I would need an angle.

I would need something truly unique and different from all the others before.

I knew the thirtieth anniversary of the club's memorable world championship season was approaching, so the timing was good to begin work on a project about the team.

Still, I needed more.

Then I thought, *What if I actually went out and visited the players where they are today—in their homes, in the dugouts they currently coach or manage in, or in the bars they might frequent? I would interview the men who'd made up this magical team, find out what happened to them after their glory days were behind them, and explore the impact they as individuals and as a team had on the fans and the organization—then and now.*

It would be a Herculean effort, as I would need their cooperation, need to get scheduled into their busy itineraries, and need a whole lot of luck along the way. The one thing I had going for me, however, was Mookie's blessing on the project. Nobody from that team is more highly regarded or has the respect Wilson receives, so the fact that I had cowritten his autobiography and that he offered to help brief some of his teammates on what I was doing was like being given carte blanche from the players. I could be trusted.

So now I was on to something.

Still, the idea of doing a profile on each of the twenty-four players from the 1986 World Series roster might make the book run too long and even seem mundane at times. I also didn't want it to come off as one of those "Where Are They Now?" magazine articles you often see at the supermarket or online. Nor did I want it to look like a yearbook, with a lot of boring, generic "surface" material.

I wanted to go deeper, because this team and their riveting lives—both on and off the field—deserved more.

I would need to narrow my focus.

To do the project justice, I decided to concentrate solely on what evolved into the fourteen men from that team who had, in my view, the most compelling lives, who had had to overcome major challenges before, during, or after their careers ended—and some during all three periods.

This book would delve deeper into the obvious, well-documented travails of players like Doc Gooden, Darryl Strawberry, and Lenny Dykstra, with their revelations of combating the demons of drug addiction, battling cancer, and starting anew after incarceration, as well as the lesser-known stories of Kevin Mitchell, Ed Hearn, and Doug Sisk with their stories of dealing with the tragic murder of a child, chronic illnesses, and getting death threats from disillusioned "fans."

It would share the thoughts of those like Wally Backman and Mookie Wilson, baseball-lifers and two of the most intelligent men in the game, who have long been inexplicably passed over for greater roles in the major leagues. It would profile Keith Hernandez—the greatest defensive first baseman in history—perhaps unjustly denied induction into the Hall of Fame because of drug use early in his career, and Bobby Ojeda, who resurrected his life after being the lone survivor of a fatal boating accident, by becoming one of the finest baseball analysts in the business.

There would be the largely untold success stories of Danny Heep, who went on to become one of college baseball's most successful managers of all time; of Howard Johnson, who made several comeback bids in a display of his love of the game; and Rafael Santana, who has for the last two decades been as great a cog in the Dominican Republic's incubator of major-league players as anyone.

And, of course, this book would include the story of the shocking, premature death of the very last man on that twenty-four-man roster anybody thought would be the first to pass away—Gary Carter—as told to me by his widow Sandy and his Mets teammates.

The book would also attempt to downplay the typecasting of the '86 Mets as a wild fraternity that, while largely based in fact, overshadowed how they were also a collection of some of the most astute, dedicated, and talented men to ever grace the baseball diamond. When they drank and partied, they usually did so while breaking down that day's game and strategizing how to get better.

And the stories would be told as a narrative, giving my own thoughts and experiences on the road with the team.

| | | | | | | |

My nine-month journey by planes, trains, and automobiles would cover over thirty thousand miles, leading me to places as culturally different as the players themselves: Shawnee, Kansas, and Los Angeles, California; San Antonio, Texas, and Long Island, New York; Jupiter, Florida, and Las Vegas, Nevada; San Diego, California, and Columbia, South Carolina; Poulsbo, Washington, and

White Plains, New York; St. Peters, Missouri, and Boston, Massachusetts.

I dealt with the elements of snow, ice, floods, and heat waves to make my meetings with the players.

With a nod to the Beatles, it was my own *Magical Mets Mystery Tour*, with me never knowing for sure where my travels or the players' stories would ultimately lead.

Despite their differences, I discovered how much many of the '86 Mets shared in common with one another. They've authored books (or, as with Hernandez, Gooden, and Strawberry, written several). They have sons that have played professional ball. They've found religion. They watch the MLB network incessantly. They are outspoken, with strong opinions. They are deeply disappointed with the direction the Mets have taken in recent years. [Author's note: This book was completed just prior to the Mets' late-2015 season surge.] They live with chronic physical pain. And they desperately want Wally Backman to get a shot at managing the team.

Some have gone bankrupt, while others, at times, have lost the will to live.

In putting this project together, I wanted to keep the players' thoughts and comments as unplugged and intact as possible, allowing them to give their unfiltered points of view. When reading this book, I hope you will hear their voices, their tones, and take in their unique personalities—some abrasive, some softer, but always direct. They will range from the brashness of Lenny Dykstra and Bobby Ojeda to the sweetness of Doc Gooden and Mookie Wilson, which helps illustrate the true diversity of personalities on that team.

When approaching the former players for interviews, I generally asked for an hour of their time. The average meeting ended up lasting over four hours, with two of them going a marathon-like seven. The emotions of the players ran the full gamut of laughter, anger, and even tears. It was enjoyable for some and more therapeutic for others. But one thing remained consistent: Once I got them talking, they didn't want to stop, which shows how passionate they were and remain about their baseball lives.

Not surprisingly, talk of 1986—when the Mets ruled baseball and were a metaphor for the city in which they played: cocky, feisty, exuberant, resourceful, and tough—always brought a sparkle to their eyes.

After all, the team they were a part of was historic in so many ways. They had 108 wins during the regular season, capturing the National League East by twenty-one and a half games. Then, to showcase their character, they put together stunning comebacks in both the NLCS against the Houston Astros and in their World Series showdown with the Boston Red Sox.

They remain immediately recognizable thirty years later simply by their nicknames—*Nails, Mex, Kid, Straw, Doc, El Sid*—an element largely missing from the game today.

"The Mets' phenomenon," was how Tim McCarver, the team's celebrated broadcaster, described it all.

But they were also the darlings of New York, while their swagger and curtain calls made them the ultimate villains everywhere else. They used the psychologies of intimidation and fear, never backing down from an opponent, leading to four bench-clearing brawls during the '86 campaign. And they popularized the fist pump well before the cast of *Jersey Shore*.

They also played in a very different era than today, which likely made them the most visible and most watched team of all time. Back then, there were far fewer entertainment options, making Mets games a hot ticket and must-see television. These were the days before the Internet, before PlayStation, and, unless you were Gordon Gekko, before cell phones and all the apps you can have on them nowadays.

Everybody remembers exactly where they were when they saw Mookie end Game Six of the 1986 World Series with the slow roller through Bill Buckner's legs. And they're not lying. That game was the highest rated World Series broadcast ever to that point, with a stunning 52 percent share.

Two nights later, Game Seven, with the cemented memory of Jesse Orosco dropping to his knees and reaching to the heavens after the final out, would shatter that record with a remarkable fifty-five share.

It seemed like *everybody* watched the World Series back then.

By comparison, these days, the World Series barely averages above a ten share, its popularity at a near all-time low.

It's a far cry from the days when a Doc Gooden start or a Mets postseason game could literally stop New York City.

While the Mets did hold a sustained run as one of the better teams in the sport throughout the mid-to-late eighties, the team that their general managerial genius Frank Cashen built surprisingly never won even another pennant, much less another World Series, after their dominating 1986 season. Some of it, of course, was self-induced, first by not bringing back World Series MVP Ray Knight or future National League MVP Kevin Mitchell, and then by having Doc Gooden begin the '87 season in drug rehab. It was a little like watching the fall of the Roman Empire. The '86 Mets were like a shooting star, a candle in the wind—perhaps too combustible to last.

It dawned on me more than once while doing this book how truly fortunate I was and how surreal it all seemed to be invited into the living rooms and inner circles of some of the greatest baseball players of modern times and have them share their intimate thoughts. Several of my friends would say things like, *You call that work? How lucky you are!*

And they were right, of course.

The game ultimately left this team, as it does all great teams, to the ages. They're older now, mostly a little heavier and a little grayer, as are the millions of fans who adored them. But their intriguing stories of yesterday and today keep the flame alive for generations past and present.

And despite the problems and challenges some have encountered, along with the aches and pains of middle age, in our hearts and minds, the Kings of Queens will remain forever young.

DOC TAKING IT ONE DAY AT A TIME

God's working through me. He's using me and that's part of the reason I'm still around because people have lost their lives for a lot less than what I've done and how I've lived my life. So I truly believe I'm still here for a reason.

—DOC GOODEN
ON USING HIS OWN EXPERIENCES TO HELP OTHERS
(METS PITCHER, 1984–94)

It was a damp and drizzly early autumn day in Westbury, New York, a village situated thirty minutes east of Manhattan on Long Island's North Shore. The legendary onetime Mets pitching phenom Dwight "Doc" Gooden and I met after nearly four months of trying. The baseball season is Doc's busy time of year, as he had kindly explained to me several times on the phone throughout the summer, but we had finally made it happen.

Doc had just recently moved into a new house. Unpacked boxes were scattered about the living room and kitchen. He apologized to me for the way the place looked for my visit and then gazed out a window to his in-ground pool in the backyard.

"Ahh, I wish we had moved in when the weather was still warm," Doc said. "But it's going to be great for the summer."

By "we," Gooden referred to himself and two of his adult

children that had moved in with him, as well as a third that was to move in the following month.

"There's Ashley, she's twenty-four and actually works for the Mets in their Marketing Department," Doc said proudly.

"Then there's Dwight Jr.—he's an agent who runs his own company called Best of the Best Sports Management and also works for this branding company where he's bringing back the throwback Dr. K T-shirts, caps, and sweatshirts. But I help him more with being an agent. He has some minor-league ballplayers he represents, and I help him deal with them because I can talk to them from both ends—as a player and as someone who worked in the front office for Mr. Steinbrenner for six years. I tell Dwight that, unfortunately, baseball players are very spoiled. They have a lot of needs, a lot of wants, and you can't promise them something that you can't come through with. The best thing is to just be honest with them.

"He saw my troubles, so that gives him an edge. He's caring, and it's not just about working with the best players to make the most money. He cares about them as human beings first, and then getting them the best contracts and moving them forward. So I like that aspect of what he does.

"And finally, I'll soon have my nineteen-year-old son Devin here as well."

Devin, I'm told by Doc, is fresh off graduating high school along with his brother Darren.

"Wow," I said. "You're going to have three of your kids here. How do you feel about that?"

"It helps me so I can put them to work and keep busy," Doc says with a hearty laugh. "Because technically, I'm supposed to be retired, but with a total of seven kids and three grandkids, you can never really retire."

"Dr. K's a *grandfather*?! How does *that* feel?" I asked incredulously, with the lasting image of that skinny nineteen-year-old who set the baseball world on fire in '84 still embedded in my head like it was just yesterday.

"It's fun," Doc said without pause. "You know, it's fun because I love kids and seven kids is *more* than enough."

We shared a laugh as we sat down at his kitchen table, and it was obvious to me very early in our get-together that he was very much at peace with his life after so many years of tumult. There is a warmth to Dwight that you see in his eyes, a boyish charm about him. He is a very tall and strong man, though I also sensed a shyness and an eagerness to please. And when he talked about his love of children, it came across as genuine, as he seemed to intimate that he wished he could have even more of his own but doesn't want to be selfish about it.

"My youngest is four, and once she got to be three I was thinking about how much I miss it when one of your children takes that first step or speaks their first couple of words," Doc said. "I truly miss that. But then again, I think about how it wouldn't be fair to have more kids at my age now that I'm fifty. By the time I would be seventy, any more children I had would be seventeen, eighteen, and maybe twenty, and that's not fair to them. So now I can replace that [desire] with my grandkids. And the great thing about grandkids is that when I get tired, I can give them back to their parents!"

Doc let out another laugh, before adding, "But it's really fine and I really enjoy being a grandfather. Plus, my grandkids are around the same age as my youngest daughter, which makes it fun."

Doc spoke at length about how being a family man now is the most important thing in his life and keeps him in constant motion. Like many professional athletes, he missed out on seeing his oldest children grow up. And then throw in his battles with cocaine and alcohol addiction, and he was clearly trying to make up for lost time.

"The main thing is, obviously, my kids," Doc said. "I have two boys that just graduated high school in Florida. I have two other small children in Maryland and just went through a divorce with their mother, but I get along well with her—there are no problems there. And I have my adult children living with me. I'm trying to be there as much as I can, because when I played ball I missed a lot. I missed all the kids' school activities. I missed all the Little League stuff. So now I'm able to, the best that I can, put my kids' activities first."

Our talk moved on to the *other* important challenge in his life—dealing with his recovery and helping others in the process. When Doc delved into this subject, he gave it long and thoughtful reflection, his pace very quick but soft-spoken, yet I sensed a fierce determination on his part to continue fighting the good fight.

"I go to a lot of meetings," Doc said, appearing very comfortable with the topic. "As often as I can, I go to meetings. I have a sponsor. I have a good support group. I speak [about the perils of drugs and alcohol] at high schools and colleges throughout the country. I share my story, not only to help them, but to also help *myself* as well. I'm really proud that now I can accept who I am, that I can accept the disease I have, the issues of drugs and alcohol."

"You mentioned that you still have a sponsor. Is it still the former boxer Gerry Cooney?" I asked.

"Not now," Gooden said. "We're still very good friends, still stay in contact and talk with one another. But we have schedule conflicts because he's a very busy guy, does a lot of charity work, and he lives pretty far away from me now. Normally, with a sponsor and the person he's sponsoring, you have to spend a lot of time together. So it just doesn't work for us anymore. But I have a good sponsor now—'JT'—and we spend a lot of time together. But Gerry's still in my support group."

| | | | | | |

Talking with Doc about his recovery, how he came to grips with his weaknesses, and his need to be strong in his fight against addiction, I was struck by how incompatible that seemed to be with the image of the pitching giant who struck fear into the hearts of opposing hitters during his career. Gooden was undoubtedly one of the best pitchers I've ever watched play. And in the 1980s he was a New York hero. "One of the parents of a kid that I coach asked me who was the greatest pitcher I ever saw," I told Doc. "My response was that over a career, maybe it was Pedro Martinez. But the greatest *season* I ever saw pitched was by you in 1985. However, you were also terrific for at least a four-year period during the mid-eighties. Did you realize at the time how great a pitcher you were? Or, because you were living in the moment, was it something you couldn't comprehend?"

"That's a very good question," Gooden replied. "When I was going through it, I was not aware of the impact I was having on the fan base. I was nineteen my first year, twenty years old in '85. It was basically a childhood dream. I was aware that I was—and I hate to use the word—*dominating* at that time. And I knew that I was doing so against professional hitters, some of them future Hall of Famers. But I was just out there having fun pitching, trying to help my team win."

Doc then recalled the intense media presence around him and how it became an "event" on the days he pitched at Shea.

"There was a lot of attention paid when I pitched," he said. "I remember the Mets stopped me from doing interviews before games.

Only *after* games that I pitched would the Mets have me give interviews. They had to take place in the Jets' locker room to accommodate all the reporters. A rare exception would occasionally happen with *60 Minutes* or when something major like that would come along. So I knew I was different. But when I took the field I wasn't aware of the magnitude. It was only in retirement, at signings and different events, when people came up to me and said things like 'I just want to thank you for the joy you brought into my house.' Or 'No matter what I was going through, for those two and a half hours you pitched, everything was forgotten and everyone was glued to the TV.'

"I've also heard everybody say that the city stopped when I pitched. But at that time, I wasn't aware of all that. I knew there were more people in the stands when I pitched, but I was just a young pitcher having fun, going out and trying to compete, doing the best I could.

"But now that I can sit back and watch film and talk to others about it, I can kind of see the impact that I actually had and the joy my pitching brought people. It's almost like it was surreal, not quite like it was someone else, but when I see certain highlights now I'm amazed and think, *Wow, that was me doing that?* Because during the time you're going through it, you're really not aware of the impact you are having on others by going out and playing the game that you enjoy. Sometimes I think, *Did I really bring that much joy?* It's amazing."

Doc went on to tell me how he hopes he can now bring that kind of happiness to those who can gain strength and wisdom from his words.

"While I never want to forget about all the joy my pitching brought people—which is a good thing, a blessing—I hope that talking about all the struggles I went through will help others and maybe bring them the same amount of joy as I brought for others when I pitched. If sharing my struggles with someone—even if it's for one of their family members, a friend, or somebody they know that's going through the things I went through—can help them, well, that's all I can ask for."

If anyone could send a positive message of hope to those struggling with addiction, it would be Doc. After all, he still has a hold on Mets fans as great as when he starred in New York. Anytime he's at Citi Field and they show him up on the scoreboard, he always receives a huge ovation. And whenever the latest Mets phenom comes up through their system, the inevitable—and unfair—comparisons to the "gold standard" that is Gooden are usually made. I asked him, knowing how his fans still feel about him, even with all the off-field challenges he's had, if he could send them one message, what would he want to convey to them?

Doc had a lot to say.

"Well, the first thing I would like to do is thank them. If I could thank each and every one of them it would be great because they have no idea not only the energy they gave me as a player, but the energy and support they've given me off the field with my struggles. It's been a tough time. It's been a long journey of twenty years of battling this disease back and forth. March 11 gave me three years clean and sober. Life is good now.

"And I'm still making that transition from major-league baseball player to Dwight in corporate America. It's a great challenge, but part of it is just being myself and the fans allowing me to be myself. I think that's what they appreciate the most when I speak. I'm not trying to be someone else. I am who I am. I've shared my ups and downs. And making the transition to corporate America is putting the baseball part of me aside and dealing with different types of people. What I really enjoy is just sharing my story. And it's more important to me when people ask how I'm doing and how my life is going now than about my baseball career. That's because even though the great memories are there, the baseball part of my life is behind me now. The most important thing for me is to talk about my life changes and how I can touch lives."

"Doc," I said, "all of your Mets teammates I've spoken with about you not only wish you well, but even still, to this day, look back and wonder if they should have seen the signs that you were using and wish they could have done something to help you. Mookie Wilson, while we worked on his autobiography, reminded me how you were just a kid when you came up and how you both had similarly reserved personalities. That's why he sometimes thinks that he, of all people, should have picked up on your drug and alcohol problem. Do you think, looking back, that there was anything any of them could have really done to help? After all, they couldn't watch you around the clock."

"It gives me goose bumps to hear that," Doc said after a slight pause and a smile. "It means a lot because we were such close teammates and what you said really lets me know how they truly felt about me. But there was nothing they could have done because, like with Mookie, we used to go out and eat a lot, talk a lot, and get our families and kids together often. But Mookie never went through what I did and didn't have any experience with it, so he wouldn't be able to recognize the signs. Plus, I wasn't completely honest with Mookie about what was going on in my life. I didn't know how to share that part of my life with him because he wasn't involved in any of that stuff. He was a Christian, a very dedicated family man, didn't drink, and didn't hang out. So I didn't feel comfortable sharing that part of my life with him, even though we were good friends and still are good friends. So I feel bad when I talk to him about it, but he can't put any blame on himself at all.

"It's almost like with my mom," Gooden continued, in a slow, deliberate way. "She feels bad at times. But nobody could have done anything differently about the life I had coming up. Besides, I had the support of the players back then, the way they gathered around me when I went down. The support was there. I totally blame myself for not reaching out when I should have. And I could have gone to Mookie and talked to him about *anything*, knowing whatever I told him was going to stay right there. I knew he had my best interests at heart, but I didn't open myself up to that, so there's nothing he or any of my teammates could have done differently to save me. It was all my doing. It was just me making bad choices, bad decisions."

"I really get the sense that Mets team of the mid-eighties was like a second family to you," I said. "Plus, they were a colorful cast of characters. What was the atmosphere in that clubhouse like and how might it compare to one today?

"*Totally* different," Doc immediately replied. "Mookie and I have talked about that a lot, like when we had the all-star game here. Yes, our team was known as a wild bunch, a crazy bunch, with guys that loved to party. That's true. But we also had a lot of intelligent baseball guys on the team, guys that loved baseball, loved talking about baseball, and had a lot of knowledge about baseball. And those things kind of get overlooked and it really pisses me off. After Sunday games at Shea Stadium [in the eighties], you remember what the traffic was like, right?"

"I sure do," I responded. "Gridlock. It took forever to get out of the parking lot."

"Well, after Sunday games I would spend time with at least fifteen of our guys and we just talked about baseball," Doc said. "There might have been a game on TV, but we talked about *our* game, what we could have done better, what we needed to improve. The knowledge about baseball that we had in that room was incredible. Then there was also the amount of time we all spent together away from the field and the time our families spent together. Well, towards the end of my career, you didn't see that anymore. We had two guys going one way, two other guys going another way, one guy's got his entourage, another guy has his personal trainer. I don't know if it was just a generational thing, but things had changed. I have never been on a team as close as that '86 team."

"I have definitely gotten the message about the baseball intelligence of the '86 Mets loud and clear from your teammates I have spoken with," I said. "They really don't want people to think of that team as mostly some wild fraternity, as has been widely reported in media outlets."

"You could be crazy and all that stuff, but also intelligent baseball players," Doc said. "The thing is, in the eighties, from talking with other athletes from that time, whether in baseball, football, or hockey, wherever, everybody was partying, everybody was doing stuff. But we got pointed out because we were in New York, we were having success, so we were the ones that were singled out. And that's what happened."

"I guess the thing that many people point to is how if the Mets had had more discipline they may have had more success," I said. "That '86 Mets team won more games in a single season than any other team in baseball during that decade. Did you believe at the time, like a lot of your teammates, that your club had another two or three championships—"

"*Oh, no doubt, no doubt about it!*" Gooden hastily replied before I even finished asking the question. "We won one with the guys we had. There might have been some room for a tweak or improvement, but you figure with our main guys, the core guys that were coming back, we should have been winning championships for a while. We should have had a run like the Yankees had in the nineties. In '87, we had the pitching staff go down with injuries, and then in '88 we were right there, but unfortunately, the Dodgers got hot at the right time. You can't turn back the clock, but I just wish we had the wild card back then. It could have been different if we had."

"Oh, with the dominant starting pitching your team would have had for a short series, it would have been very different," I said.

Gooden nods.

"But, anyway," Doc continued, "I definitely thought we could have won more, but it just goes to show you how hard it was to win that one. You just never know and you can't take anything for granted. But I don't take anything away from what we did accomplish. I always tell the guys that when you win championships, you're *never* ex-teammates, you're *always* teammates."

We had begun to switch gears, talking about how the trade for Gary Carter following the 1984 season was instrumental in getting the Mets to the next level, when Doc got emotional thinking about "Kid" and how he was one of his teammates who always supported him, right up until the day he died.

With tears welling in his eyes before he excused himself to use a tissue, Gooden let out a big exhale, unnecessarily apologizing for temporarily losing his composure, and said, "I'll always remember Gary's last days. He said to me, 'Doc, I have this thing. I'm fighting it. I'm going to fight it, because I want people to know you never give up the fight. And what I want you to do is fight your disease as well. Let people know that you never gave up and that there's a better way. And if you can promise me that, we'll take that with us.'

"That was the last conversation I had with Gary. Seems like it was yesterday."

It had been nearly three years.

| | | | | | |

I reminded Doc how it had been four years since we had met briefly at an event in Scarsdale, New York.

"You had put on quite a bit of weight around then," I said delicately.

"*Oh man!*" Doc said while laughing.

"But you look terrific *now*," I was quick to add. "What caused the weight gain and how did you get back into such good shape?"

"Well, back then, I was going through a rough time," Doc explained. "Eventually, the news came out about the child endangerment issue. [Author's note: Gooden was arrested in New Jersey for driving with his five-year-old son Dylan while under the influence of Ambien and traces of cocaine in his blood.] I put on a lot of weight and was very depressed. I wasn't dealing with it. I stopped going to meetings and I was living in Maryland going through a tough time with my girlfriend. Life was just miserable. It was the first time I left my family and my kids in Florida, so I had all that going on. I didn't know anybody in Maryland, was drinking, and then eventually started using.

"Then we moved to New Jersey, got married, and actually everything was great with the marriage. That wasn't the issue, just myself—*I* was the issue. I was missing everything. I was eating out of control. I was basically isolated from everybody unless I had to go to work or something like that. And the next thing I knew, I was two hundred eighty-five [pounds]. I'm six-three-and-a-half. And I'll tell you how the disease works. I would look in the mirror and I was like, *I'm not that bad*. But then I played in the Yankees' old-timers' game in 2010 and on the back page of the *New York Post* they had a picture of me. I looked at that picture and thought, *Wow, what happened? What happened?*"

"Wasn't that around the time you were getting inducted into the Mets Hall of Fame?" I asked.

"Yes, it was," Gooden replied.

"That must have been great for your spirits at that time," I said. "How did you find out?"

"I got a call from Jeff Wilpon telling me the Mets were going to induct me into the Mets Hall of Fame. At that point, I said to myself I had to do something [about my weight] because that's something I *have* to go to and I can't look like a mess! So I had to start working out. Even though I wasn't going to get down to where I wanted to be, I had to do something. I started going to this outpatient program in New York City. It was okay, but it really wasn't what I needed. I was getting on track, but was still using. I was drinking, too, but not as much as before.

"I was able to get clean two weeks before the induction ceremony, which was a great event. For me, it gave me closure. I always wanted to go back to the Mets and right the ship since 1994 [when the Mets didn't resign him and he became a free agent]. I, at least, wanted to come back for even just a month to finish my career with the Mets. Unfortunately, I didn't get to do that. But by having the induction, it gave me two things. First, everything was okay again between me and the organization. And secondly, I would be connected to the Mets forever. And because the fans are a part of me, I said in my speech that I was taking them into the Hall of Fame with me.

"And from that day on, between the fans, the ovation I got, and the whole celebration, it gave me the opportunity right there to make life changes. It kind of jump-started me. That was in August 2010. I still had my struggles, going back and forth with drugs and alcohol, but I finally got to the point where I figured out I couldn't do this anymore or else I was going to die."

"Were there any other factors or breaking points that made you serious about stopping your use of drugs and alcohol for good?" I asked.

"I remember waking up after a three-day binge, being in a hotel because my ex-wife and I had split up again. She went back to Maryland and I didn't see or talk to my kids for six months. I was going through a very depressed time. So for three months I'm in a hotel room, and for some strange reason, I woke up one morning and there was a gospel song on. The artist's name is Marvin Sapp. His song 'Never Would Have Made It' was playing. So I'm listening to the lyrics, and when he sings, 'He's seen the worst of me, but he's seen the best of me,' that really stuck. I called a good friend of mine, Ron Goldstein, and I said to him, 'Look, you've got to get me to rehab *right now*. If I don't go now, I'm *never* going to go.' And Ron said, 'No, just wait, you'll be okay. Just sleep it off and call me when you get up.' But I said, 'No, you don't understand. You've got to come right now.'

"He came to get me and I went into an inpatient facility in Manhattan."

"I read in your autobiography, *Doc*—an excellent book by the way—that it was the work of Dr. Drew Pinsky and his three-week program at the Pasadena Recovery Center that ended up helping you more than any of the other treatment centers you attended, including Smithers and Betty Ford. So how did you get involved in his reality show, *Celebrity Rehab*, and how did the experience play into your recovery?"

"Well, after my time at the inpatient facility," Gooden explained,

"I was having lunch with Ron and Lenny Dykstra in Manhattan and we were looking at the *New York Post*. On the back page, there was mention that Amy Fisher, Mike Lohan, and myself were going to appear in the next series of *Celebrity Rehab*. None of us knew where this news came from. I told Ron and Lenny, 'I'm not going on that show.' Lenny agreed and said, 'You don't need to. You're fine.'

"So three days later, I get contacted by the show. I realized I still needed help. But first, part of me going to rehab was to get the okay from my mom and my kids because I would have to relive all those dark moments. They were okay with it, so I flew out to California and checked in."

"So then why did Lenny famously try to get you out of there?" I asked.

Dwight smiled and told me, "Well, I guess Lenny was talking to Ron about it, and he thought they had *hypnotized* me into going on the show because I had just told him I wasn't going. So Lenny came out to California one night. A lady at the facility came to get me and said they had Lenny Dykstra there to see me. I was asked if I could just talk to him a little bit because they didn't want to call the police and have him arrested.

"I said, 'No, don't have him arrested.'

"But then I started thinking, *Okay, I know this TV stuff. This has to be some kind of stunt.* The lady said there were two guys with him and they were serious about getting my bags and getting me out of there. Anyway, I went to see him.

"Lenny told me, 'This is not the place for you.' But I told him, 'No, I'm fine.' So Lenny said, 'Well, give me one of your bags and then tomorrow let me know and I'll come and get you out of here if you want.' But I said, 'There's no problem. I appreciate it. But tomorrow we can talk. You can't be here now.'

"But then Lenny became persistent, telling me, 'I'm not leaving until you come with me.' So I had to convince him that I was okay and would call him. The next day, someone from the show was talking about Lenny and asked me if I thought he would be willing to be on the next episode. I just laughed and said, 'Wow.'"

"It seems like Lenny really cares a lot about you to have gone through all that trouble of trying to get you out of that facility," I said.

"People don't realize we go back to the minor leagues together," Doc explained. "We played together in A-Ball, and when Lenny first got called up to New York, he stayed with me. We've been great friends since. I loved Lenny then and still love him today. I'll always love Lenny. He'll always be like a brother to me."

"So getting back to the Dr. Drew show," I said, "how did it exactly help you and why was it different from other treatments?"

"I just basically wanted to come onto TV and tell my story, talk about how I felt when I was going through my problems, so people could hear *me* say it as opposed to some media guy writing this is what Doc felt," Gooden said. "I put my face out there, which was the best thing I could have done."

Doc continued, giving some more specifics about what helped him.

"Part of me going there was for myself, so I could talk. I was in total denial that I had this disease with drugs and alcohol because I don't know if it's an athlete thing or an ego thing—*I don't have that disease* or *I can stop if I want to.* But you can't stop unless you make certain life changes. Everything has to change; that's the only chance I had of stopping it. It's like a cancer patient—they have to go for chemo. With the disease of drugs and alcohol, my 'chemo' is lifestyle changes—people, places, and things—a support group, having a sponsor, doing the twelve steps. If I don't do those things,

I don't have a chance. You can't go to rehab for twenty days and say you're cured. You're *never* cured. I'll never be cured of this. But it gets better as long as I continue to do the things I need to do and let someone know how I feel and keep myself out of danger's way. And when things come up, 'triggers' come up, I have to call someone and let them know how I'm feeling and get to a meeting. If I don't, I'm asking for trouble."

Dwight was extremely convincing that, at last, he was on the right track. He seemed so in tune with his recovery and what it's going to take to stay on the straight and narrow.

"Doc, with the Dr. Drew show being such a positive experience, with the millions of viewers watching you on television, what happened when you left California and the lights from the cameras were no longer on you? Were you at all concerned about going back out into the real world?" I asked.

"Well, right after the Dr. Drew show, I did an outpatient program at Bergen Regional Medical Center in Paramus, New Jersey. Once I got there, things really got rolling. I started working out, started eating right, going to support groups, going to meetings, getting on track, and my life started changing. My appearance started looking better. I started feeling better about myself. I began spending time with my kids, building a relationship with the youngest ones. My ex-wife and I started getting along well enough to the point where we actually reconciled and got back together for a time. Life just started getting better just from making those changes. I never look back [at the dark days]. I still keep those memories there, but I don't dwell on them. I just remember what can happen if I let my guard down or even worse."

"Okay," I said. "I've got to talk to you about your book, *Doc: A Memoir*, because you were very open about your challenges in it, just as you have been with me this morning. Like I said earlier, a really great read and your introspection is admirable. I wouldn't even call it a baseball book, but rather a book on life. But this was your second autobiography. Why did you decide to write another one?"

"Because when I did *Heat*," Doc explained, "I was in Cleveland, and a gentleman [and Gooden's onetime representative] Ray Negron and [sportswriter] Bob Klapisch came to me and said I should do a book. So I agreed to do it. Part of my downfall was people-pleasing. Another part was putting myself in positions where I shouldn't be because if this guy's gonna be happy, I'll make myself happy. So what I'm trying to say is when I did *Heat*, they came to me and said it's a great time to do it. I said okay, but my heart wasn't in that book. I hate to say it, but while I took part in it, a lot of it was more of guys putting stuff in my mouth. They would say, 'You should put this in there,' and I was like, 'Okay, that's fine, that's fine.'

"But with *Doc*, I look at that as probably my first true, real book that came from *me*. So I remember doing the twelve steps with my sponsor, and I was running down things in my mind that bothered me—missing the [1986 Mets] World Series parade was a big one. Other big ones were missing my kids' birthdays and showing up high to my kids' games. And as I'm doing this, I'm thinking, *You know what? This here would be a good book. This book could help others and be good for me, as well.* So, *Doc: A Memoir*, basically came from my twelve step stuff that I was going through personally that kept me sane.

"But then I thought, *Do I really want to put this out there?* So I prayed about it, and talked it over with my older kids and my mom. My mom said if it was going to help me and help others, she backed it. In the book, I talked about my childhood, like what I went through when I watched my sister get shot. And then another time, watching my mom shoot my dad. Stuff I never dealt with that I never knew was traumatic until I was in therapy. For example, when my sister got shot, I hid in the bathroom; I didn't realize until therapy that anytime I would get high, I went to a bathroom to do it. Those things I had to deal with I put down on paper and thought it would be a good book. So I talked with Ellis Henican, who cowrote the book with me, and we discussed how to do it. It was unbelievable therapy for me."

"You wrote in the book how you still keep in touch with a lot of your old Mets teammates," I said. "Yet you wrote rather strongly how you had a falling out with Darryl Strawberry and how some of his actions towards you didn't befit a friend. You two came up to the big leagues a year apart and were always linked together, especially early in your careers. He was supposed to be the next Ted Williams and you were supposed to be the next Walter Johnson—just two incredible talents that were destined to be the cornerstone of the Mets' organization for many years. So now that Darryl has his own ministry and it seems like he has really turned things around in his life, have things gotten any better between you two?"

"Yes, things have gotten a lot better," Doc said. "It was a situation with Darryl where, like you said, when we were playing, a lot of people linked us together, made us out to be closer than we were. And for a couple of years we were close. But I think a lot of times we allowed others to influence us; we believed people who told us of things he or I may have said that may have not been true. And we never got together to talk and ask one another, *Hey, what's going on?* We had the opportunity to do that on several occasions, to talk about it, but didn't. But most important now, Straw's got his ministry. He's touching lives. With my recovery, I'm hopefully touching lives in a different way by sharing my stories. Our relationship is great. We have a lot of respect for one another. We talk a lot. And our relationship couldn't be any better than it is now. It's better than it's ever been. That's because it's *real* as opposed to when it was *planned*. Now it's genuine. The drugs and alcohol are behind the both of us and we talk about life issues. We don't talk much about our baseball careers and what could have been. We just talk about things we're doing now and moving forward post–baseball career."

"That's great to hear, Doc," I said. "It sounds like you have even more in common now than when you were teammates."

Gooden nodded in agreement.

"You mentioned earlier how you always wanted to return to the Mets after your final season with them in 1994," I said. "Did you ever reach out to them, and if you did, what stance did they take?"

"I really understood why they wanted to cut ties with me in 1994," Doc explained. "But I always wanted to come back and do it right. I thought I would play my whole career with the Mets. So when they wanted to cut ties, it hurt. But after playing with the Yankees for two seasons, and before joining Cleveland, I called the Mets and told them I wanted to come back. But Steve Phillips was the general manager and told me, 'No, but we wish you the best.'

"Then, after the '99 season," Gooden continued, "I was a free agent and called the Mets again, but they still didn't want any part of me. So in 2000, I ended up with the Houston Astros, pitched one game, got traded to the Tampa Bay Devil Rays, and was released after eight games. I called the Mets again, saying I would even go to Triple-A. Still, they wanted no part of me. So I ended up signing back up with the Yankees."

"Ahh, yes," I said, "and you ended up getting a chance to return to Shea to pitch against the Mets!"

"I sure did," Gooden said, grinning. "I was pitching in Rookie Ball with the Yankees, and I remember Billy Connors calling me into an office. I was thinking, *They're probably going to release me.* But instead, Billy told me the Yankees needed a pitcher to pitch up in New York against the Mets for a day-night doubleheader. I knew I wasn't quite ready, but I couldn't say no. So I thought, *Well, at least this gives me my chance to go back up to Shea Stadium one last time, which is all I ever wanted.* But I pitched well over five innings and beat them. A lot of people forget about that day game at Shea because the night game at Yankee Stadium was when [Roger] Clemens hit [Mike] Piazza in the head. So my game kind of got pushed under the rug a little bit. But, still, it was weird for me coming out of the visitor's dugout and walking to the visitor's bullpen at Shea Stadium."

"That was a huge game for you, Doc, in so many ways," I said. "First, the Mets were a good team that season. And it also kind of set up the incredible possibility of you facing the Mets in the World Series."

"Well, the first thing it did was allow me to stay with the team," Doc explained. "And we had the possibility of making the World Series. I always imagined going out and taking the mound again in a World Series at Shea. And when the Subway Series happened, there I was in a Yankee uniform playing against the Mets, something I just could never picture. But, unfortunately, I didn't get into any games in the Subway Series. That would have been the *ultimate.*"

We both paused to consider how "Hollywood-like" his pitching against the Mets in the Fall Classic would have been.

"I always felt the baseball gods missed two great opportunities," I said, breaking the silence. "In the 1986 World Series, Tom Seaver was a member of the Red Sox and in their dugout throughout the seven games, but was inactive due to a knee injury. Had he been healthy, he likely would have pitched in Game Four in place of Al Nipper. It also would have been Seaver's last game of his career. The same would have applied to you had you pitched in the Subway Series, as you retired after 2000. Two legendary Mets going out against the team that made them famous."

"*I agree, I agree!*" Doc said excitedly. "But basically, you never know. There was nothing personal against the Mets in 2000, but it was just the way I kept going back to them again and again [and to be turned away]. And while I completely understand them not taking me back, you might say I wanted bragging rights. To win during the regular season against them at Shea and then if I could have beaten them in the World Series and then call it a career, that's the way to go out, I think."

"Your time with the Yankees was when owner George Steinbrenner was in his prime and ruled the club with an iron fist," I said. "Anything less than a world championship was considered a disappointing season. What was your relationship with him like?"

"George was great," Gooden said. "I remember in 2000 I was with George when he signed me, and he said, 'Look, if it works out, fine, if not, you come work for me.' So at spring training in 2001, I actually hurt my knee, and I said to him I thought I would retire. So I worked for George that first year of retirement helping with the minor-league pitchers that came to big-league camp, and I also got invited by him to some meetings. He saw that I knew more than he thought about pitching and that baseball was my passion since I was a kid. He saw that I brought something to the table where I could really help and evaluate the minor-league pitchers and free-agent signings, as well as do some scouting. So I had a lot of roles. It got to the point where I only had to answer to him, and for six years there were many times I would fly up to New York with him on his private plane. He was like a father figure to me.

"I got to really know George the person," Doc continued. "He had a great heart for people. The stuff he did in the community and how he helped others was really great. I saw him do a lot of things he didn't want anybody to know about. He always told me that when you're doing charity work, or when doing something from the heart, if more than two people know, it's not from the heart. He also told me to always put family first no matter what—even if sometimes they piss you off. Because while you can change your friends, you can't change your family."

Doc went on to tell me how he actually first met Steinbrenner way back in 1978. Dwight joined his nephew, the future major-league star Gary Sheffield, on a trip to Yankee Stadium. Sheffield played for a team that went to the Little League World Series that year, and The Boss flew the whole team up from Tampa to get introduced on the field before a game.

Doc then recounted a story about The Boss and the importance he placed on always being there for your family.

"My dad was very, very sick in 1997," Gooden said. "I used to go to the hospital in Tampa to see him a lot. One time, George had a meeting at the Yankees' [Tampa] minor-league complex. George asked someone at the complex how my dad and I were doing. He was told I was at the hospital with him and that my dad was not doing well. He was also told he had some of his baseball people that had been waiting for over two hours to meet with him. George said, 'Well, tell those guys I'll be right back.' He came to the hospital, spent an hour and a half in the room with my dad and me. Dad ended up passing days later, but the fact that George took the time out, putting his meeting on hold, to come and spend time with us, that's something I will *never, ever* forget."

Doc let out a sigh and continued.

"I loved the guy. Of course, he got on me at times when I

deserved it. But at the end of the day, he would tell me what his expectations were, how I let him down, and why he did what he had to do. I understood that and had a lot of respect for him. I remember I was in Las Vegas doing a signing with Pete Rose when I found out that he had passed. It felt like I was reliving my dad's death all over again. He was that close and meant that much to me."

| | | | | | |

"So you called it a career with two hundred wins, a .634 winning percentage, a no-hitter, a Rookie of the Year Award, and a Cy Young Award to go along with three world championships," I told Doc. "Those numbers and achievements alone would bring you into the Hall of Fame conversation. Do you still think about what could have been if your career hadn't gotten sidetracked? Do you ever look back?"

"I'm glad you bring that up," Gooden replied. "I used to look back all the time when my career was over. I used to say, 'Wow, man, I could've done this or that. I should have won three hundred games with the start I was off to. If it wouldn't have been for *drugs*, if it wouldn't have been for *alcohol*, if it hadn't been for my *lifestyle*, what if? And then it all led up to 2006 when I was in Gainesville incarceration. [Author's note: Gooden served time for violating probation for cocaine use; Gainesville is a minimum security facility that specialized in drug rehabilitation.] It was there that I played over my career of what could have been and this light came on. Even though there would be more downfalls after '06, at Gainesville I said to myself, *Hold on. Wait a second. Who am I to beat myself up over what I could've done and other people's expectations of what I could have been?* That's because my own expectations going back to 1984 when Davey Johnson said, 'Congratulations, you've made the team,' were just to stay healthy, have a long career, and have fun. I never thought about any awards. Obviously, you think about winning the World Series as a kid, but I never thought about making the Hall of Fame or any of that stuff.

"So I look back and I won every award a pitcher can win. I was blessed enough to get three World Series rings—all in New York. To accomplish some of the things I did, what more can I ask for? So I had to stop asking what could have been, and start enjoying the things I *did* accomplish and the career I *did* have. The only reason I had to do that was because it was keeping me sick and I was continuing to beat myself up, continuing to use and drink over what could have been."

Still, despite no longer dwelling over the idea of not having a plaque in Cooperstown, he couldn't help give his opinion on whether or not he belonged there.

"Regarding the Hall of Fame, I can't really say who deserves to get in and who doesn't because it's the media's decision and they look at different things. But while I can say I'm happy for the players that go on to the Hall of Fame, and they deserve it, a lot of them are players I had a lot of success against. It was a privilege to play against those guys and I had a great career of my own. Look at the numbers I *did* put up. You could argue that they make me belong or not belong in the Hall of Fame. You could argue that I only won so many games, but if you take the top pitchers of my era who may get in or are already in the Hall of Fame, look at how many starts they had and look at how many I had. Look at winning percentages. If you compare things that way, my numbers are there. The guy that wins three hundred games, how many more starts did he have than me?"

"Like a Don Sutton," I said.

"Right, like Don Sutton," Gooden agreed. "How many more starts did he have over me? So when I look at it like that, I think, *You know . . .*

"But at the same time," Doc continued, "I have nothing to hang my head about. It used to bring on a lot of *depression*, a lot of *guilt*, and a lot of *shame*. Things that kept me sick. But I'm glad I'm finally over that."

Listening to him talk, I couldn't help but recall how truly amazing he was and how he was on track to becoming the greatest pitcher in Mets history. But the hard truth, in my mind, was how he could also just as easily be dead right now. He got a second chance, I thought, with his biggest "game" being played out today.

"Doc, when you were granted a five-year probation in 2011 instead of facing more jail time for the child endangerment charge we touched on earlier, you were given another chance to make positive change in your life," I said. "What have been some of the steps you have taken to *stay* clean and send a positive message to others?"

"I think the most important thing," Gooden replied, "has been to be honest with myself. Because I can tell you something and I can tell somebody else something, but I can't lie to myself. And once I accepted that I have this disease of drugs and alcohol, and there are procedures I have to follow—one day at a time, an hour at a time—it's the only way I was going to make it. You talk about jails, institutions, rehabs, and cemeteries. I've done all of them but the cemetery. I was right there, and the only thing that was waiting for me was that cemetery."

"Any advice for others?" I asked.

"My advice is that you have to do it for yourself. You can start off by saying, *I want to do this for my kids*. That will only get you so far. It boils down to doing it for yourself. The one thing that kind of jumped out at me was when I once told someone, 'Well, I wouldn't want my kids to live with knowing their dad died from an overdose. Or that their dad died from crashing his car because he was high.'

That got me in the door. But once I got in the door, it was about me. I said, 'This comes before my kids, my mom, the Mets, because if I don't take care of the things needed in my recovery, and put that first, everything else I'm going to lose anyway.'

"But if I can handle my recovery first, not only do I get the best of what I have and develop my relationships with my kids, my family, and rebuild the trust and get their support, but I can touch lives just by being myself and just living a life. It's one thing talking, but it's another thing living it. And where I am today, I don't take anything for granted. Things that I didn't enjoy as much, like watching my kids' games, I now have such joy from that. And the things I thought I really enjoyed, I enjoy more now. I cherish every moment with my mom, with my church, every one of my kids. And I enjoy just being alive. Because I know looking back at my life and the situations and things I've been through, I could have been gone a long time ago. So, I know I've been spared for a reason. I'm figuring out that reason now as I go. At the same time, I just make sure I take care of myself first and then everything else will take care of itself."

"So what does the future hold for you?" I asked. "Do you think you might like to get back into baseball as a pitching coach or something along those lines?"

"I'm not quite sure yet," Doc responded. "I have some things that are going on in my head that I would like to do in the future, but at the same time, I have to stay within the things I can control right now. I just have to keep it simple because I'm a big dreamer. My passion is really kids. I would like to one day open a center and help kids who have been through any type of abuse, who have struggled or are in tough situations. But I also want to help kids that are fine and doing well and help them stay on the path of success.

"I really don't see myself getting back into baseball as a

full-time job," Doc continued. "I did it for a while with the Yankees and loved it, but again, I found out that I was doing it because everybody was telling me I should be a pitching coach, or doing this or doing that. I love baseball, don't get me wrong. But my *true* passion is kids."

The gracious Doc thanked me for stopping by and showed me out his front door. He decided he was going to take a walk around the neighborhood. It may still be gloomy outside, but for the once-troubled legendary pitcher, there is now sunshine in the forecast.

·2·

THE HEARNS: PROFILES IN COURAGE

I feel really tired. I feel like I'm eighty four instoad of fifty three. I feel like I should be sitting in a chair in some retirement home looking out at some palm trees. But this journey has given me a gift that I know I'm supposed to use.

—ED HEARN
(METS BACKUP CATCHER, 1986)

It's late one evening in 1994 and Ed Hearn, feeling extremely weak and deeply depressed from a failed kidney transplant, is sitting in an old reclining chair in his basement watching a videotape recording of his major-league debut. The May 17, 1986, *NBC Game of the Week* from Dodger Stadium is a contest between the Mets and the Dodgers. In a day game after a night game, Mets manager Davey Johnson is giving his all-star catcher Gary Carter the afternoon off and inserting Hearn into the lineup.

The hard-throwing right-hander and future Cy Young Award Winner Bob Welch is on the mound for the Dodgers. Hearn, who singled in his first at bat that afternoon, follows that up in his second plate appearance by drilling a long fly ball to deep left center field for a stand-up double.

As Hearn stands proudly on second base, the announcers Vin

Scully and Joe Garagiola discuss how Hearn must feel as if he's on top of the world.

Upon hearing those words, Ed musters all the energy he can and jumps out of his chair, kicking the television off its stand and sending it crashing to the basement cement floor. With tears running down his cheeks, he sits down beside his workbench and starts writing a "final note" to his wife, Tricia.

Sorry Trish. I've become too much of a burden for you. Forget about me. Remarry and be happy.

Ed then looks up and sees an old photo of himself as a boy playing ball with his father. Then another photo of his wife as a ten-year-old girl catches his eye.

He begins another note, this one to his baby boy, Cody.

Cody, I've never been a quitter, but the "bean balls" have been too much. Don't be like me, son. Keep swinging for the fences regardless of life's curves. Ya' gotta face the curves if you're gonna be a big leaguer in life.

Ed puts his pen down, walks over to his gun rack, and pulls out a .357 Magnum revolver. He loads a single bullet into the chamber, closes his eyes, and takes a deep breath. He cocks the hammer back with his finger on the trigger before taking one last look at the photos.

Then, in what would have been the last moment of his life, he begins to think about his faith in God and how taking his own life would affect Tricia. Ed puts the gun down, choosing to keep battling his daunting health issues, and live another day.

| | | | | | |

Shawnee, Kansas, is a lush, green, middle-class suburban town with roughly 62,000 residents. With its serene lakes and parks, and its close proximity to Kansas City, Missouri, *Money* magazine recently ranked it seventeenth in its "Best Places to Live" survey.

There was some question on whether or not I would get to see Shawnee, the home of former Mets' backup catcher Ed Hearn, as my email exchange with him became an exercise in gaining his trust.

"Much has been said and written about the '86 Mets," wrote Hearn in one email. "So before you were to take the trouble flying out here, I would be interested in hearing a bit about your angle on this project. I'm no longer enthused about much of today's purposeless, slap-stick media."

I eventually gained Ed's trust by emphasizing how I intended to humanize each of the '86 Mets profiled by visiting them in their current surroundings, thus greatly enhancing the quality of the book for the reader in the process. He liked how that sounded and invited me to his home.

Several weeks later, I was pulling into his driveway about twenty minutes later than I had intended.

"So what do you think about our Kansas City traffic, dude?" Ed said grinningly as I got out of my rental car.

"No kidding," I said. "I'm glad I called you before I left my hotel."

Ed's greeting was warm as he shook my hand and welcomed me into his house. He seemed happy and content, unlike anyone that I would imagine ever having contemplated suicide. Once inside, I was introduced to his wife, Tricia, and their nineteen-year-old son, Cody, a polite young man who has battled stage 3 non-Hodgkin's lymphoma the last few years. After some small talk, Cody excused himself to watch a local baseball game with friends as Ed, Tricia, and I adjourned to their kitchen table. While Ed spoke in a low, yet soft and sometimes even breathy, voice, I found Tricia's to be surprisingly strong and authoritative despite how pretty, petite, and feminine she looked.

"She's a stubborn-ass first generation German from Long Island," Ed took delight in pointing out a couple of times during the visit. "Both of her parents are from Germany. You better do things *her* way."

I would come to understand what made Tricia so strong: not only had she been Ed's caregiver for well over twenty years, but she had also been dealing with Cody's cancer battle since he was seventeen.

"You've had to be strong for this family, haven't you?" I asked her after they began telling me about some of the health issues Ed and Cody had endured.

"I think my strength has kind of progressed over the years," Tricia explained. "While I think I was meek as a teenager, growing up in New York made me stronger over time. I started working in a bakery at sixteen, and New Yorkers are known for being difficult to please. The experience helped make me more assertive, and I learned to stick up for myself.

"And with Ed, I think my being a professional nurse really helped. As a wife you want your husband to have the best care. If I didn't think he was getting it, or if I felt I could do it better, then I would do it myself. The stronger you are, the more likely you are to get what you need and want. I always try to do it in a nice way, but if I don't get what I need, I just get more and more aggressive."

As I listened to her speak, I couldn't help but think that if there was ever an embodiment of the wedding vow phrase "in sickness and in health," it would be Tricia's devotion to Ed.

Ed would certainly agree.

After Tricia was done speaking, he turned to me and glowingly described in great detail the circumstances surrounding how he met his wife during the much happier times of the Mets' 1986 world championship season.

After eight and a half years of minor-league ball, Ed was called up by the Mets to be the backup catcher to Gary Carter. He was more than capable in the role, hitting .265 with four home runs in limited action. And when "Kid" went down with an injury that August, Hearn confidently declared with true '86 Mets bravado, "It's *my* team now," and helped the club to an 11–4 record in Carter's absence. His time behind the plate that year was highlighted by a home run he belted off of the great Fernando Valenzuela. But the greatest connection of his life came near the end of the season.

Ed was shagging fly balls in the outfield at Shea Stadium with pitcher Randy Niemann, whose wife had just had a baby the night before. Ed offered his congratulations, and Randy talked about how he couldn't wait to get back to the hospital to see his new baby. As the conversation slowed, Ed asked an innocent question that would eventually change his life.

"I jokingly asked Randy if there were any good-looking single nurses up on their wing," Ed said with a smile. "I've always had a soft spot for nurses. Most of them seem to have a genuinely caring personality that I had come to like during my many visits to the hospital for one surgery or another."

Niemann was more than happy to give his teammate a scouting report. As Ed told it, "He said, 'Hey, there is this really cute-looking gal my wife has gotten to know pretty well. She's a *real* looker! Petite and slender, brownish blond hair, and brown eyes. And she seems really sweet. My wife really likes her. And best of all, she doesn't even have one of those New York accents. But the only thing is, they wear those surgical scrub outfits, so I can't tell if she's got great boobs or not! Yeah, you've got to come on down to the hospital and meet this gal.'"

As intriguing as this may have all sounded to Ed the bachelor, he was hesitant about going out with another New York woman, finding them to be too fast for, as he called himself, "an ole Southern boy."

"In New York, everything and everybody is always in high gear—including the women!" Ed explained. "So I had basically decided that since we only had a few more weeks left in the season, I would just wait it out until I could go back home to find a nice Southern belle."

But after hearing more accolades about this pretty young nurse, Ed got Tricia's phone number and set up a lunch date.

At the time, Ed was casually dating Red Sox relief pitcher Calvin Schiraldi's sister, Rhonda. Prior to the World Series, this courtship wouldn't have raised an eyebrow and would have made total sense. After all, Schiraldi and Hearn had been roommates together while playing minor-league ball in the Mets' organization at both Jackson and Tidewater.

But when the World Series between the Red Sox and the Mets began, to say it became a bit of an awkward situation would be an understatement.

"Rhonda came up from Texas to Boston to see her brother pitch in the World Series," Hearn explained. "We were down 2–0 and Calvin got her tickets to the three games at Fenway. Well, after the games in Boston were over and we were now down three games to two, Rhonda decides she wants to come to New York. She hits me up for a ticket [to Games Six and Seven], so I'm thinking I can find one more, so why not? But she also wanted to fly down on our team charter flight back to New York, which was usually a no-no during the regular season, but our GM, Frank Cashen, allowed wives and girlfriends to travel with us during the postseason. So Calvin Schiraldi's sister was on the Mets' flight to New York with the World Series on the line."

As I listened to Ed tell the story, I couldn't help but wonder what some of the players thought of this arrangement.

"Anyway," Ed continued, "I had just met Trish a few weeks earlier and had given her a ticket to Game Six as well. Each player received a dozen or so tickets to each game. So Game Six arrives, and my parents were wise enough to put Trish on one end of the row and Rhonda next to my dad on the other end. That solved one issue. But another was created when Calvin was giving up the Red Sox lead during our tenth-inning rally. My dad was cheering like crazy while Rhonda was freaking out and just bawling for her brother. My father told me afterwards if I ever put him in a situation like that again he'd kill me."

He never did. Ed and Tricia were married a year later.

Hearn's career appeared to take a turn for the positive late during spring training in 1987. While he relished the role of being on a defending world championship team, a trade to Kansas City in exchange for pitcher David Cone would make him the Royals' everyday starting catcher.

He told me he immediately fit in and had fun with the core players from that Royals team—guys like George Brett, Bret Saberhagen, Buddy Black, and Kevin Seitzer. In fact, Ed tried to bring over some of the antics like the "hot foot" from the Mets, but they didn't exactly catch on with management.

Ed, after letting out a big exhale, explained.

"*Ahhh*, one day I plugged in the *Let's Go Mets* video for a few of the guys, to show them how Roger McDowell and Howard Johnson made the perfect hot foot. Well, Saberhagen, in particular, was really into trying it out. So since the most frequent Mets' hot foot victim was first base coach Bill Robinson, we decided to give our own first base coach, Ed Napoleon, one. 'Sabes' and I fixed a hot foot for him and it went off superbly. Mike Macfarlane was at the plate, and just before the third pitch was thrown, it goes off. Napoleon kicked his legs almost to the level of his shoulders as the flame went off!"

"So management didn't share your enthusiasm?" I asked.

"Not exactly," Ed began. "After the game, our manager, John Wathan, sent word to call Sabes into his office. Now, even though we both were responsible for giving Napoleon the hot foot, Sabes was a Cy Young Award winner. So he swung by my locker on the way to Wathan's office and told me he was going to have the blame pinned squarely on himself."

But Ed said he wasn't about to let Saberhagen take the fall. He felt no need for somebody to cover for him.

"I almost ran Sabes over as he was coming out of the manager's office," Hearn said. "I was going to set things straight. I told Wathan, 'Sabes was totally wrong and, while he was involved, I showed him how to do it. But I'm going to tell you right now that if we can't have some fun, then that's just a sad case of treating us all like soldiers. I apologize for today, but I think we need a chemistry-building environment around here. I won't do it anymore, but I'm disappointed.'

"So I left his office wondering why they traded for me. Wasn't part of the reason to bring a world championship chemistry to Kansas City? But the Royals just didn't get it at that time. It seemed like they cared more about how you wore your uniform than how you did at the plate."

But the premature death of the hot foot in Kansas City would be the least of Ed's problems.

Just two weeks into that 1987 season, a major shoulder injury, followed by reconstructive surgery, was sadly the beginning of the end of a once promising major-league career. Ed would play his final big league game on October 2, 1988, despite agonizing come-back attempts over the ensuing three years.

Of the over four hundred trades the Royals have made since their inaugural year of 1969, the Ed Hearn for David Cone one is often listed as the worst they ever made. That's because while Hearn's career was derailed for good less than two years after the trade was made, David Cone went on to have a spectacular one, winning 194 games to go with a Cy Young Award and a perfect game.

While Ed has accepted this unfortunate piece of baseball trivia and even uses it as a part of his motivational speeches today, there were times when mention of it was hurtful.

Still sitting around their kitchen table while their yellow Labrador, Homer, now rested his head on my right pant leg, Tricia went into how poorly timed a *Kansas City Star* feature story entitled "Kansas City's 15 Biggest Mistakes In Our 150 Year History" had been. While Ed was fighting for his life awaiting a kidney donor, the paper ranked the Hearn-for-Cone trade at number four.

"Ed was eight months into dialysis treatment after his second kidney transplant failed," she said incredulously. "What were they thinking?"

Ed added, "This was no blog. This was the *Kansas City Star*, man."

Not surprisingly, the *Kansas City Star* was inundated with letters, faxes, and emails from outraged readers coming to Ed's defense. In talking about the support they gave him, he paused often while choking back tears.

Hearn's medical history is the worst I have ever heard of.

He said he currently takes between twenty-five and forty pills a day, and he figures that, since 1992, he has taken nearly a quarter of a million. He's had three kidney transplants, scores of radiation, and more than three dozen carcinomas that in one instance nearly cost him an ear and in another forced him to have his entire lower lip reconstructed.

"I've struggled hard with depression," Ed explained. "It was induced shortly after my first transplant by one of the numerous immunosuppressant medications one must take to keep the body from rejecting the new organ. Depression and mood swings are just two of the countless potential side effects of these meds. Obviously, it probably didn't help matters that I almost hyperspaced from being a ballplayer to suffering with three serious conditions at one time and the offspring of those conditions."

I must admit that I was shocked by what Ed had suffered through over the last twenty-five years. The reason being, he doesn't look all that sickly. In fact, his appearance is that of a mountain of a man, one of great strength. I brought this up to Ed and he chuckled.

"When I asked George Brett to do the foreword to a book I wrote years ago," Hearn said, "he asked me, 'What are you going to write about?'

"Brett knew how I blew out my shoulder two weeks into my first season with the Royals, how I battled for the next three seasons to come back, and about the dialysis, but to him, I appeared perfectly healthy."

Tricia interjected, "I think that many people suffering with chronic illness and not an apparent physical disability may appear normal to other people. It was the same with Cody. All the attention was on him from his friends when he was bald from the chemotherapy. He felt terrible and his friends rallied around him. But once he regained his hair and put some weight back on, even though he didn't feel much better, his friends treated him like he was normal again. When people no longer see the signs of sickness, they perceive the person to be in good health.

"And Cody has never known a healthy dad," Tricia continued. "Because of that, I think there are positives and negatives. The positive is that Ed has been around a lot. But the cause of that, particularly when Cody was only seven or eight years old, was because his dad was on dialysis in our house for two and a half years. But I think the experience made Cody stronger, because he watched Ed's blood coming in and out of that [dialysis] machine and it got to the point when, even as a little boy, he helped me with it."

Tricia then smiled as she reminisced about one instance she and Cody shared with the machine.

"Cody and I were joking how if Ed had a successful transplant, we could get rid of the noisy dialysis machine and have a 'kicking party.' When we thought that was going to be the case in 2001 during Cody's tae kwon do days, we *did* start kicking it. Well, the transplant failed, but that was a good memory for him to have. I believe the experience helped make him stronger when it came to his own battle with cancer later on."

Ed interjected, "You know, Cody has never seen me sleep without a BiPAP machine [a device that assists and monitors breathing at night]," Ed pointed out. "But we've still done so much together. I got to coach his seventh and eighth grade youth baseball teams. The kids came from all walks of life, sort of a Bad News Bears kind of group. Well, we ended up winning the 2008 Kansas State championship at our level. Our vagabonds beat teams with kids whose parents pay three or four grand a year to travel halfway across the country to play in tournaments. That team of ours did some great things together."

Ed's voice and pace started picking up. He told me entertaining stories about how he handled the players and their parents and only picked coaches that didn't have children on the team to avoid any conflicts of interest. It was easy to see how much he enjoyed coaching and sharing the experience with Cody.

"Cody was a good player with great hand-eye coordination," Ed said. "And he loved the game, but didn't take it too seriously. He played for the joy of playing and had a knack for keeping the game fun. On at least three or four occasions, an umpire would come over to me and say something like, 'That kid behind the plate, he's hilarious. What a sense of humor.'

"So one time I told one of them, 'Well, that's my kid. Would you please tell him to shut up and do his job?'"

Laughter filled the room, and Ed grew more animated as he talked about his relationship with Cody.

"Did I tell you the Father's Day story yet?" Ed asked me.

I told him he hadn't.

"Well, my first major-league home run was at Shea Stadium on Father's Day, 1986, and my parents were in the stands," Ed began. "One of the grounds crew exchanged a bat for the home run ball with the fan who retrieved it. So I was able to give the ball to my dad after the game. That meant everything to me because without his time and dedication to helping me pursue my dream of being a professional athlete, I would have had no chance of being where I was that day. Giving my dad that ball was a very small token of thanks, but I think it meant the world to the both of us. It was one of those teary-eyed special moments.

"So fast-forward to when Cody was in a fifth grade baseball tournament and one of the games was played on Father's Day. I was driving Cody and one of his teammates to the field when Cody lowered his voice and told his buddy about how I hit my first big-league home run on Father's Day and gave the ball to my dad. Cody told him, 'Wouldn't it be so cool if I did that and gave the ball to my dad?'

"Well, lo and behold, in his third at bat of the Father's Day game, he hit a shot to right center that went all the way to the wall, and he raced around the bases for an inside-the-park home run. After the game, Cody ran over to me with the same kid we drove to the game with, held the ball he hit for the home run, and said, 'I finally did it. I know it took twelve years, but I did it, just like you did. So I want to give you this ball!'

"It was a *Field of Dreams* moment for the two of us," Ed said. "Just so touching."

We had already talked for several hours at Ed's house when, at nearly nine o'clock in the evening, we drove over to a nearby steak house for dinner. On television sets strategically installed throughout the restaurant, the major-league all-star game was on, the kind of game I normally wouldn't want to miss. But the Hearns were far more engaging and I hardly glanced up from them to catch the score.

"I hope you're hungry," Ed said to me.

I smiled at the comment as I began reading the menu, but I really didn't have much of an appetite. I was in a good deal of discomfort from a kidney stone I had at the time. But I didn't dare complain about it, knowing that compared to what Ed had endured and continued to battle in his life, my situation was almost insignificant.

The topic turned back to Cody, and the Hearns talked more about his health issues.

I asked Ed and Tricia what their son's reaction was—as just a seventeen-year-old—to learning that what he thought was a nagging case of "tennis elbow" from playing golf was actually Burkitt's, a form of non-Hodgkin's lymphoma in which cancer starts in immune cells.

Ed said he and Tricia sat in the living room with Cody and explained the situation to him. When they were done, they didn't know what to expect as a reaction, but their son courageously asked, "Well, when I beat this, will I be a cancer survivor?"

It was, they said, typical Cody.

As Tricia explained, "He is a very compassionate person. He's got a lot of heart. He's the type of person that when we went to a nursing home and an old person needed assistance with their door, he had no problem helping him out. Or another time when there was this sick kid that didn't have a lot of family, Cody stayed with him the night before he died. Most kids back off from those types of things, but not Cody."

Still, Tricia went on to explain how the ensuing two years after the diagnosis were very challenging ones for Cody, to say the least.

"Cody was diagnosed with cancer when most kids were maturing, becoming independent, and spreading their wings," Tricia said. "Finishing high school, his senior year—he was sick through all of that. Thankfully, with the help of his school, he was able to graduate on time with his class. From there, he went straight into an internship for an engineering firm while umpiring Little League ball in the evenings. All the while, he was battling headaches from the spinal taps, dealing with something like six or seven chemo-related issues, and seeing countless doctors."

If all of this sounds about as bad as it could get, that would almost be correct, except for the fact that because Tricia was so diligent in getting the proper diagnosis of Cody's problems right from the start, they caught the Burkitt's in stage 3 instead of the much more frequent stage 4 for his kind of cancer.

"Our oncologist said 98 percent of the time when they discover lymphoma, it's almost always in stage four, which means it's in the brain or spinal cord," explained Tricia. "The only reason we found it was because I was so aggressive in getting a diagnosis and not waiting around. The lymphoma grew so quickly that from the time the initial X-ray was done showing nothing to three weeks later when the MRI was performed, a significant part of his bone had been eaten away."

Ed and Tricia would also tell how the original diagnosis from a nurse practitioner at the local children's hospital was not lymphoma, but instead the very fatal Ewing's sarcoma. So for a whole day, they believed their son had the same form of cancer that had taken the lives of two of his friends, children named Kori and Justin, one of which had lost his leg before dying.

"I pulled off to the side of the road after getting the news," Tricia told me. "I was hysterical."

"But the nurse practitioner wasn't convincing, even saying they weren't *totally* sure," Ed said incredulously. "I wasn't going to wait. I knew at that moment we weren't going to assume he was right with his diagnosis. I had been making connections with people around the country who could help. I knew someone at Children's Hospital in Philly. I knew a guy at Johns Hopkins. So I got the specimen myself and got things going."

Cody's specimen was sent to a different pathologist who, sure enough, diagnosed Cody with Burkitt's lymphoma.

"I think it was almost a blessing to think it was so bad for a day and then to find out the correct diagnosis was lymphoma," Tricia said.

The couple would say they learned their lesson of being sure to get second opinions from several of Ed's misdiagnoses over the years and from living in the relatively small market of Kansas City, which has a much smaller sampling of cases compared to the Mayo Clinics of the world.

"Tricia was trained on me and became what every patient needs, their own advocate," Ed said. "I don't like to make waves. But Tricia? She's a pit bull!"

Laughter filled the room and broke a level of tension that had risen while the two described all the angst and frustration they had gone through with Cody's health scare.

"Hey, I'm from Long Island!" Tricia reiterated with a smile, to more laughs.

While Tricia's role was clear, it dawned on me that Ed had experienced the rare combination of both patient and caregiver. I asked what I thought was a near-impossible question for him to answer: whether it was harder being the patient all those years or a caregiver to Cody.

But Ed didn't hesitate.

"I think it's harder being a caregiver, especially when it's your own child with a life-threatening illness. If you're the patient—sick and hurting—you no doubt can be pretty hard to deal with. Even just a broken arm can make you grouchy. So the caregiver needs that unique, God-given spirit of compassion, especially for those that they love the most. It's hard because the person you're caring for doesn't necessarily act the same as they do under normal circumstances. That's a hard thing to cope with.

"In the first few years after my initial transplant, I used to tell Tricia repeatedly to take me out behind the barn and shoot me. Well, eventually she told me how much that hurt and asked that I please stop saying that. But it was just the state I was in—as much as I appreciated all that Tricia was doing for me, I sometimes didn't act lovingly and thankful towards her, but instead was just frustrated about my predicament. My demeanor was affected immensely and not in a good way. That's why the divorce rate of chronic sufferers is around seventy-five percent, about the same percentage as professional athletes. Well, we have lived both of those categories. But I was one of the lucky ones. God gave me a nurse."

"It was destiny," Tricia said, smiling.

I asked Ed about his motivational speaking, which he has been highly successful at for almost twenty years and for which he has been awarded the prestigious Certified Speaking Professional (CSP) designation from the National Speakers Association. Only 8 percent of speakers throughout the world have received this distinguished honor.

"Believe it or not, my speaking started just *a few days* after the loaded pistol incident," Ed revealed.

I must admit this revelation floored me. I thought, *How could a man come so close to taking his own life and then, less than a week later, stand in front of an audience and openly share his life's challenges with them?*

Ed explained.

"Dave Lindstrom, a former Kansas City Chiefs football player, was a member of the Overland Park Rotary Club and was given the task of getting speakers for their weekly meetings. A scheduled speaker canceled out on him shortly before their next meeting. Scrambling to fill the last-minute void, he called me begging to pinch-hit for him. I tried my best to politely decline by telling him I wasn't feeling well, without sharing with him the depths of despair that I had only days earlier. But finally, I gave in, figuring I could tell a few baseball stories for twenty minutes and help a friend in need. But on that day, shortly after stepping up to the lectern, I discovered something about myself in front of those people. I realized that I had a gift of being very authentic when I speak. I'm very open, and my talk that day went beyond baseball and into my personal challenges. Without planning to, I felt I even shared a few personal philosophies on life learned from the ups and downs of my journey to that point."

Ed had a look of disbelief on his face as he described what came next.

"As this entire room of Rotarians rose to their feet when I concluded my remarks, I was almost in shock by what my intended talk about baseball had turned into and how well it was received. As the meeting adjourned, it seemed as if nearly every person in attendance had stopped by to express some form of appreciation. And to my surprise, it wasn't so much about the baseball, but more about my openness, the perspective and encouragement they had gleaned from my presentation."

Ed then said that the owner of a national speakers bureau offered to take him under his wing and introduce him to the business.

"But my response was thanks, but no thanks," Ed said, pointing out where he was emotionally just days before. "How could I empower others when I could barely empower myself?"

But six months later, after Ed had worked hard to see past his circumstances to a future opportunity, one with *real* impact and not just entertainment, he called the owner of the speakers bureau back to inquire about his offer.

Within a year, Ed was speaking full-time. At his peak, he was giving eighty to ninety speeches a year.

"You know, I could have probably played ten years in the big leagues had I stayed healthy," Ed reflected. "But then I wouldn't have had the opportunity to impact the lives of people like I have."

Hearn added that the irony of having played his only season in New York on the '86 Mets was not lost on him.

"If I didn't get that ring, do you think I would have had the opportunities I've had? No shot," Hearn began. "And how we won it all? The championship series against Houston, coming back like we did in the sixth game. If we had lost, there was no shot at beating Mike Scott in a seventh game. I would have bet my life on that because our key guys—Hernandez and Carter—were just 'buffaloed.' We would have had no chance against Scott. Then what happened in Game Six of the World Series with Mookie's ball going under Bill Buckner's legs? I mean, a ground ball rolls through a guy's legs, I get a World Series ring on my finger, and it opens doors down the road for opportunities to be significant.

"It wasn't until I began speaking and helping people that I realized that there was a 'plan' for me. Maybe this will sound narcissistic, but did that ground ball go between Bill Buckner's legs so that one day Ed Hearn could go around and touch lives? *Big stretch.* But we have a big God and He has plans we can't comprehend. Maybe that's a stupid thought, but I didn't make much money playing the game. If it wasn't for speaking, what would I be doing? I would have been trying to make a living instead of making a life."

There's a framed slogan on his office wall that reads, "Keep Swinging for Life's Fences." Ed says it's also how he inscribes copies of *Conquering Life's Curves*, a book he wrote in 1996.

"That phrase means perseverance to me," Ed said. "It's kind of a personal slogan of mine that evolved into a longer version I used for a while: 'Keep swinging for the fences regardless of life's curves.' My latest version, and one that I now use in some of my lectures, is: 'Keep swinging for HIS fences.' It's the bottom of the ninth in our society and a lot of people are beat up. So you better keep swinging!"

Still, despite all the people he has helped and inspired by his motivational speaking, Hearn is human and continues to grapple with an internal struggle. It was near the end of our long evening together that I asked him if he thought it was a miracle that he was still alive today.

Ed glanced down and, after a long pause, looked right at me, and said, "Do I consider my being here a *miracle*? No, the '69 Mets were a miracle. But there have been times when I have felt so worn down and beaten up, to the point where I wanted to stay in the game but was definitely ready to be called home by the Great Skipper in the sky."

There was a slightly uneasy silence at the table before Tricia broke the tension, turned to Ed, and said, "Instead of a *miracle*, how about a *blessing*? Would that be a better word?"

"You know, a lot of days I wonder," Ed said with the sound of resignation in his voice.

But Tricia, the woman who had been by her husband's side since the day they married, was quick to remind Ed about how there are good days as well as bad days and how great it had been that he was able to watch Cody become a young man.

I turned to Ed and added, "You know, I can't imagine or relate to how difficult your life must be every day. But I see you have a beautiful family, a great home, and so many other blessings. Are you ready to go because you feel comfort in believing you're going to a better place in heaven after death?"

Perhaps trying to lighten things up a little bit, Ed perked up and, with some humor, told me, "Now you're getting the game plan, Erik. Darn straight. There sure better be that brand-new, pain-free body hanging in my locker waiting on me or else I'll be in the Coach's office chewing His ear about the promises He made about heaven many seasons ago in the playbook."

Tricia nodded knowingly at me and said, "I think you need to understand that we're worn out. Almost anything that happened to Ed was what medical professionals would tell him ninety-nine percent of the patients won't have. Ed was *always* the one-percenter."

"We've had enough," Ed added. "I sure as heck don't need any more material for my speaking!"

So what keeps Ed Hearn going? I asked him.

"Every once in a while, somebody will come up to me after a speech I give around here and say something like, 'You know, Mr. Hearn, you joke about the Royals making the worst trade of all time to get you for David Cone. Well, you know what? After hearing you speak today, you might be one of the best trades we've ever made.'"

Ed began to get emotional again and, swallowing hard, told me in a slow and deliberate way, "It's those types of sentiments that are the best medicine I can ever take. No pill, no doctor, will keep me going any longer because, as the legendary Jackie Robinson once said, 'A life is not important except in the impact it has on other lives.' Because, Erik, after going from the penthouse to the outhouse and back, it's the *back* that truly matters to me the most, and hopefully to others."

In the game of life, Ed Hearn remains a world champion.

·3·

THE COMEBACK KID

Probably the best thing that can be said for that group was that we were in every game. Players never held back. Davey never held back. The front office never held back. We had an opportunity and we took it. We played our butts off every night. It was fun to be a part of that group.

—HOWARD JOHNSON
ON THE '86 METS
(METS THIRD BASEMAN, 1985–93)

It was one of those impossibly beautiful mornings in Boston's Back Bay. The sun shone brightly in the bluest of skies. The morning dew glistened off the perfectly manicured green grass of Fenway Park. A slight chill in the air served as a reminder that autumn was near. It was still several hours before an afternoon game between the hometown Red Sox and the visiting Seattle Mariners. The only sounds in this jewel of a ballpark were the voices of a local high school choir practicing the singing of the National Anthem in the stands.

Howard Johnson and I could have met at his home in Nashville, Tennessee, or at his regular season residence in Seattle, where he currently serves as the hitting instructor for the Mariners. But we decided on Boston's Fenway Park as the most appropriate venue, the site where the Mets' 1986 World Series comeback began after the club lost the first two games at Shea Stadium.

Three decades since the Mets' glory days, "HoJo," as he is commonly referred to by friends and fans alike, is immediately recognizable. He still has his trademark light brown mustache without any hint of gray and is only slightly heavier than his playing weight.

I was sitting at the distant end of the visitor's bench when HoJo appeared outside the tunnel leading up from the clubhouse. He walked by a couple of Spanish-speaking coaches and said a few words to them in their native tongue while holding a fat cigar in his right hand. He greeted me with a warm smile and asked if I minded if he smoked. I told him my father was a smoker and didn't mind at all.

"The World Series memories," HoJo began as we sat down for our talk. "I was sitting right here watching Dykstra hit one around the foul pole in right field leading off the first game here. And then Carter hitting the ball up over the Green Monster twice the next night. Now they have seats up there, but back then there was a net."

I asked HoJo if this was his first trip back to Fenway since the '86 World Series. He seemed to read into the way I asked the question that I desperately hoped, for the sake of our interview, that it was.

"Ahhh, it's actually my *second* time back," Johnson said with a smile. "When I was with the Mets in 2010 [acting as their hitting coach], we played here in an interleague series against the Red Sox. It was cool to come back and kind of walk around and see everything again."

HoJo didn't see action during the three World Series games at Fenway, but the memories came flooding back.

"I was enjoying those games," Johnson recalled. "I mean, we had a pretty good rivalry with those guys. They had come off a big series with the Angels and we had come off our own with Houston, so there was a lot of excitement and stuff on both sides."

I reminded him of his reputation as a bench jockey despite

appearing to be a really quiet guy. He laughed and then recalled Game Three and trying to get under Red Sox starting pitcher Oil Can Boyd's skin.

"I had known Oil Can for a long time," HoJo recalled. "He was pretty flamboyant on the mound, very exuberant, a lot of body motion and things like that. So you tend to get into it with him when he's on the hill. We all came here with a job to do, so I felt like I wanted to contribute any way I could."

HoJo did start at third base in one of the World Series games, taking the field in the much-hyped Game Two dream matchup of Doc Gooden and Roger Clemens. Gooden had nothing in that game, and the Mets left New York down 2–0 in the series.

"What was the mood like for the Mets after getting smoked 9–3 in Game Two?" I asked.

"Oh, that's easy," HoJo replied. "I remember walking through the tunnel into the locker room at Shea and all the guys were like, 'Hey, we got this. We got this.' And on the bus we were talking loudly to each other and saying stuff like, 'We've been through this before, so we're going to go up to Boston and kick their ass and come back here to New York. That's what we're going to do!'

"And I had no doubt that we were going to do that. No doubt at all because we were a little tired from that Houston series both physically and emotionally—and then there was the flight home, of course!"

HoJo's eyes twinkled as he chuckled at the thought of the wild flight back to New York, then continued.

"But seriously, just the mental drain from that [Houston] series . . . Game Six took a lot out of us. But we just knew what kind of team we had, and we knew that we were going to come here to Boston and do our job. And when Lenny led off Game Three with a home run around the right field foul pole, we were off. I knew we were going to take care of business. And while I couldn't predict the outcome of Game Six, I was certain we would be coming back to Shea to play it. The rest of the guys sincerely felt in their hearts we would be going back to New York as well."

"You bring up going back to Shea to play in what is now a historic Game Six," I said. "It's easy to forget that you were in the on-deck circle when Mookie was at the plate during his famous at bat. There was a real possibility that Mookie was going to draw a walk as the count was full for several pitches of his ten-pitch at bat. If he had, you would have come to the plate with the bases loaded in a tie game. What was going through your mind at that point, with the World Series on the line?"

"The biggest thing was the situation," Johnson said. "The wild pitch tied the game up, so really all the pressure was off us at that point. We felt we had dodged a major bullet. So quickly my thoughts were going to [Bob] Stanley because I had faced him before when I was in the American League. So I knew what he was all about and I was thinking, *Okay, I know what I'm going to get here. If I get to hit, I know what I'm going to look for. I got this guy.* So my whole thought process was to just watch Mookie, watch Stanley, and to just mentally prepare for my at bat. It never occurred to me that Mookie was going to walk. I thought he was going to get a hit or something [else] was going to happen."

"Was that because Mookie was such a free swinger?" I asked.

"Yeah," HoJo answered. "At that point in his at bat, he had really done a great job of kind of shrinking his swing and just kind of being protective, putting the ball in play. I just felt something good was going to happen. And I was ready. I was very confident if

I was to hit against Stanley, I felt I would get a good pitch to hit and I was going to put a good swing on the baseball."

"How about Calvin Schiraldi, the fire-balling Red Sox closer who actually started the inning? Down two runs, did you think you could beat this guy?" I asked.

"Oh, *one hundred percent*," HoJo said without pause. "We knew Calvin from the time he pitched for the Mets, knew his makeup. He was a little bit tentative at times. I know some guys were up in Davey's office, but I was in the dugout and remember a couple of us saying, *'It can't end this way. It's not going to end this way.'* And Carter was going up and down the bench, repeatedly saying, 'I'm not going to be the last out of this World Series.' He kept saying it over and over to everybody. As the inning progressed and Carter got up with two outs, he kept battling and battling before he got his base hit. And so the feeling was that we were not going to go down. It wasn't going to end. So when Kid got that hit, I was thinking, *Okay, we can do this.* It was just amazing that things happened so fast. When you're watching it after the fact, it seems like it takes forever. But when you're in it, it's actually like *boom, boom, boom, boom, we scored!* I remember Schiraldi being out there and the crowd was chanting his name and stuff. It was just pretty crazy. But the feeling was there that we could do it. Absolutely."

"I have heard the use of the word 'swagger' by some of your Mets teammates to best describe what made the Mets so tough to beat in '86," I said. "But I also hear a lot about how much fun you guys had on that ball club, yourself certainly no exception. After all, you and Roger McDowell brought a greater awareness to the 'hot foot' around baseball that year. Are you and your old partner in crime still in touch these days?"

Reflecting back on the high jinks, HoJo takes a puff off his cigar, lets out a hearty laugh, and talks about his former teammate, a current Atlanta pitching coach.

"We played the Braves this year, so I got to see him from the other side of the field. But last year I talked to Roger a little bit. I know he had one of his knees replaced because he was struggling with that, but he's calmed down quite a bit since those days. Coaching will do that to you! He's gotten serious. *Very* serious. Almost *too* serious, you know? I usually see him on TV, and he just doesn't seem like the same Roger McDowell that was always pulling practical jokes. He's really serious about his job now. People watch the videos from that '86 team and see that we had the hot foot and all that stuff. And you look at him now and go, *Is that the same guy?* But it is. Roger's still in there."

I agreed with HoJo, having noticed the same body language from McDowell.

"I love that one video of you two demonstrating how to make the *perfect* hot foot," I told HoJo. "It's classic."

Johnson became animated, as if he couldn't wait to let me in on a secret wish of his.

"I've actually thought about getting ahold of Roger and trying to re-create that video!" HoJo revealed excitedly.

"Oh, you've *got* to do it!" I exclaimed.

"Like exactly the way we did it then," HoJo said. "It was pretty awesome. We had some good times with the hot foot."

HoJo then glanced down at the bench we were sitting on and made an observation.

"Ha! This is a good bench for the hot foot, by the way. It's good because you need space—just like there is under here—so you can sneak up behind some unsuspecting guy."

Johnson then leaned back, took another puff off his cigar, and said rather nonchalantly, "You can't take the fun out of this game. Guys are going to do what they want to do. It's good fun."

But it was clear that other teams around the National League didn't share the Mets' sense of frivolity as New York rampaged through their '86 schedule. The opposition didn't enjoy losing to New York and then watching all the fun the Mets were having in the opposing dugout. The result was four bench-clearing brawls.

"When other clubs started head-hunting or sliding spikes high into you and some of your teammates, you guys never backed down from a fight," I said. "And you had enforcers like Kevin Mitchell and Ray Knight to lead the charge, so to speak."

"Mitch would fight at the drop of a hat," HoJo said incredulously, shaking his head. "He was a great guy and one of my best buddies. And Ray had a great season in '86 and was an enforcer, a leader. He was at the end of his career. He knew it, but gave it all he had. That was the kind of attitude I tried to learn from. It was just one of those things where maybe if they were around [after '86] we would have won again, but who's to say? It just wasn't meant to be."

I then asked HoJo what it was about the '86 season that he thought separated it from the others that came up short during the mid-to-latter part of the eighties.

"I would say there were two main things that happened," HoJo began to explain. "The first was when we came out of the gates in '86 with a record of two and three. I remember we had the *Welcome Home Mets* dinner after starting the season on the road, and Keith went up [to the podium] and said a few words. He said that nobody should panic, that we were going to win this thing. I distinctly remember him saying that.

"And then the other thing was when we went into St. Louis to start a four-game series later that month. In the first game, I hit a home run to tie the game in the top of the ninth off their closer Todd Worrell. We won that game in extra innings and then won the next three for a sweep. At that point, we separated ourselves from the Cardinals, who we always felt was our main competition. So from that point on, we were kind of like, *Okay, we're on this track now to go.*

"Those two things showed what kind of team we had in '86 against other years."

By the young age of twenty-five, HoJo could lay claim to having won world championships with two different teams—the '84 Detroit Tigers and the '86 Mets, easily the two most dominating teams during the decade of the eighties.

"Okay, so who would win a World Series if those two clubs faced off against one another?" I asked Johnson.

HoJo let out a howl.

"Oh! That's a tough one, boy!" Johnson exclaimed. "If the '86 Mets were to play the '84 Tigers, I would probably give the edge to the Mets because our starting pitching was deeper. And maybe our bullpen was a little deeper, too. But after that, it's just a toss-up. I mean, certainly we had the edge with, say, Mex at first base, but Trammell was the better shortstop. Whitaker was steady at second base. It's not a knock at our guys, but those guys were solid players."

As I listened to HoJo, I found it interesting that he referred to the '86 Mets as "we" and the '84 Tigers as "those guys" despite playing on both of those teams.

"The '84 Tigers?" Johnson said. "That was my first full year in the big leagues, and just to be a part of that group and lockering next to [Kirk] Gibson and watching him get ready to compete was amazing. I tried to learn from that as much as I could. But the one guy on the pitching staff that really made it work was Jack Morris.

When he had the ball, he competed his butt off, and he won and pitched late into games. He wanted to be out there and beat the other team, and that was the kind of attitude our guys had."

It dawned on me while we spoke that HoJo was the poster child for the age-old question of whether it's better to have personal stardom and all the accolades and inflated contracts that go along with it or team success. In Johnson's case, while being a pivotal member of both the '84 Tigers and '86 Mets, he was not a full-time player for either one. That distinction began for Johnson at the start of the 1987 season, when his all-star career really took off.

"At one point, you weren't a regular but had two World Series rings," I said to HoJo. "But then you became an all-star without winning any more championships. How were those two stages in your career different from one another in terms of satisfaction?"

HoJo laughed and didn't hesitate in his response.

"I'd trade the all-star part of my career for the rings any day," he said. "It's all about winning and it's all about feeling that camaraderie that you get with a group of guys that you battle with throughout the season. And when you reach the highest level, the top peak, and you win the whole thing, there's no way to describe it. That's why guys want it so bad.

"When you get a chance to play every day, certainly from a personal standpoint, it's an opportunity for you to do something for yourself and your family and make some money and be able to do different things, which is great. Every player has that desire inside of them. But at the same time, it's about winning. I know all about having a good year and being on a losing team and how hard that can be. While you do get the accolades and people remember you for certain personal achievements, I still love the fact that I was a part of two championships."

Perhaps it is ironic that the two best teams of a generation—the '84 Tigers and the '86 Mets—haven't won a World Series since. That bitter taste was not lost on HoJo, particularly when it came to the Mets, whom he joined in 1985.

"We should have won at least one more, especially in '88," HoJo said in a serious tone. "We just ran into a buzz saw with [Orel] Hershiser in the Dodgers series. And Oakland ran into the same buzz saw against them in the World Series that year. So it just wasn't meant to be. Fate wasn't on our side. It wasn't that we didn't play hard; it's just that things can happen in a short series that you just can't foresee. In '87 all of our starting pitchers went down with injuries at some point. But '88, we should have won.

"And then the front office started to break the team up after that. It was kind of sad to see that happen. I remember when McDowell and Dykstra got traded. Then Keith and Gary and everybody just kind of left a little at a time. It was just one of those things where we had our window and for some reason it closed quickly. It's sad. I remember it so clearly, the feeling of losing and not living up to the expectations. It was very, very painful."

Of all the great Mets on the 1986 team, HoJo was the one whose talent seemed to be the least appreciated. He was easily the superior offensively to Ray Knight, the Mets' primary third baseman, but either Davey Johnson didn't realize yet what he had in the young HoJo or he was transfixed by the chemistry and veteran leadership Knight brought the team.

"At the time of your retirement," I said to HoJo, "you held two National League switch-hitting marks and were a three-time member of the 30-30 [30 home runs, 30 stolen bases] club. In the history of the game, only Bobby Bonds, Barry Bonds, Alfonso Soriano, and yourself have reached that mark at least three times. Now, you were in your fifth major-league season in '86 but still not starting. Was it just a case of your talent going unnoticed, or did you make some adjustments following the championship season that helped make you a prolific hitter?"

HoJo didn't hesitate, believing his all-around game had always been there, but was kept under the radar.

"Well, in '86," Johnson began, "I had two hundred and twenty at bats. Ray Knight played mostly at third, and I ended up playing some shortstop as Davey wanted to get me in the lineup. But my at bats weren't as high as if I was playing every day, so I ended up hitting ten home runs that year and had thirty-nine RBIs. I remember the day they decided not to re-sign Ray Knight, and they were going to give me the third base job, and Lee Mazzilli called me and said, 'Hey, guess what? You're the third baseman of the New York Mets!' I told him I couldn't wait.

"So at the end of spring training the next year, Davey told me I was the guy after I went out there and competed and had a good spring. But I kept saying I expected to hit twenty home runs and drive in eighty runs. They would ask me how I came up with those numbers. I would say, 'Well, I had two hundred and twenty at bats last year and hit ten home runs and drove in forty, so if I get more than twice the playing time by being out there every day, then I should probably be able to hit my goal. I ended up surpassing those numbers that year.'"

HoJo was being modest, which is not unusual for him. He ended up having a breakout campaign, belting thirty-six home runs, driving home ninety-nine runs, while stealing thirty-two bases for the first of his three 30-30 seasons.

Besides his offensive prowess having been kept under the radar, he also attributes part of his big season to working harder at being a switch-hitter.

"I worked very hard on my right-handed hitting," Johnson explained. "That had been a big weakness for me and I knew that going in. But that's what helped me have the kind of year I ended up having."

At this point in our conversation, HoJo noticed some of the Mariners come out of the tunnel to warm up on the field. He talked about how he uses his own experiences to try to make them better.

"What I try to teach younger guys that don't have a lot of experience is that other teams will exploit the weaknesses that they have. That's what opposing teams do. So if you ask me what I try to teach our guys, a lot of it is the mental side of the game. If you have an issue and can't do something, the other team will find out about it real quick, especially in today's game because of all the videos, computers, and other things going on. So it's important to work on your weaknesses, not just your strengths. In fact, make your weaknesses your strength. If you can do that, you will become a great player."

It was clear to me how much HoJo enjoys helping younger players. But considering the two comeback attempts he made after his initial retirement, I couldn't help but wonder if his true motivation for coaching was mostly to stay involved in the game he loves.

"I've heard it from a number of players I've interviewed," I said to HoJo. "After they retire, they go back home, and then when late February or early March comes around, reality hits hard, and they realize that for the first time since they were a little kid they won't be playing baseball anymore. It's a bitter pill to swallow. How did that reality first affect you and did it lead to you wanting to make a comeback?"

"Well, after the '95 season, I decided that I just wasn't going to be able to do it physically anymore; I just couldn't go out there and compete," HoJo said. "I had kind of lost a little bit of the passion for the game because when you go out there and your body's not a hundred percent—and I'm not saying you have to play at one hundred percent all the time—it's mainly harder to get on the field and perform at a high level.

"So '96 came around and I started coaching in the Devil Rays' organization. My first coaching job was in Butte, Montana, and I really enjoyed it. But during that time, I started taking some swings during batting practice. I felt like, *What the heck, the guys wanted to see it.* So I would do it. And I still had a little thunder left in the bat, and I began to think, *You know what? Maybe I should try to play again.* That's probably what you're talking about because when you're not playing, coaching is the next best thing to playing. But when you're not playing, you do miss the competition on the field. So you do start thinking, *Can I do it again? Can I do it again?* And that's when I decided to go back and try and give it a shot and see what I could do the next year. But you're definitely right: it's difficult when reality hits you that you're not actually out there competing against somebody. Instead, you're on the bench trying to teach these guys how to compete."

Johnson made his first of two comeback attempts during spring training in 1997 with the Mets, but abandoned the idea after a slow start.

"So after aborting your initial comeback attempt, did returning to coach and doing some scouting help fill the 'emptiness'—a word I have heard used countless times from retired players?" I asked.

"Absolutely," HoJo responded. "After spring training in '97, I didn't have anything going on. I was home. I was playing golf. I just shut it down for good. I had come to grips with retirement and that I wasn't going to play anymore. But it helped that I was still kind of involved with the Mets at that point. They just said to go back home, take my time and enjoy my summer. And that's when I started scouting, which was my next venture. Mentally, I had to move on from playing and get on to something that was really satisfying and kind of fill that baseball void because no player wants to stop playing and feel like they still have something to offer. I think that's the emptiness you get. It's not that you're not playing and that you're not in uniform, but rather you want to still contribute to the next generation of players. All of those experiences you've had you want to share with somebody. You want to pass that on to others."

"So your legacy lives on, right?" I asked.

"Yeah," HoJo responded. "Because when you see players in the big leagues that I know I've coached in the lower leagues, it's great to see them having success in the majors. I think, *You know what? I had a hand in that kid's development.* It's a sense that you passed on part of yourself to the next guy. It's not that it's about you, but it's just like the things you learn you want to pass on to somebody and hopefully it will help them."

"That's a great way to look at your coaching, Howard," I said. "That said, I've got to get back to the theme of your comeback attempts with a story I just love—your *second* comeback attempt at age fifty. In 2011, as a member of the Rockland Boulders, a professional team in the Can-Am Independent League, you played a couple of games on the same club as your son Glen. What was that experience like for you and Glen?"

"Probably the coolest thing I *ever* did in a uniform," HoJo said without hesitation. "And that's a hard thing to say because when you've played in a World Series, you think that's the greatest thing. But when you're on the same field as your own son when he's trying to achieve something, that's a rare thing. Fathers usually impart knowledge to their sons, but it's different when you're actually in the game with them, watching them hit, and being able to talk about things during a ball game. So that was really fun for me and I know it was really a cool thing for him, too."

"You see so many former ballplayers who have sons in professional baseball now," I remarked. "What's the biggest piece of advice you gave to Glen?"

"What I tried to pass on to him was the value of practice," HoJo said "And it's not just teaching him to catch, throw, and hit; but to me it's about the time you put in away from the game itself, what you do between games to make yourself better. My father taught me that, and I wanted to pass it on to Glen. I try to do that with all the kids that I coach, teach them the value of putting the work in to try and get better. I'm not saying to spend hours and hours in the cage or fielding a thousand ground balls. I'm talking about understanding what you're trying to do, practice it, work on it, think about it, and try to execute it. Those are the lessons I've tried to teach Glen."

"So how is he doing now?" I asked.

"He's doing good," Johnson said. "He stopped playing because he just couldn't stay healthy. He reached a point where he had to make a decision on baseball, and he decided to go a different route. He's a very smart boy. He's good with numbers and math and he's finishing a financial degree. He's got like three majors going on with school and he coaches baseball, imparting his knowledge to his players. And I've got two other children. My oldest daughter, Shannon, lives in Nashville, where we live now, and I have a grandson through her and a granddaughter on the way. My youngest daughter, Kayla, is in New York City after graduating from the University of Florida last year.

"It's great to be a grandfather," HoJo continued. "When I first heard Shannon was going to have a boy I was like, *Oh man, this is awesome because now it's another person, another life you can impact directly in a positive way—such a blessing.* My wife and I are just so excited to have grandchildren. My job is going to be to teach them to play some baseball."

"And how about your other 'kids'—the young players on this Mariners team that you help become better hitters?" I asked. "What are some of the things you've implemented to help this Mariners team make such a marked improvement over previous years before you arrived on the scene?"

"Well, I was with some of them at Triple-A and it's fun to see some of the kids come up through the system," Johnson said. "I'm excited to be with them now in the major leagues. What I do is take lessons I learned when I was with the Mets, refine them a little bit, and also use what I've learned from [Mariners manager] Lloyd McClendon on how to communicate certain things to the guys. Sometimes you learn to not say so much, but sometimes you have to say more. You kind of learn what's important and what isn't. And that takes time to learn. This team has been really good. There are a lot of young players and it's been challenging, but at the same time it's been most rewarding."

Listening to HoJo, hearing about all of his experiences and successes in coaching, I wondered if he had his eye on becoming a big-league manager someday.

"Howard, I have your coaching résumé here," I said. "The Brooklyn Cyclones, St. Lucie Mets, Binghamton, and the North Fork Tides. You've won championships coaching with *all* these teams. And now you're having great success with the Mariners as their hitting coach. Is managing at the major-league level a part of your future?"

"Not in my immediate future," HoJo said. "But maybe down the road I wouldn't mind giving that a shot. Still, I'm very happy with the job that I have, and enjoy doing it. Until another opportunity comes along, I'm a firm believer that you do what you're good at. If you're comfortable in a certain position and you know that's where your strengths are, then stay with that instead of always trying to go beyond what you're really good at, especially with players, because they're going to know. Lloyd is a great manager. It didn't take guys long to realize that. He was a hitting coach at one point, but you can tell he's got the mentality of a manager, and that's the kind of thing that I think he's perfect for. And right now, I'm very well suited for what I'm doing."

"I must say, you seem happy and energized to be working with this young, up-and-coming team. Do these Mariners in any way remind you of the Mets of, say, '84 or '85?" I asked.

"They remind me a little bit of both teams," HoJo replied. "We've got great players out there. We've got a lot of young guys, too. On the '86 team, some of our young guys were me, Kevin Mitchell, Tim Teufel, and Danny Heep, all bench guys that were really, really good. Mitch went on to Frisco after a stop in San Diego to lead the league in home runs in '89. And then I led the league in '91. So you had two guys on the bench on the '86 team that went on to have these years that were really special. You just don't see that nowadays. Still, with this group I see a Brad Miller, a Chris Taylor, and a Mike Zunino, and these other young players that I know will eventually have big, big seasons. And that's what makes this group so exciting. It's challenging, but at the same time it's also pretty special."

Howard Michael Johnson, cigar now exhausted, thanked me for stopping by, walked up the dugout steps, and returned to his tutelage of the upstart Mariners, a team that makes its home 2,871 miles from where Shea Stadium once stood, to continue passing along that old Mets magic.

[Author's note: Since the time of this interview, Johnson has been reassigned to work in the Mariners' minor league system.]

· 4 ·

THE THUG WHO WASN'T

All these years, people used to think I was the bad one. Never. When I came up to the Mets, I started drinking. But I never did anything like Doc and Straw. And once I left the Mets, I ain't had a drink since.

—KEVIN MITCHELL
(METS INFIELDER/OUTFIELDER 1984, 1986)

When I telephoned Kevin Mitchell to set up our interview, he was tending to his Japanese garden after a morning of giving one of his regularly scheduled free baseball clinics to a group of young children at San Diego's Brickyard Batting Cages. His demeanor was warm, cordial, and accommodating, his voice that of a person at peace with his world.

It was a typical day in the life of a man who once had the profoundly inaccurate reputation of being a thug during his days in the Mets' organization.

"Mitch," as he is called by nearly everyone who knows him, went out of his way, driving an hour to meet with me at my hotel overlooking San Diego International Airport near Old Town a few days later. It was one of those typically pristine days in Southern California—brilliant sunshine, blue skies, and a light breeze. Mitch had a noticeable limp as he stepped out of his large, white Tahoe SUV, the result of hips in desperate need of surgery from fifteen years of playing major-league baseball. He wore flip-flops to ease the pain.

"I'm bone-on-bone right now," he would explain. "That's created nerve damage from the shins on down."

We sat in a courtyard near a pool, where children enthusiastically splashed while playing a rather loud game of Marco Polo, and ordered breakfast. The noise didn't bother either of us, particularly not Mitch, who adores children.

"I work with a bunch of kids at the Brickyard—mostly nine- and ten-year-olds," Mitch said with a sparkle in his eyes and a smile that showed off a shiny gold tooth in the middle of the upper row. "It means a lot to me to help them do well and stay on the right track. Some of the parents come up to me and give me hugs for what I'm doing. It's a lot of fun. And I care. I *really* care about the kids. A lot of people don't have money, man. A lot of people out here are charging a lot of money to help kids improve their game. I'm not trying to do that. I'm doing this on my own. I've had opportunities to get back into baseball, including a good one with the Giants, but I don't do it because my passion is here. I prefer working with kids. God has a plan for me."

We weren't more than five minutes into our discussion before Mitch voluntarily brought up the "eight-hundred-pound gorilla in the room," the subject I was told to avoid at all costs by a colleague who said to me beforehand, "Whatever you do, *don't* bring up Straw's story about the cat. Kevin gets very upset about it."

What the colleague was alluding to was the urban legend that, at some point during the '86 season, Mitch had decapitated a girlfriend's cat during an argument with her. The story initially appeared in Dwight Gooden's first autobiography, *Heat*, but had now resurfaced years later when Darryl Strawberry, answering a question during an interview to promote his own latest book, *The Imperfect Marriage: Help for Those Who Think It's Over*, corroborated the tale, telling a *HuffPost Live* reporter, "That's a pretty good story . . . Kevin Mitchell did do that. He's a great guy. Super teammate. Great person. Though he was from San Diego and he was affiliated with gangs quite a bit, and I guess he figured his girlfriend was acting a little crazy so he thought, *I'll kill her cat*."

Perhaps it was Mitch being preemptive, wanting to clear the air on the controversy surrounding him, because he started right in on this topic before I even got to my first question of our interview.

"I got a couple of calls from New York," Mitch began, "and I'm wondering why reporters from New York are calling me. I'm thinking, *What is this?* They're asking me about coming on talk shows. Then a couple of friends called me and said stuff like 'I didn't know you cut a cat's head off.' So then some families of kids I help train at the Brickyard were very concerned and start asking me about it. So I go over to a friend's garage and they're watching the news about it on the Internet. I told them, 'I don't know what's going on. I'm calling Straw.'

"I reached him and asked, 'Why are you mentioning my name on national TV? We've been in the trenches together. Man, I thought we had a good relationship.'"

Mitch explained to me that he could understand how Gooden could have put a story like that in his book: "I don't know what he was on when he wrote that," he said. But Straw's comments deeply hurt him.

"I said, 'Straw, you're a minister, homie. My mom and dad are ministers, you know what I'm saying? You're sitting there lying to God and you're lying to yourself saying I cut a cat's head off. Can you verify my girlfriend's cat and you were standing right there? Bro, I was a young "thundercat." Why would I have one girlfriend in New York when there were like fifteen hundred "J. Lo's" in the city?'

"So I just got on his case," Mitch continued. "He apologized to me and said he was caught off guard. But I said, 'Caught off guard? Bro, you should know what you're going to say when you're talking with people.'"

"So how about now?" I asked. "What would you like Straw to do to fix things?"

"I would like him to go on national TV and tell people the *truth*!" Kevin said without hesitation.

Mitch then took a breath before continuing—calmer now.

"You know, I never mentioned his name in any of *my* interviews," Mitch said. "I would tell the reporters that if they wanted to talk about Darryl Strawberry, they should go talk to Darryl Strawberry. And when I did talk to the press about Straw, it was only in a positive way. It was also always the same with Barry Bonds. I didn't know what Barry was doing off the field. It was his private life. I'd tell reporters 'We're good friends and go out to eat, but if you want to talk to that man, go talk to him.'

"When the cat story came out here in San Diego, there was a lot of negative stuff said about me," Mitch continued. "That's *crazy*, man. I'm an animal lover. How easy would it have been for Straw to just say 'I don't know anything about it'?"

When the infamous story first appeared in *Heat*, Mitch, infuriated, told me he threw his copy of the book away right after reading it. He said he even considered suing Doc over it.

Worse yet, he remembered sports talk show host Jim Rome ripping him about it on his program.

"I called Jim Rome and said, 'You ain't in the jungle. Come to the real jungle down here in Southeast.' He said, 'You think I'm kidding, but I'll come down there.' I said, 'Come on down here and bring your crew and see what happens.' But a guy from his station called me back on the phone and tells me Jim wasn't coming down."

I mentioned how Rome had always had that tough-guy image on his show and brought up the infamous Jim Everett interview when, after baiting the former Rams quarterback by repeatedly calling him "*Chrissy* Everett," the two came to blows right on the air.

Mitch practically jumped out of his chair.

"*I was there!*" Kevin shouted out. "Me and Andre Rison. I thought [the Rome-Everett tussle] was planned. But when the studio guys ran over to try to help Jim [Rome], I knew it was real. I was standing right there, and I told Jim Rome not to do that to me because I'll hit ya! Oh man, he's terrible. He's got bouncers behind him, too."

Mitchell sighed, seemingly resigned to the idea that people are going to believe whatever they want to believe.

"You can't beat the media," Mitch explained. "They're going to say what they're going to say, bro. They can talk all they want about me. As long as my friends and family know what kind of person I am, I'm on top of the world. I don't care, man. Anytime they write something bad about me, I'm famous. And I know I ain't getting no good stuff about me right now."

Because of the gang-infested environment he endured as a teenager in San Diego—one which would later take the life of his stepbrother Donald in a shootout while Kevin played at Triple-A Tidewater—the Mets were reportedly wary of how Mitchell might negatively influence some of the team's other young stars. So, despite his having played only one full season with the Mets in 1986, a year in which he finished third in the Rookie of the Year balloting, showed limitless potential, and brought an intimidation factor to the club, soon after the World Series ended the Mets' front office dealt Mitchell to the San Diego Padres for the talented, yet swaggerless, Kevin McReynolds.

I reassured Mitch that all of his former Mets teammates I had interviewed universally agreed that he had nothing to do with the ill-advised associations and drug and alcohol problems that were encountered by Gooden and Strawberry. But I brought up the popular theory that the Mets' general manager, Frank Cashen, was always leery about him because of his rough and difficult youth. Mitch jumped right in, countering this premise by naming other exceptional athletes who went on to become positive role models despite their original surroundings.

"I grew up in a gang environment," Mitch said, "but so did Marcus Allen, who I played football against. Terrell Davis is another. He grew up with us. All of us down here in San Diego."

I asked him if it was true what I had heard from writer Jeff Pearlman about him *still* having some shrapnel in his back from a gunshot wound he suffered as a part of that gang violence he lived through.

"Yes, I think I still have a little bit left in there," Mitchell said. "But I don't know if that is why my back is bothering me now. I never had back problems my whole life, even when I was playing. Maybe it's because I'm getting older."

Mitch then reflected on the day he got shot.

"I was just in the wrong place at the wrong time," he lamented. "I wasn't the only one that got hit. A friend of mine got hit and lost his arm. I was standing next to people they were probably shooting at."

I suggested to him that baseball may have saved his life, putting him on a path away from the gang lifestyle.

"I'll be honest with you," Mitch told me. "I wanted to play *football*. I was a running back. And I was hanging out with three other guys—all great football players—with promising futures. But they all ended up doing time for robbing dope dealers. They got caught up by the police one day and started to tell on each other. I thought they were going to tell on me. But I was able to sign a baseball contract with the Mets and get away from that life."

| | | | | | |

Once in the minor leagues with the Mets, Mitchell was surrounded by some of the biggest prospects in baseball. Years of last place and near last place finishes by the Mets replenished their farm system with high draft picks.

"We were special in the minor leagues," Mitch remembered. "We made the Triple-A World Series. Played with Straw Man. Terry Blocker. La Schelle Tarver, a good left-handed leadoff guy. Lenny [Dykstra]. In fact, I played with Lenny since Lynchburg. We knew we were going to be special coming up."

I told him I was driving up to LA to see Lenny the next day.

"He's talking better now," Mitch told me. "I saw him a couple of months ago after he got out of prison. I heard Lenny provoked a deputy in Orange County jail and got his teeth knocked out. You *can't* do that. They *hate* that. They will hurt you bad, man. They'll put you in a rubber room and work you over."

As for the Straw Man, Mitch reflected back on his first encounter with him in a 1981 pickup basketball game at an Instructional League training facility in St. Petersburg, Florida, and how he gained immediate "street cred" with his new professional teammates.

"They asked me if I wanted to play," Mitch began. "It was only my first week and I hardly knew any of them—not even Strawberry. In fact, before meeting him, I thought he was white. They kept calling him Straw. But I did know Randy Milligan, having grown up with him, and he knew how tough it was in San Diego.

"Anyway, every time I got the ball, I shot. So Straw kept calling out my name, calling me a pussy. Then he kept calling out Crenshaw Crips on me, like he was with the Crips gang in LA. I said, 'Hey man, I didn't come up here to deal with that stuff. I've come too far.' He then called me a motherfucker and pushed me and it was on from there. I picked up Straw and threw him on his back. Mike Davis, Lloyd McClendon, and some of the other guys grabbed me. I felt like if Straw were on top of me they wouldn't have grabbed *him*. So I went back to my room to grab a bat.

"While I was gone," Mitch continued, "Milligan told them they were messing with the wrong guy, saying, 'This guy's got a reputation.' Anyway, I was ready to go. But then I was called into Davey Johnson's office. Davey asked me about Straw, and I said I didn't know nothing about him. He said, 'You don't know who you were fighting? He was the first-round pick in the nation.' He then asked me what happened, and I told him he pushed me first, grabbed my head, and brought up the Crenshaw Crips. I said I didn't know nothing about no Crenshaw Crips. I was from San Diego. I grew up in a Blood neighborhood, man. You throw Crenshaw Crips in my face like Straw did and I had to do something."

Mitch then grinned when reminiscing some more about how he took Straw down and how the fight had become legendary.

"Straw still won't admit it. Like when I came over to play in the American League, Derek [Jeter] and some of the other Yankees came over and asked me if I really had a fight with Straw. I told them, 'Go ask Straw. He knows what happened. He won't admit it, but he got beat up.'

"But we're good friends now," Mitch said with sincerity, "and we don't talk about what happened anymore. And because we're good friends now, it's why the cat story hurts me."

Another longtime teammate of Mitchell's both in the Mets' farm system and on the '86 team, Ed Hearn, said there was no other player in his entire career he would have wanted in his foxhole more than Mitch. I asked Mitchell what he believed were some of the elements that make up a good teammate.

After a long pause and then an exhale, Mitch said, "We had a lot of teammates you could learn from in New York. No matter what happens on the field, you have to have the backs of all your players. And we all did. That's what made us such good players and gave us the chemistry we had. I learned a lot from playing with those guys. The veterans like Keith, Mookie, George Foster, and Gary Carter were positive every day.

"When I played with Keith," Mitch continued, "he would say stuff like 'Mitch, we've got a little game we're going to play today: "Who's going to hit the first home run?" or "Who's going to get the first base hit?"' He played those games with me and gave me the motivation to go out there and get them before him, even though I was going up against 'Super Max'! That's what I called Keith—*Super Max*."

I ask Mitch if he meant "Super Mex," as "Mex" is the common nickname given for Keith despite the fact he is not of Mexican origin (Hernandez is Spanish-Irish).

"No, 'Super Max,'" Mitch said. "Super *Maximillian*! I called him that because he was like a superhero. I never saw a guy play first base like he did. He always knew before a play what he was going to do. Unbelievable. And he still looks good!"

Mitchell went on about how even though he represented a threat to the playing time of much of the roster—Kevin played six positions and received the nickname "World" from Carter because he could play everywhere—his teammates were eager to help him out.

"When I first came up in '84," Mitch said, "I had a lot of help from Hubie Brooks in the infield. But in '86, Ray-Ray [Knight]— or 'Trap Dog' as I liked to call him because when he got mad his cheeks looked like trap jaws—really helped me out at third base and shortstop."

I brougth up how he and Knight were widely considered to be the "enforcers" on the '86 Mets, giving the club an element of intimidation to go along with their talent when facing off against opponents.

"*Intimidation*. That's part of the game," Mitch told me. "I always teach my kids that. Mentally, you've got to be strong. You've got to be like you came up from South Beach [San Diego]. Look at Adam Jones, another guy from San Diego. He's not intimidated by nothing, man. He goes out and plays the game hard because of where he grew up at. Intimidation is so important. You *need* that type of personality."

Mitch continued, saying he would try to teach that intimidation factor to his teammates, though sometimes unsuccessfully.

"Take Sid Fernandez," Mitch said. "When I was in New York, I always used to sit on the bench with Sid, and he would say to me how he hated pitching inside because he was afraid he might hit somebody. And I was like, 'Sid, you've got to pitch in to establish the ball away. You've got two pitches—a fastball and a curveball. If you're not getting one over, you've got to do something.'

"Then when I was with the Giants, and I faced Sid," Mitch

continued, "I'd come out of the clubhouse in Candlestick when he was warming up and I'd tell him, 'I've got one off you today.' That meant I was going to hit a home run off of him. I used to tell him that all the time. And I *would* take him deep by putting that in his head. The game is so much about intimidation, man. That's why Pedro Martinez was so good. He knew he didn't have to hit, so he'd talk crazy on that mound and throw at anybody. If he was pitching in the National League and had to hit, I'll bet he wouldn't be acting like that."

The Mets got into four bench-clearing brawls in 1986, and Mitch was in the middle of all of them, helping defend his teammates and their turf. To this day, he is remembered as the quintessential teammate by nearly every member of the team, including manager Davey Johnson.

"I was at the opening of Straw's restaurant about five years ago and I was sitting next to Davey," Mitch told me. "While someone was taking a group photo, Davey said in front of everyone that he regretted the Mets trading me. He said he never wanted to trade me. He wasn't speaking for Frank Cashen, but for himself."

I asked Mitch what his player-manager relationship was like with Davey, having played for him first with the Mets and then later with the Reds, and he used an anecdote dating all the way back to his first time in a big-league spring training camp at Al Lang Field in 1984 to best describe how the relationship was always a strong and loose one.

"Near the end of camp, I got sent back down to Tidewater," Mitch began. "After I found out, I went into Davey's office and I took a knife in there. I said, *'If you cut me, I'll cut you!'*"

Mitch started laughing after looking at my shocked expression.

"It was just a joke!" Mitch assured me, still laughing. "'Uncle

Bill'—Bill Robinson—wanted me to play a joke on Davey. I eventually told Davey, 'Me and Uncle Bill are just playing a trick on you. Don't press charges against me!'"

Mitch said the three of them had a good laugh about it.

"When Davey [finally] gave me the chance to play," Mitch went on, "I was just thankful to be there playing with a bunch of great guys."

I wondered aloud how the Mets—with otherwise astute baseball people running the club at the time—could have moved forward with trading Mitch, along with Shawn Abner and Stanley Jefferson, to San Diego for Kevin McReynolds.

"Because they thought I was a bad influence on Darryl Strawberry and Dwight Gooden," Mitch answered. "But how could I be a bad influence on those guys when they were in the big leagues before me? I was a young kid. I wasn't the one on alcohol and drugs. I was the scapegoat. I thought I was going to be a Met forever. But even now, they don't do anything for me, not one thing. They don't invite me back."

It's hard to comprehend, but Mitch's single to keep the Mets alive in the bottom of the tenth inning of Game Six of the '86 World Series was to be his last at bat as a New York Met. I brought it up, and there was first sadness in Mitch's eyes, which shortly was replaced by a gleam.

"I was talking with Wally Backman in the kitchen one day late that ['86] season," Mitch told me. "Wally said, 'We're going to the World Series this year. Mitch, they ain't never getting rid of you. You're one of their prospects.' But then shortly after arriving home in San Diego after the World Series, I was going over to my grandmother's house, the only address the media had for me. Channel 10 and Channel 8 News were there. I thought something had happened. But the press was in there talking with my grandmother about how I had just been traded to the Padres. I loved being at home, but in that situation, I didn't want to be playing there."

But then, recalling the at bat when he came to the plate with the Mets down 5–3 with two outs and Carter on first, his spirits picked up again. But first, he wanted to make it clear that contrary to rumors over the years—while he was, in fact, back in the clubhouse making airline reservations home to San Diego when he was called to the plate, he was *still* in his uniform, unlike the stories that have circulated that he was already changed.

"People say I was in there either undressed or in my street clothes, but that's not true," Mitch said. "All year long, I hadn't faced a right-handed pitcher, only lefties. Now all of a sudden I'm called on to hit against [right-hander] Calvin Schiraldi. I think it was Mookie who came into the clubhouse to come get me, told me I was hitting for Rick Aguilera."

I agreed with Mitch that I would have been as surprised as he was, because the only viable left-handed reliever for the Red Sox was Joe Sambito, and there was no chance he would come into the game in that situation.

"Yeah, it was just weird," Mitch said. "I think they were trying to set me up for failure, to make the last out of the World Series."

"*Really?*" I asked, intimating that that may have been unrealistic.

"That's how I took it," he said. "They hadn't had me hit against right-handed pitching all year. They've got me playing just against lefties, and all of a sudden you're going to put me in against Schiraldi?"

But if there was ever a right-hander that Mitch felt good about coming up against with the World Series on the line, he was about to face him. It was as if Kevin knew what Schiraldi was going to throw.

"Schiraldi was my roommate on the road in the minors with the Mets," Mitch said, "and sometimes we would sit in our room and he would tell me how he would pitch me if we ever faced each other. He always said, 'Fastball in, slider away.' So the first pitch he threw to me was a fastball in. So the next pitch I was looking for a slider. He gave me a slider and I got a base hit. I had remembered our talks since we were in the minor leagues together."

I brought up the idea that maybe Davey had that information and that was why he used Mitch to hit in that situation.

"No, only Schiraldi and I knew," Mitch answered. "I actually watched Schiraldi on a talk show following the series and he recalled those conversations we had. I was so locked into his throwing a slider that if he had thrown anything else, I would have been hit because I was leaning over the plate so much."

Knight would follow Mitch's single with one of his own to score Carter and cut the Red Sox lead to 5–4. On the play, Mitch took a chance and ran hard to third by running on a ball that dropped into right center between Dave Henderson and Dwight Evans, who had a rifle for an arm.

"It didn't matter which outfielder was going to get it, I was going. I could run a little bit, man," Mitch said, grinning.

Mitch taking third turned out to be a pivotal play in the game. With Mookie Wilson coming to the plate, Red Sox manager John McNamara brought in Bob Stanley to relieve Schiraldi.

"As soon as I get to third and see that Stanley was coming in," Mitch said, "[third base coach] Buddy Harrelson tells me, 'He's known for bouncing balls. Be prepared. He's going to bounce one.' If you're a rookie like I was and your coach is telling you something like that, the first thing you think is *Why would the pitcher want to bounce a ball in that kind of situation with a man on third?* But sure enough, he bounces one and I score the tying run. I'm in the dugout telling guys, 'This guy [Harrelson] read Stanley's mind. Buddy told me he was going to bounce one. It's like he had him in his pocket or something. I can't believe he just said that!'"

And then Mitch smiled a similar grin to the one he had in the dugout after scoring the tying run moments before Mookie's famous ground ball got past Bill Buckner to win the game.

| | | | | | |

So much has been made about how the character of the Mets changed after they traded Mitchell away and then basically allowed Ray Knight, the reigning World Series MVP and one of the clubhouse leaders, to walk as a free agent after a lowball salary offer. I asked Mitch if he believed they would have had another world championship in them had the team been kept intact.

"*Another* world championship?" Mitch asked rhetorically. "Yes, indeed! The team chemistry, the fun we had, our Mets team would have won a *few* more! That's because everyone on that team was a *player*. We didn't have any average guys. We had a bench that could go out there and play nine positions. You could put a whole new team on that field and win. And we had *fun*! We weren't tight at all. We loved the game. The veterans made it fun. The older guys made us who we are today. As younger players, we watched those guys. They made us the players we became.

"And if I hadn't played in New York City," Mitch continued, "I probably wouldn't have become the player I was. Because by playing in New York, I knew I could go and play anywhere else and it would be a piece of cake."

Mitchell was right. He soon became one of the most feared hitters in baseball shortly after leaving the Mets. After the Padres misguidedly traded him to San Francisco, he would go on to capture the 1989 National League MVP Award by leading the senior circuit with 47 home runs and 125 RBIs in helping the Giants reach the World Series.

Kevin had transformed himself from a line drive hitter with the Mets into a slugger with the Giants. I asked him how he was able to do that, especially in a notoriously terrible hitter's venue like Candlestick Park.

"Dusty Baker and Willie Mays," Mitch answered without a pause. "They told me where the wind tunnel was at Candlestick— right center field. So I learned to hit the ball to right center. You hit it well there and it's gone. Whenever we were down a run, I used to try to hit the ball to that part of the field. I hit twenty-four of my forty-seven home runs to right center field in my MVP season of '89. And when the opposing pitchers pitched me inside, I pulled it to left. It was like a pinball machine."

We then talked about Johnny B. "Dusty" Baker, his manager with the Giants. I had met Dusty when I cowrote the autobiography of Glenn Burke, one of Dusty's Dodger teammates and friends. In my experience, I found Baker to be a talented baseball man and a true gentleman. I told Mitch that no matter how busy Dusty might have been preparing for a game, he seemed to always make the time to speak with me either behind the batting cage or in his office, about baseball or whatever I was writing about at the time.

Mitch smiled and agreed.

"Dusty, he's the top, man. That's *Papa*! He's awesome, bro. Dusty could make the most average guy be the best player in the game. The way he talks, man, it's like E. F. Hutton; everybody stops what they're doing and listens to him!"

Mitch then talked about how Dusty taught him about the mental part of the game.

"Sometimes when watching a game with my friends," Mitch said, "I play a game of calling which pitches are about to be thrown. After guessing correctly a bunch of times in a row, one of them might ask how I knew those pitches were coming. I tell them it's all about situations and counts on the hitter. You learn what a pitcher is going to do. He's trying to trick you and you're trying to trick him. Dusty used to tell me if a pitcher's throwing a bunch of sliders, just swing ugly on the next one you see. Ninety-nine percent of the time, they're going to come back and throw you that same pitch. Then you know what's coming and what to do with it. That Dusty is a smart man."

Mitch then brought up an example of the tough-love part of Dusty and the special interest he took in him.

"I once hit two home runs in a game and Dusty pulled me to the side and told me we needed to work in the cage that night. I said, 'Dust, I just hit two home runs.' He said, 'Well, I see something in your swing we need to work on right away.' So after everybody's gone, we worked on my hitting. Dusty was just like that. That's why I loved him, man."

I told Mitch it broke my heart when the Cincinnati Reds fired Baker following the 2013 campaign, especially after he'd had his third ninety-plus-win season in four years. Word was he wouldn't lay blame on his coaches to the front office and it cost him his job. But I speculated that perhaps Dusty wanted some time off or else another managerial job surely would have found him by now.

"Well, yes," Mitch agreed. "I think he just wants to concentrate on his son, Darren. Man, he can hit."

I asked if that was, by any chance, the little three-year-old Giants' batboy that, in the 2002 World Series, famously raced to home plate to collect a bat and nearly got knocked over by J. T. Snow, who scored on a hit.

Mitchell started laughing.

"Yep," he said. "He ain't no little kid anymore. Good left-handed hitter and throws right-handed. Really great!"

[Author's note: Baker still works with Darren on his baseball development, but became the new Washington Nationals' Manager on November 3, 2015.]

Hitting wasn't the only thing that brought Mitchell fame in San Francisco. Once, while playing left field in St. Louis in 1989, he made one of the most unbelievable catches you will ever see in a baseball game. Racing back and toward the left field line, he reached up to make a bare-handed catch and snare a ball hit by Ozzie Smith. It is shown all the time at ballparks and is a huge hit on *YouTube*. I asked Mitch why he didn't use his glove on that play.

"When I was a kid, I grew up in all the boys' clubs," he explained. "We played Wiffle ball a lot, and that's what you did—catch balls with your bare hand. At the time, it wasn't a big deal to me. I didn't even realize what I had just done. After I made the catch, all I was thinking about was getting up to the plate to hit against John Tudor [after the inning ended]. I remembered facing him before and doing well. And I ended up hitting a home run. As I came into the dugout after circling the bases, our catcher, Terry Kennedy, came up to me and said, 'Mitch, do you realize what you did?' I said, 'Yeah, I hit a home run.' Kennedy replied, 'Mitch, you caught a ball without your glove!' I simply told him, 'It's just something that happened.'"

Everyone was pretty awestruck, Mitch told me.

Except for one man.

"Willie Mays called me and said he didn't teach me that," Mitch explained. "I don't want to say how Willie *really* said it and sit here and cuss. When the Giants moved me from the infield to the out-field, Willie worked with me, and wasn't too pleased with the bare-handed catch. But for a while, every field I went to after that, the fans booed me for using my glove. Some told me to throw my glove to them in the stands. Man, they would get on me."

The father of the children who were splashing around in the nearby pool overheard us talking and asked if the gentleman I was speaking with was Kevin Mitchell. Mitch nodded with a big smile, shook the man's hand, and couldn't have been more gracious if he tried. The man brought his wife over and told all of us how he'd had a baseball card of Kevin's in a protected plastic sheet for years.

While Mitch will forever be remembered as a member of the adored '86 Mets in New York, his greatest seasons were played in California.

Mitchell finished out his career in 1998 with the Oakland A's, his ninth professional team including a one-year stint in 1995 with the Fukuoka Daiei Hawks in Japan. He ended up with a .284 bat-ting average, 234 major-league home runs, and 760 RBIs. But he still looks back sometimes at what could have been with the Mets and is surprised today's team doesn't make more use of the expertise from that great '86 club.

"I tell everybody that I just don't understand it," Mitch said. "I do see Tim Teufel out there [coaching third]. Teufel's an awesome guy and I love him. He was my bench guy. But I don't know why they distance themselves from other players from that team. I mean, why do you fire Mookie? Mookie is the nicest guy. There's no reason you should fire him. And then they hire guys from outside of the organi-zation. A lot of the young players they have are coming into New York not knowing what to expect. If you're average in New York, you're going to get highlights. You do well, and you're going to get stars and lights over your head. Gary Carter should have had the manager's job. Or Wally Backman—that guy's a winner. Wins everywhere he goes."

So I asked Mitchell if he had any theories on when the '86 team began to get shunned from any positions of importance within the Mets' organization.

"What I've heard is it started when Steve Phillips was the GM [from 1997 to 2003]. Steve played with us [in the Mets' farm system]. He couldn't hit his way out of a wet paper bag, and I think he was mad at all of us. This is what I've heard. I didn't even know that it was Steve at first when he became their general manager, because of all the gray hair. Mookie told me it was him. I said to Mookie, 'That's the Steve Phillips that played in the minor leagues with me? He went gray young.'"

I told Mitch how the fans desperately wanted to see that '86 Mets team represented on the field or in the front office—and use the enthusiastic support that Backman is receiving to one day pilot the team—and he jumped right in.

"Everybody had swagger on that team," Mitchell said. "*Everybody.* Even quiet Mookie had that swagger, that walk, that little tippytoe walk. Everybody had a different swagger, but when we stepped between the white lines, no matter who was on the field— Danny Heep, Mookie Wilson, George Foster, Lenny Dykstra, me—it didn't matter. Even when Kevin Elster came up, even *he* had that swagger. And when we took a loss, we still had it. We knew we'd come back the next day and beat up on everybody, no matter what happened the game before."

| | | | | | | |

Today, in addition to his baseball clinics, gardening, and an active church life, Mitchell owns two hair salons—the one he runs is called, appropriately enough, Homerun Hair Design, while his girl-friend Celeste manages Ohh Girl.

I asked how those businesses are doing.

"Oh, very well. Black people want to get their hair cut," Mitch said with a laugh. "Not me, though. I don't have any hair left, so . . ."

We shared a laugh and started talking about how the barbershop and the African-American culture have merged in some hilarious cinematic comedies. We referenced the *Barbershop* movies starring Cedric the Entertainer and Ice Cube, but I told him my favorite barbershop scenes were in *Coming to America* with Eddie Murphy playing several different characters.

Mitch agreed and jumped right in.

"Oh yeah. When they go into the barbershop and the guy tells the prince, 'You need to get one of those good Christian girls,' then cuts his little ponytail off. *So funny!*"

Mitch said many of his customers come in every two weeks.

I asked, "Because they want to keep it tight, right?"

"Yes, especially in San Diego," Mitch replied. "You get a perm, you're going to sweat it out in this heat. It's gonna be quick. I used to have a perm back in the day. Rollers and everything."

| | | | | | | |

While life is good for Kevin Mitchell at middle age, it has not been without its share of problems. For one, he claims his last agent burned him for a good deal of his savings on bad investments.

And then there was a run-in with a golfer on a course a few years back that resulted in Mitch getting sentenced to probation and anger management classes.

"What the heck happened with that?" I asked.

"This short guy and I were going at it for three or four months,"

Mitch began. "So one day while I was golfing we got into it and he kept calling me the N-word. Somebody told me he might have a gun. So when he reached into his bag, I pushed him. He tried to get me to go away [to jail] for four years."

But nothing could possibly compare or prepare him for the heartache of losing one of his four daughters, nineteen-year-old Bethany, back in 2010.

Mitchell, with a heavy heart, explained:

"While my daughter was attending college up in San Mateo, she was strangled in her house by a live-in boyfriend. I knew nothing about him . . . didn't even know they were living together. Not long before it happened, she slept at my house one weekend and told me she had a girlfriend as a roommate. I found out later the police had been called to [her and her boyfriend's] home several times before because of domestic disputes."

Not long after his daughter's death, Mitch experienced more emotional misery. He was miffed that his estranged brother Tommy didn't show up at Bethany's funeral, but soon found out the reason why.

"The last I heard, Tommy was married and worked as a bouncer in Reno," Mitch explained. "He was playing baseball in a men's league for a team called the Reno Stars. I hadn't seen him in twenty years. Soon after Bethany's funeral, one of his friends called me and says, 'Your brother gave me this number a long time ago and said if something ever happened to him to call you. Well, I found him lying on the floor . . . he can't walk or leave the house.' I said, 'Are you talking about my brother? My brother's a good athlete, used to run every day, what are you talking about?'"

Mitch continued with understandable sadness in his voice.

"Turns out no one was taking care of him. So me and my mom drove up there. We opened the door and there was my brother, but we hardly could recognize him. I told my mom, 'That's not my brother.' We put him in the car and drove home. He was suffering from brain cancer. He said the reason he didn't show up at my daughter's funeral was because he didn't want to be a burden."

Kevin then recalled Tommy's last days in hospice.

"The day before he died, stuff was coming out of his eyes, he was bleeding through his stomach. The doctor told me he wasn't going to live past nine o'clock the next day, a Friday. I saw him that Thursday for an hour. He was just eighty pounds, but he was so strong. He was trying to take his catheter and other things he was hooked up to out. The nurses tried to grab him. And I'm sweating like a hog, holding his arms, trying to hold him down, but *he's* tossing *me* around! I couldn't understand how he was still so strong. He couldn't talk as the tumor was coming down his throat, so I don't know why he was trying to pull everything out.

"The next morning a little after nine o'clock," Mitch continued, "my mother calls me from the couch in hospice to tell me he was gone. He was only forty-eight years old."

And then, Mitch's sadness in talking about Bethany and Tommy was replaced by the only real display of anger that he showed all morning.

"Tommy's wife shows up at the funeral after leaving my brother in that state," Mitch said, voice rising. "She ended up getting money from his death. She got a *brand new truck*!"

After a pause and a seemingly empty glance toward the pool area, Kevin became melancholy again in talking about how he'd handled those deaths.

"In my mind right now, I still don't think Tommy's gone," he said. "And, you know, with my daughter, I didn't cry or nothing. It hasn't hit me yet. When my mom calls me and starts talking about my brother, I get pissed about it. I don't want to hear it. I don't even have pictures of my brother or daughter in my house. I want to remember them like they were. I was always the strong one in the family, the lion. So if something happened in the family, everybody called me. I have always taken care of family and friends—that's the kind of person I was. But I can't do anything now. I've got to take care of myself now because I'm hurting."

These days, Mitchell also must take better care of himself physically. Despite his pleasant demeanor, Mitch deals with chronic pain.

"I know I've got to have surgery on these hands," he said, looking down at them. "I've got carpal tunnel syndrome from all those years swinging a bat—they hurt so bad. And again, my hip problems from playing ball have caused nerve damage down my leg."

Mitch rolls up his pant leg slightly to show me an affected part of his leg.

"See that?" Mitch says. "I have atrophy in this one. It's been too long with the nerve damage—nothing can be done about it now. I've contacted Major League Baseball to take care of the hip surgery I need through their insurance. I'm trying to get them to take care of it, man. I never had a job. I didn't ever type or play on the computer. All this happened from playing ball. Three whole years have been spent trying to get it taken care of. I lost two toenails—they just fell off. Another one's turning black, too. All from the nerve damage. I can't wear shoes. Everywhere I go I have to wear flip-flops. I went out and got a lawyer. I shouldn't have to pay."

Our meeting ended, and as we walked slowly back to his SUV, Mitch told me how much he enjoyed our talk and then, taking note of what he called my laid-back style, said, "Hey man, you don't seem like you're from New York."

"I get that all the time," I told him. "People who don't know me often think I'm either from Florida or California."

"I can see that," he said with a smile.

And with that, one of the greatest, most misunderstood ball-players of his generation drove off.

· 5 ·

LENNY LONGS FOR NEW SEASON

I see myself on top. That's the place I've always been. I won't
be in the mill, I guarantee you that.

—LENNY DYKSTRA
ON WHERE HE SEES HIMSELF IN FIVE YEARS
(METS CENTER FIELDER, 1985–89)

I was sitting comfortably on a plush couch with oversized pillows in
the lobby of the Hotel Palomar, an upscale, swanky hotel on Wilshire
Boulevard in the Westwood section of Los Angeles. To my right, a
fireplace was encased in a marble wall, and I wondered why such a
source of heat, while decorative, would truly be necessary in this city.
To my left, a well-heeled couple appeared agitated about being kept
waiting an extra few minutes before meeting with a hotel representa-
tive to plan an event there. Outside, it was just another typical sun-
splashed early fall afternoon in LA.

I was there to meet with Lenny Dykstra, the three-time all-star
and the onetime perfect baseball player for both the Mets and the
Phillies, for a three o'clock interview. Lenny had been hard to find
for this meeting. Nobody, not even the Major League Baseball
Alumni Association, seemed to have any contact information for

him. He had been out of a federal penitentiary for a little over a year, after having served time after pleading no contest to charges ranging from grand theft auto to filing a false financial report, and was keeping a low profile in trying to rebuild his life.

But then Heather Quinlan, a filmmaker and friend, suggested I reach out to one of Lenny's longtime associates, Marc Falcone, to see if he could put Dykstra in touch with me. Falcone, a personable gentleman from Philadelphia with an easy laugh, has acted as a kind of guardian angel to Dykstra, helping him with some of his business dealings and making sure he gets to his appointments on time. Falcone could have certainly been of some assistance to Lenny on this particular day.

As three o'clock became three-fifteen, I called Lenny on his cell phone to see if he was on his way down to the lobby.

"Dude, I'm so sorry, man," Dykstra said. "Can we meet at four, instead?"

Lenny seemed genuinely sorry for the delay and I happily agreed to the new time. I was actually somewhat amused by this, as earlier in the day one of Lenny's former teammates had laughed after being told I had an appointment with Dykstra, saying, "I hope you have a few hours to wait for him."

Four o'clock became four-thirty, and then, at last, after a couple of more calls up to his room, at five o'clock, Lenny appeared before me in the lobby, having chosen to go with the untucked button-down shirt look, with the sleeves rolled up and cell phone headset buds dangling around his neck. The light brown hair with the slight curl on top that he'd sported during his playing days had been replaced by a look more suited to a banker—straight, salt-and-pepper in color, and combed perfectly to the side. His speech had improved markedly over past interviews I had seen him do on television, when it was slurred and slower, almost like that of a punch-drunk boxer.

Lenny and I entered BLVD 16, a dimly lit lounge on the other side of the lobby, and he led me to a cornered off, off-limits section in the back. We took a table anyway. Dykstra immediately set up his Mac laptop and inserted his cell phone earbuds, forewarning me that he would have to take some calls during our meeting. He pulled out a can of Monster Energy drink from his computer bag and, while multitasking, began interviewing *me*!

"When is this book coming out?" Lenny asked.

"Spring of 2016," I said.

"Is that how long it takes, about a year for a book?"

"Oh sure, it takes time to write a book of this length."

"What do they raise now for books? I heard that the market went down."

Lenny was more than interested in the publishing process, telling me he was in the beginning stages of an autobiography.

Then Lenny reversed course.

"You know, I got all my teeth knocked out in prison."

"What happened with that?" I asked.

"Ohhhh! We're suing, man. They're fucked!"

By "they," Dykstra was alluding to the LA County Sheriff's Office for alleged abusive violence toward him and others while he was incarcerated.

"They got indicted by the FBI. You know that, right?" Dykstra asked.

Lenny quickly punches up one of the stories on his laptop and shows me an article under the headline LOS ANGELES COUNTY SHERIFF DEPUTIES INDICTED IN FBI INVESTIGATION.

"It happened in the LA County jail," he said. "I am the poster child. They got indicted, dude, for exactly what they did to *me*—beating jail inmates. They arrested them, dude! You have to understand something: What they did to me, they covered it all up. They lied. So on one hand, they got the best of me in prison, but that's a whole different story."

"Did the punishment fit the crime?" I asked, referring to the allegations that put him in jail.

"No, there's no crime, dude," Lenny said. "For selling two pieces of furniture? No crime. The crime was that I was going to expose the whole bankruptcy system, dude. I was one hour away from exposing the whole system. It's very complicated."

According to the U.S. Attorney's Office, Dykstra sold furnishings and fixtures from his mansion for cash at a consignment store without the permission of a bankruptcy trustee.

"Dude," Dykstra continued, "they knocked my teeth out and I was in the hospital for five days. They lied about it to cover it up. They threw the video away and everything. But I can't talk much more about it because of the lawsuit."

At this point, I shut off my tape recorder for the first of several times at his request, as he shared some of the more disturbing details of his time in prison and other details of his life with me, off the record. I respected his request, and we built a trust with one another over the rest of the three-hour meeting. I sensed it was therapeutic for him on some level. He told me a couple of times how the eye contact we had with one another was important to him. He also seemed a little self-conscious about his appearance, asking me, if I hadn't known in advance about his missing teeth, if I would have noticed their absence. I told him the truth: that I wouldn't have unless he showed me.

The waitress arrived and Lenny glanced quickly at the menu before ordering us nacho chips and fondue. We changed the subject.

"How are your sons doing? They're doing well in baseball, aren't they?" I asked.

"Yeah, they're awesome," Dykstra replied. "Cutter just made the all-star team in Double-A. He signed with Washington and is going to big-league camp next year. And by the grace of God, I got out and was released in time to spend the whole high school senior year with Luke, who just got drafted by the Braves. What I've done since I was out was spend time with him and was there for him every day, worked with him, and kept him straight, all while doing my community service work. They had me do five hundred hours of community service."

"You were mostly serving food to the homeless, right?" I asked.

Dykstra nods, then takes a business call.

Watching Lenny work the phone, I can tell that he is serious, perhaps even obsessed, about regaining at least some of the wealth and respect he earned in his post–baseball career business life, before everything came tumbling down.

Just how successful was he?

A 2008 financial statement by one of Dykstra's creditors says he was worth fifty-eight million dollars. A source close to Lenny said the figure likely peaked at nearly one hundred million. He owned a chain of highly successful car wash businesses, then had a terrific run in the stock market, with none other than CNBC's Jim Cramer calling him "one of the great ones in this business."

Lenny then started a company called The Player's Club, designed, ironically enough, to help current and former athletes with their expensive lifestyles while securing financial freedom for the rest of their lives.

His residence?

A $17.5 million estate he purchased from NHL superstar Wayne Gretzky in Thousand Oaks, California. The four structures, pool, two hot tubs, and the requisite tennis court were built on seven acres of property surrounded by the Santa Monica Mountains.

His toys?

They included both a Maybach and a Rolls-Royce for driving around town and a Gulfstream II private jet for flying around the country.

But then in a spectacular fall, Dykstra claimed to be a victim of bank mortgage fraud, which forced him to file for Chapter 11 bankruptcy protection. In 2009, his bankruptcy filing showed he had just $50,000 in assets and $31 million in debts.

When our food arrived, Lenny asked the server, "So, hey dude, fondue is *this* stuff?"

"Yes, cheese fondue."

"Okay, thank you," Lenny said, as he began dipping a nacho chip into it.

He was interested in talking about the Mookie Wilson autobiography I coauthored, and then pointed out how it was difficult for him sharing center field with Wilson.

"It became hard," Dykstra said. "When I first got to the big leagues, I knew I could play every day, and when I couldn't, it became frustrating. Obviously, I proved I could play every day. I led the league in hits two years after [becoming an everyday player]."

Still, he was quick to point out how he has nothing but the highest regard for Wilson.

"Mookie was just respectful, man," Dykstra said. "He made me feel good. He never was disrespectful to me, ever. Mookie's a class act. I was popular with the fans and so was he, so it was kind of a weird deal. But he and I never got sideways. I don't know what he told you."

"He told me it was very hard for the two of you because you

both felt you should be starting," I said. "But still, when you came up from the minors, he wanted to help you."

"He did," Dykstra said. "Not only did he want to, he did. Like I said, a class act. But also a good husband, a good father, a good person to be like. He lived right. No drugs. That's the right way to live. I don't know if there's any taller compliment than that. I mean, I come up to take his position and he treats me with respect."

"If the roles were reversed, how would you have handled that situation?" I asked.

Lenny was quick to answer.

"Not as good as him. Oh, and I loved watching him run."

The platoon between Lenny and Mookie lasted five seasons before Dykstra was shipped to the Phillies along with Roger McDowell for Juan Samuel in 1989.

"One of the many fucking bad moves the Mets made," Lenny said regarding the trade.

"Was it a surprise to you?" I asked.

"That was a weird deal, man," Dykstra recalled, "because we were playing at Philly and I always fucking raked it at that yard, man. I was playing that day and was having a good game. And then in the seventh inning, Davey said to me, 'You're done.' And I'm like, 'What the fuck? What do you mean I'm done?' But Davey goes, 'No, you're done.'

"So I got pissed, went up the runway, and sat in front of the TV in the clubhouse. I hear Harry Kalas, the greatest guy on the planet, the best announcer, say, [Lenny breaks into a dead-on impression of Kalas] 'A lot of action today at The Vet.' So I'm sitting in a cubbyhole watching the game, just waiting for the tap when somebody says, 'Davey wants to see you in his office.'

"I get in there to see Davey, and the nudist dude was in there, too."

"The *nudist* dude?" I asked.

"The general manager. Joe McIlvaine."

Lenny was alluding to how, following his time as the Mets' general manager, McIlvaine was arrested for public lewdness for nude sunbathing on Jensen Beach in Florida.

"So Davey and the nudist called me in, and Davey said, 'Thank you for your service and what you did for us, helping us win the World Series. You've been traded to the Phillies.'

"I said, 'Wait, isn't that the team in the other clubhouse? So do I walk over there after just beating the fuck out of them?'

"It was kind of a very tricky moment, dude," Dykstra continued. "So the Phillies' general manager ended up meeting me and bringing me over there."

Lenny is still a fan of the Mets, though he isn't pleased with the way they've gone about their business in recent years. [Author's note: The interview took place prior to the Mets' National League championship season.] His passion was evident.

"The Mets aren't even on the map," Dykstra said. "Who are the Mets? Are they still in the league, even? I don't understand. I mean,. why isn't Wally Backman the manager of that team? It's fucking crazy. How long has he been managing in the minor leagues now? Twenty-five years?"

I agreed with Lenny, offering that all Backman does is win in the minor leagues. But aside from the Arizona Diamondbacks once hiring him and then firing him four days later, after a background check revealed he had two arrests and past financial issues, no team has given him a shot at the big leagues in more than a decade.

After a pause, Lenny reflected back on playing in the Northeast.

"The Mets, New York, man, I loved playing there," he said. "In fact, I was blessed by the grace of God to play in the two best fucking sports cities on the planet—New York and Philly. For me, it didn't get any better because I'm not a pussy. I want [the fans] to bring it. You play, you fuck up, they bring it. You know what? That's what it should be like. Here in LA, these fucking fans, man, are a bunch of pussies. They leave in the seventh inning and don't care what the score is."

Lenny was on a roll now, not to be stopped.

"And the Mets' manager now? Who's this clown?"

"You mean Terry Collins," I replied.

"I mean, are you *kidding* me?" Lenny asked incredulously, his voice rising. "I can picture all the kids and parents at home saying, *Hurry, get in the car! We don't want to miss watching Terry Collins bring out the lineup card!* When [Jeff] Bagwell and [Craig] Biggio hate him, something's wrong. [Author's note: Collins managed them both in Houston from 1994–96 and, at that time, had a reputation in baseball circles as an old-school manager who was inflexible and unwilling to adapt to the modern-day player. To his credit, he has become far more player-friendly and patient in his current managerial stint.] Those two are the greatest dudes ever—those are *gamers*, man. Collins? I don't even know the guy, but I know he's a pussy. You don't want to go to war for him. And the Mets *re-signed* him? And passed on *Backman*?! The business they're in is the business of putting people in the seats. *Entertainment!* So if you're going to be in that business, get people to entertain the fans and have them pay money to watch people play. I mean, I don't know what their attendance is."

"Around twenty-five thousand paid a game," I said.

Dykstra then tried to be optimistic.

"As bad as they are, I think they have some young guys coming up, but I don't know," he said with resignation in his voice.

"They do have some good young pitchers," I noted.

"Well, I'm just talking about what I've seen the last five years," Lenny said. "I don't know what's coming."

If Dykstra seemed harsh on the Mets, it was nothing compared to the attack he was about to make on his other favorite team.

"I *do* know what's coming for the Phillies," Dykstra said emphatically. "It is almost like the owners called in Ruben Amaro, the general manager, and said, *Listen, Ruben, we're making too much money. We need to take losses. We need you to fuck this organization up as bad as you can.* And [Amaro] couldn't have done a better job. [Author's note: Amaro would be fired by the Phillies late in the 2015 season.]

"That organization is five years away from being anywhere near competitive. *Five* years. The players are all in their mid-thirties. They get a year older and they have nothing in the minor leagues. So the future in Philadelphia for baseball is not just dark, it's *Alaska* dark. Twenty-four-fucking-seven.

"They get these thirty-year-old players. Don't they have the charts that I have? I can pull up a chart right now and show you a player at thirty years old and he goes straight down. It's not like maybe, no. The peak is twenty-eight, twenty-nine, or thirty on average. There's a lot of things involved. Number one, your body's beat up. Number two, you've got a guaranteed contract. Number three, you just don't have the same killer attitude. I mean, it's called the *human factor.* It's like when you get older, do you want to fuck as much? It's all the same thing. When you get older, you don't want to fuck or play as hard. It's just human nature. It's not anyone's fault."

By this point, the prepared questions I had weren't worth the paper they were printed on. It was pretty much going to be Lenny-unplugged the rest of the way. And that wasn't necessarily a bad thing at all. Say anything you want about Lenny Dykstra, but even his detractors would have to concede that he is entertaining.

"So where are you staying tonight, bro?" Lenny asked me.

"I have to drive back down to San Diego," I said.

"What, you've got some pussy there or something?" Dykstra said with a mischievous grin, before adding, "Why San Diego? *Mitchell?*"

"Yes, I met with Kevin Mitchell yesterday," I replied.

"He's a bad motherfucker!" Lenny said enthusiastically. "That dude was an *athlete*. I mean, you could put him anywhere. That guy was one of the most underrated players ever. He had the MVP year and, remember, that was all *without* drugs. With everyone else, it was with drugs. The guy next to you juiced up, so, okay, let him make thirty million and you go home with sixty thousand and be miserable. *Really?* It doesn't sound stupid, does it?"

I agreed with him on Mitchell's superior talent and how he put up big numbers the right way. And I also told him I understood the temptation that players of his era faced with respect to steroids. I then tried to shift the conversation toward the '86 Mets and everything they accomplished.

"Let's talk about the '86 World Series," I said.

Dykstra interrupted before I could go on, and said with a smile, "You mean the reason we won was because of *me*?"

We shared a laugh, and I said, "You're going to like this question. I interviewed Howard Johnson, now with the Mariners as their hitting coach, and—"

Dykstra jumped in again.

"*Finally!*" Lenny said excitedly, his pace picking up. "HoJo got to the big leagues! That's *awesome*! HoJo was a *great* guy. Isn't he a great guy?"

"Yes," I said. "He is definitely a great guy."

Again, I began a question—this time about the role Lenny played in jump-starting the Mets in the pivotal Game Three of the '86 World Series, when the Mets trailed Boston two games to none—and Lenny dived right in like he used to in center field.

"For one of the few times in my career, I told myself and actually told my wife, 'I've got to take the fans out of play. I'm actually going to try to go up and hit a bomb. I'm going to try to put up a fucking crooked number right away. Change the momentum.' And Oil Can Boyd threw me a fucking tog shot, dude, and I fucking wrapped it around the foul pole and the party was on! I actually *tried* to hit a home run to try to take the crowd out early. I also wanted to give [Bobby] Ojeda a little bit of confidence with a run already."

After Dykstra's leadoff home run, the Mets would score three more times in that first inning, to cruise to a 7–1 victory and make it a series again.

"How about the big home run you hit in Game Three of the NLCS against the Astros. Were you also *trying* to hit a—" I started to ask before Dykstra chimed right in again.

"No. Complete opposite," he said. "We were down a run. Backman was on second. I was trying to get a hit to tie the game up. Then Dave Smith threw a basketball up there."

The home run gave the Mets a critical two-games-to-one lead made all the more important by the fact they would now have the opportunity of facing the invincible Mike Scott in just one more game instead of two if they closed the series out in six games.

"Didn't Davey want you to stay away from trying to hit the long ball and go more for the singles?" I asked.

"I *did* go for the singles," Lenny said. "I hit .290 or whatever every fucking year. I was with Davey Johnson a few months ago. Me, him, and Ray Knight. It was so funny. We were doing an appearance back east and we had to drive in a van together. So Davey was cool as fuck, man. We were laughing. It was a long drive. I said to him, 'I think I've talked to you more on this fucking ride than I talked with you the whole five years you managed me!'"

I asked him what they talked about.

"Everything. Life. Davey's cool, man. Now, he's cool. When I played, Davey didn't talk to me."

"Do you think it was because he was your boss and wanted to keep some distance?" I asked.

"I don't know what it was and I don't care, either," Dykstra replied. "The last time we were together, we had a great rap, dude."

Lenny then wanted to talk about something else from his playing days he is very proud of.

"You know I was voted the most *hated* player in the league five years in a row, dude?"

"You were?" I asked. "According to whom?"

"They poll the players," Dykstra said. "The opposing teams. It's an honor to me."

"Like a *badge* of honor?" I asked.

"If they like you, what good is that?" he asked rhetorically.

Lenny's cell phone rang again—this time a call from a friend.

"What's happening, man?" Lenny answered.

"I'm sitting here with this dude, Erik Sherman. He's writing the big book about the Mets, dude. And he said I got a couple of key hits there to help. I mean, *really*? They kind of put the fucking five-foot-nine runt on the map, didn't they?" Dykstra said glowingly, tongue-in-cheek, smiling over at me.

He then excused himself to take the call away from the table when the talk turned to visiting the set of one of Lenny's best and most famous friends, Charlie Sheen. Keeping in character with his sense of humor, Lenny gave me a deadpanned glance, then a wink, and said, "I've got to talk about pussy right now, so I've got to step out."

I grinned and told him I understood.

Upon his return five minutes later, he went straight to his Mac and pulled up a story on the Internet under the headline THE 10 BEST POST-SEASON HITTERS EVER.

"So let's see how many Hall of Famers are on here," Dykstra says. "Oh yeah, here's a Hall of Famer, here's another Hall of Famer. And number eight . . . *Lenny Dykstra*! I mean, pretty good company to stroll out with. George Brett, Lou Brock, and then you got this one, Lou Gehrig. The Babe. And at number one, [Carlos] Beltrán, who hit all those home runs. Anyway, I didn't make that up for you. I didn't type all that out for you."

"You didn't manipulate all that out for my benefit," I played along.

"It is what it is, dude," Lenny said.

After a good mutual laugh about it, Dykstra started quizzing me in a sort of cosmic way.

"Do you *feel* me? Can you *feel* me? Do you *feel* me, bro?"

"I feel you, man."

"That's right," Dykstra said, while nodding with a satisfied grin. "You *feel* me."

The mood was light and we were both enjoying the conversation. Lenny was being Lenny and I was just there for the ride. He was a fun guy to be around. But when it comes to the game, taking away all the profanity and exaggeration for effect, he has a seriously strong baseball intellect.

Case in point was his insightfulness when I asked him how important the mental part of the game was and if it's at times even more important than talent.

"Great question," Dykstra said. "See, here's the deal, man. I played with a lot of great players that could have been Hall of Famers but they didn't love the game. It's not their fault if they don't love the game. It's a grind, dude. It's not like what the public thinks, that you get to play baseball for a couple of hours each day. No. The emotional highs and lows, dude—every at bat you're either a hero or a loser. You have to be able to handle failure. That's what Billy Beane says. You read his book, right?"

"Sure, I read about Beane in *Moneyball*," I said.

"Some players didn't love the game, like Strawberry," Dykstra said. "Strawberry could have been a Hall of Famer. Great guy. I love him. Good man. Great man. But he didn't *love* the game. He didn't go out and attack it. If he had, he would have been in the Hall of Fame. But he's a great guy, man. I think he's doing well. He's a minister now. I mean, like, *really*? Good for fucking him."

"So does Straw being a minister surprise you?" I asked.

"I'm just glad," Dykstra said. "Strawberry and Gooden took me in, you know? It was Strawberry first when I came in, and then it was Gooden before I got called back down. I played with Gooden in A-Ball. He had 300 strikeouts in 150 innings. He just *abused* dudes. The hitters did not want to go up there. I was in centerfield the whole time. I watched this guy—it was like playing with fucking children.

"I told him, 'Doc, you're going to "The Show" next year, man.' He said, 'What's that?' And I said, 'You're going to pitch in the big leagues, dude.' And he goes, 'No, I'm eighteen.' And he was up the next year and won Rookie of the Year. Doc had some fucking gas-through-your-ass with a nose-to-toes hook. And then he had a change-up which is now the best pitch in baseball."

"Yep, and they called that curveball of his *Lord Charles*," I said.

Dykstra nodded, still reminiscing in awe over how great a pitcher Doc Gooden was at such a young age.

I then brought up the incident when Dykstra tried to spring Gooden from the Pasadena Recovery Center, the rehab venue used by Dr. Drew, to get Lenny's angle of the story, which turned out to be completely different from Doc's version.

"I did it because that's being a friend," Lenny said. "He called me, dude. He was down and out, man. I could hear it in his voice. And I said, 'Bro, what's wrong?' He said, 'Dude, you've got to get me out of here.' I said, 'Wow.' And he said, 'It's brutal, man.'

"You know that voice you hear?" Lenny asked rhetorically. "And Doc Gooden, that guy's my man, dude. Just a great guy. So I said, 'I'm going to come and bust you fucking out. I'm coming right now! I'm getting in my car and coming to get you out of there.'

"Well, I tried, but they cock-blocked it," Lenny said of the rehab center's staff. "I tried, though."

"Didn't you actually get his luggage?" I asked.

"Yeah, I almost got him," Dykstra says with a huge grin. "Did you like that? It wasn't fake. I'm like, *Let me go in the phone booth, dude, with a fucking cape on and I'm coming! I'm gonna get you, man!*"

"So he knew you were on your way?" I asked.

"Oh yeah, and I almost got him. Didn't he make a story about that? Is it public?" he asked.

"Oh sure, it's out there," I said.

"It's out there?" Dykstra said. "Man, a lot of shit's out there."

I brought up Pete Rose and how Dykstra was, in several regards, the "Charlie Hustle" of his generation. I thought it was an apt comparison, as both played the game with a take-no-prisoners, reckless abandon on the field, and had an insatiable competitive spirit off of it, as well, which, ultimately, they both paid hefty prices for.

"Watching Rose in your formative years, did he have an influence on you?" I asked.

"Not at all," Lenny was quick to say. "He was a switch-hitter. I figured out early on that baseball was a game of percentages. Everything is based off counts. Ask Curt Schilling and he'll tell you I was the smartest player he ever played with. It's not bragging, that's a fact. But when I was with the Mets—remember I was young—they didn't think of me that way.

"There's only one way to hit, but ninety percent of the hitters today hit wrong," Dykstra continued. "They don't know how to hit. They get away with it because they're talented and they hit .280 or whatever. But they should be hitting .300 or .310 if they hit right. But they're not disciplined and nobody teaches them how to hit. Once I figured out how to hit and approach each at bat, I was putting myself in the best position to succeed. I led the National League in hits twice, dude. Not the California League or the Texas League or the Venezuelan League or the Japanese League. No. I led the *National League*. The next step up is God.

"I may not have been the best hitter, but I figured out how it works. The *best* players are seventy percent losers, the ones that hit .300. I mean, Tom Glavine used to throw shit I used to want to catch and throw back at him. But because he played bright, as a pitcher, he was a seventy-five percent favorite. Pitchers like him and Greg Maddux got to walk out there with a fifteen-inch cock. Think about it, they're a seventy-five percent favorite! They just played right by throwing strikes and not walking people. The percentages are that the hitters will hit it at the fielders because that's where the balls go. They've been standing at those positions for hundreds of years for a reason. So if you don't fuck your job up, you're going to do like Maddux and Glavine throwing eighty-fucking-five miles an hour!"

I asked if, considering his baseball intellect, he thought he would ever get back into the game.

"Oh, there's no reason," Dykstra replied. "They're not going to let me back in. I mean, why would they? Why do they need that hassle?

"The bottom line is, with the public perception of me," Lenny continued, before changing direction mid-sentence and adding, "although when they see my book, that may change."

It was apparent to me that Lenny is betting the house that once he gets the chance to explain in his autobiography what happened to him, he will be able to gain redemption with the public at large.

"I'm looking forward, not back," he told me.

It was now time for Lenny to head home. He is staying with his ex-wife and the mother of their two sons, Terri, in Thousand Oaks. Lenny still speaks glowingly about her and referred to her as his wife throughout our interview.

Outside the hotel, Dykstra handed a valet his parking ticket and we both sat down on a curb after being told it would take a few minutes for them to retrieve his car. Lenny lighted up a cigarette and offered me one. I thanked him, but said I didn't smoke.

"You're a good guy, aren't you?" Lenny said with a warm smile. "Hey, I know I didn't answer all the questions you wanted to ask me," he said, perhaps remembering how he'd gone unplugged for a while. "But anything else you need, just call."

Dykstra then began talking about what it meant to him playing for the Mets.

"You know, I was blessed to be a part of that team," Lenny

began. "We were all shocked when we were told about Doc's failed drug test in spring training, '87. We had a real closeness with one another on that ball club.

"The government took away almost every material thing I had, but nobody can take away those memories."

The valet handed Lenny his keys, we wished each other well, and the onetime hard-nosed player they called "Nails" drove off into the California sunset.

·6·

THE CAPTAIN

New York fans can be tough, but there was a connection we
had with the New Yorkers. I think we were one of the most
beloved teams in New York history. I just think we had that
kind of appeal. We had the power, we had the speed, we
had the pitching, so it was an amazing team to watch and it
was an exciting team to play with.

—KEITH HERNANDEZ
(METS FIRST BASEMAN 1983—89)

For as glorious a career as Keith Hernandez had, there remain two
gaping holes—*injustices* really—in his baseball résumé.

The first should be seen as obvious. When you're the very best
fielder at your position in the nearly 150 year history of major-league
baseball—and can hit like the batting champion Hernandez once
was—you belong in Cooperstown.

Tim McCarver, the Hall of Fame announcer during Hernandez's entire tenure with the Mets, called him "the *Baryshnikov* of
first basemen." And in his book, *Oh, Baby, I Love It!* he wrote, "Few
athletes have the talent to do spectacular things routinely. Keith has
that kind of talent."

Aside from his ability to pick it at first and make diving plays to
both sides, his daringness and agility in consistently getting the lead
runner on sacrifice bunts at second or third base was legendary.

He was to first base what Bill Mazeroski was to second base, Ozzie Smith was to shortstop, and Brooks Robinson was to third base—all three Hall of Famers, all three the very best all-time defensively at their positions. Hernandez was the standard by which other first basemen should be measured.

By the time Hernandez's career was completed in 1990, there was nothing left for him to accomplish.

First and foremost, he helped lead two teams, the Cardinals and the Mets, to World Series championships. He won eleven *straight* gold glove awards, the most consecutive wins of any player in history. He set major-league records for most lifetime assists for a first baseman and the most seasons as the first baseman leading in double plays. He won an MVP award, two Silver Slugger Awards, and the aforementioned National League batting crown. He was a tremendous clutch hitter, proven statistically by his being the all-time leader in the now defunct category of Game Winning RBIs.

But most importantly for the Mets, he immediately gave them credibility not just with his gold glove and bat, but with a leadership sorely needed on a perennially losing team comprised mostly of younger players and a few malcontent veterans. He was a field manager, mentor, motivator—or, quite simply, the perfect leader for the mid-eighties Mets.

When I once asked Mookie Wilson, who wrote glowingly of Hernandez in his autobiography, which I cowrote with him, why Keith wasn't in the Hall of Fame, he rolled his eyes and said with resignation in his voice, "Oh, *please*, don't get me started on *that*!"

It was obvious from his reaction to the question that Mex would certainly have had Mookie's vote.

Yet, in the Hall of Fame balloting where a former player requires seventy-five percent of the vote from the Baseball Writers'

Association of America (BBWAA) for induction, Hernandez's highest total was just 10.8 percent. He is no longer on the Hall of Fame ballot, leaving the only means for possible enshrinement having it come by way of the Veterans' Committee.

His other missed opportunity was not becoming a big-league manager, whether he ever truly wanted that opportunity or not.

Mex was a master when it came to the psychology and subtleties of the game and used that skill to successfully energize his own teammates or, conversely, to get inside the heads of opponents. He also wrote an entire book on the strategies of the game, using more than 250 pages to break down two major-league contests, pitch-by-pitch, in *Pure Baseball*.

As a Cardinal, he no doubt picked up a great deal about managing from Hall of Fame pilot Whitey Herzog, their strained relationship be damned. And as first baseman of the Mets, Keith routinely made more trips to the mound than even the manager, Davey Johnson. He knew just what to tactfully say to a young pitcher without damaging his psyche, like telling a kid that didn't have his breaking ball on a given day that the opponent couldn't touch his fastball. Or to his infielders, advising them on where to align themselves and what to do if the ball was hit to them in different situations. He was a take-charge player, likely a skill that was in his sports DNA going back to his days as a high school quarterback, a position where the leadership to move players around is a prerequisite.

His Mets teammates had full faith and trust in him as one of their own, going to Keith in the clubhouse with the full realization that he had Johnson's ear, a bridge between player and manager. His formally being named the Mets' first team captain in franchise history, in 1987, was met with shrugs, as the players had unofficially already recognized him in that capacity for years.

In other words, he had all the tools to be a terrific manager.

But baseball as an institution can be unforgiving. And Keith, a product of his time, when cocaine use ran rampant in society and was the drug of choice for the young and successful of the early 1980s, was branded near the end of his time with the Cardinals as a recreational user. Hernandez, by his own admission, has claimed it was the angst he was experiencing from a bitter divorce that contributed to his using drugs as a kind of escape. I'm in no way defending or judging his choice in this regard, but to his credit, he took the high road, never naming other users in baseball, of which there likely were scores, and, most important of all, never allowing his use to affect his play on the field.

Still, by being one of the twelve major leaguers to be called on to testify before a grand jury about their drug use during the high-profile Pittsburgh drug trials of 1985, and later facing punishment handed down by Commissioner Peter Ueberroth, he appeared to seal his fate for possible induction into the Hall of Fame and for the option of becoming a future major-league manager. It hardly seemed to matter that by the time his playing career had ended, his involvement in drugs was ancient history.

"The only person I hurt was myself," Hernandez said at the trial.

Indeed, perhaps Keith was right about that assessment.

Still, I can't help but think of the case of Ferguson Jenkins, a future Hall of Fame pitcher who was caught possessing cocaine, hashish, and marijuana during a customs search in Toronto in 1980 while a member of the Texas Rangers.

Nor can I forget about the arrest of first baseman Orlando Cepeda in 1975 for the importation and possession of approximately 165 pounds of marijuana. Yet Cepeda would also eventually be elected into the Hall of Fame—in his case by its Veterans' Committee.

Nothing against Jenkins and Cepeda, but with their own drug-related transgressions far more serious than Hernandez's, how is it possible that they are in the Hall of Fame and Mex is not?

It just doesn't add up.

While managing would certainly appear to be out of the picture at this stage of Hernandez's life—and he likely wouldn't even entertain an offer if one came—it would seem fitting that the Veterans' Committee right a wrong by electing Mex to the Hall of Fame.

Until that happens, Cooperstown will remain one first baseman short.

| | | | | | |

I have always been intrigued by Hernandez and the intensity he brought to every game. When I played college ball, I used to time a pitcher's motion while in the on-deck circle in precisely the same manner Keith did. And I lived by his philosophy of never giving up an at bat, even in a lopsided game. I tried to always be prepared, like Hernandez was, never wasting a single opportunity on the ball field.

My initial thought about the news that he had been acquired from the Cardinals on June 15, 1983, was *Who could the lowly Mets have possibly traded to get him?*

The Mets dealt Neil Allen, a once reliable, then troubled, reliever made all the more expendable by the sudden all-star closing abilities of a young Jesse Orosco, and Rick Ownbey, a seldom-used spot starter, to obtain Hernandez. It was the steal of the century, easily the best trade in Mets history. While some would argue that the George Foster trade a year earlier gave the Mets long-awaited credibility or that the Gary Carter acquisition was the final, crowning piece to their '86 championship team, no other player in the history of the franchise changed the club's attitude, fortunes, and overall look faster and more profoundly than Hernandez.

Herzog, the Cardinals' manager who pushed Hernandez out and justified the uneven trade by reportedly dropping hints to the media, before that news was public, that Keith dabbled with cocaine, should be honored with a monument outside of Citi Field for his most charitable contribution to the Mets' franchise.

I had the pleasure of working with Keith on several different occasions while doing research for Mookie Wilson's autobiography, *MOOKIE: Life, Baseball, and the '86 Mets*, and then later, after Mex agreed to write the foreword for the book. Each time we spoke, I found that once you get him started talking baseball, he's a writer's dream. He's ultra-intelligent about the sport, brutally honest, unfiltered, ever loquacious, and a great storyteller. It's those ingredients that help make him one of the great "listens" as a television color analyst and one of the few reasons to tune in during the recent down era of Mets baseball.

I caught up with Keith over the phone on one of those occasions from his hotel room at the Marriott Marquis in New York's Times Square, where he had just finished a workout. We began talking about when he first joined the Mets and how active he was on the field—making regular trips to the mound, talking with the pitchers, giving direction to the infielders, and generally embracing the role of field general.

"Did you take on those duties with the Cardinals, as well, or was that something you did with the Mets because they were a younger team in need of more direction?" I asked.

"Lou Brock always told me that someone in the infield has to help out the pitchers when you're out there," Mex began. "I grew up with the Cardinals, they were a veteran team when I came up, and as I got older, a lot of guys I played with in the minor leagues were still there, so I never really took on that role. But when I came over to the Mets, there were just so many young players, so what Lou said really resonated with me. We had a lot of young guys and, obviously, a pitching staff that was wonderful. I had been in the league at that point around ten years, I knew the hitters, so it was a perfect spot for me to step in and kind of take on that role. As they became experienced, I eventually sort of backed off. But I was kind of an emotional player anyway, so that's just the way it was."

I tell Keith that, from my perspective, even though the record of the '83 Mets was similar to that of the '82 version, I could see signs of a turnaround.

"When you arrived from St. Louis," I said, "the Mets had just called up Darryl. So with the additions of you both, the team certainly looked more competitive than in previous years."

But Mex didn't see it that way.

"I kind of disagree with you about '83," he said. "I didn't see anything down the line. There was no Dwight Gooden—he wasn't there. There was still a lot of deadweight on the team. But I had no idea they had all that talent down in the minor leagues that came to spring training in '84. And Frank Cashen did a good job of getting rid of the deadweight. Davey was the right guy for the job. The younger guys knew him from the minor leagues, and it was a natural progression right there. Davey knew who the good players were and there were plenty of them."

"You mentioned Doc, though the Mets had another pretty good young pitcher at that time named Ron Darling," I said. "I know you've always been close with Ron, and you've shared the SNY broadcast booth with him for years now. He could have been the ace on a lot of staffs, but with the Mets, it was always Doc. In your conversations with him, did he ever mention to you that he may have felt overshadowed by Doc or was he comfortable in his role with the Mets?"

"Oh, I think Ron was comfortable," Keith said. "He got the ball every fifth day. It's just that Doc was number one and everybody pitched every fifth day, so it wasn't like they adjusted the rotation so Doc could pitch more or whatever. Everybody had their turn and they all got the same amount of starts. So no, there was never any of that. And in '84, they were all young kids just trying to make their way. That was their big opportunity. There was Ronnie when he broke in, Doc was a rookie, you had [Roger] McDowell, who was a rookie, Walt Terrell, who wound up getting traded but was in the beginning of his career. So no, I don't think Ronnie felt overshadowed at all. I mean, Doc was a rarity, like a Bob Gibson or a Dizzy Dean or any of the great pitchers. That's what Doc was. They don't come around too often."

"Regarding '84," I said, "so many Mets fans I talk to say that year was even more satisfying than winning it all in '86. There was for them, in many ways, a greater sense of accomplishment with the Mets being in a pennant race well into September in '84, considering how far the club had come over the previous seven losing seasons. How about for you? Which season gave you a greater sense of accomplishment—'84 or '86?"

"Well, we did the ultimate in '86," Hernandez recalled. "When you look in the record book, in the history of baseball, I don't think there are twenty teams that won 108 games in the regular season. But '84 was really a fun year. It was a year when the team was primarily young. There were just a few veterans on the team—Foster, Mookie, and myself. Didn't have Carter then. It was all about the young kids. And it was one of the most fun years of my seventeen-year career. It happened to be one of the best years of my career not only as far as RBIs, but also for clutch hitting. It was a good, solid year for me. It was so much fun and was the beginning of things turning around, as Frank did the right thing later on by getting Carter, Ojeda, and adding to our team."

"It always seemed to me," I said, "that after the Mets had more wins over the '84 and '85 seasons combined than any team in baseball, that winning the World Series in '86 was like a coronation. But '84 just came out of nowhere."

Hernandez, perhaps thinking bottom line, took a moment to reflect, sighed, and gave a simple final analysis of the '84 season.

"Well, we couldn't beat the Cubs that year," he said. "They were a veteran team and they wound up winning it. They happened to get [Rick] Sutcliffe who went 16–1 for them. Without him, we would have won the division. *That* would have been something!"

Talk then moved to the Gary Carter acquisition from the Montreal Expos following the 1984 season. Carter was acquired in exchange for a good deal of young talent—Hubie Brooks, Mike Fitzgerald, Herm Winningham, and Floyd Youmans—but many pundits saw this as the final piece of the puzzle for the Mets to finally jump over division rivals like the Cubs and the Cardinals. Talent-wise, Carter was a massive upgrade over Mets catchers Fitzgerald and prospect John Gibbons, but the media, not to mention some of the Mets, wondered if "Kid" might disrupt some of the chemistry that they had built up over the previous two seasons. The all-star catcher was called "Camera Carter" in Montreal by some of his teammates for his perceived never-ending thirst for publicity. Some in the media also wondered if Hernandez, the de facto leader of the team, could coexist with the larger-than-life Carter.

In retrospect, Mex could only find the positives of the trade.

"What was your initial reaction to the news?" I asked.

"My initial reaction was *elation!*" Mex answered, as if I had asked an obvious question. "Gary, not only because of his offensive numbers, but his defensive skills and, most importantly, his handling of the pitching staff, was just made-to-order. Gary called a very aggressive game. He took charge. He was the perfect guy for those young pitchers. He just fit the bill in every possible way, and he gave us another power bat in the lineup with Strawberry. So, it was *all* good. It was *all* positive."

Mex then gave Frank Cashen credit for pulling the trigger on the deal.

"Frank wanted to win," Keith said. "Cashen had already won with Baltimore. But his crowning glory of his career as a general manager was turning the Mets around into a world champion. After seven years as sellers, what he did was really quite an accomplishment. And to do it so rapidly was impressive."

We talked about how Carter was just another one of the Mets players that really appealed to New York fans at that time. The Yankees of Don Mattingly, Dave Winfield, and Rickey Henderson were very good, but didn't draw nearly as well as the Mets.

"It seemed as if even though the two clubs, with the exception of '86, had similar records during the mid-eighties, the Mets were getting most of the attention in town. Was there a 'cool' factor about the Mets that endeared them more to New York fans back then?" I asked Hernandez.

"Well, I think everybody loves an underdog," Mex said. "And the Mets had always been the little brother to the Yankees, who were still a very good team. But I think our team had mass appeal because of the characters we had. Our team played with a lot of spirit and it showed on the field. It was infectious, and I think it was

infectious to us as players. We fed off of it. We had a lot of emotional guys that played with grit, and it appealed to the fans. And I
really do feel that this is a National League town at heart. And if
the [present-day] Mets could ever consistently field a competitive
team out there, they would have the same results as the Yankees.

"You have to look at the Mets' history," Keith continued. "You
can't just look at the Mets now like my generation when they were the
'62 expansion team. They've been around now for over fifty years, and
it's been primarily losing. There have only been four [now five] World
Series appearances, with two world championships. And when the
Mets are down, they're not [even] a .500 club—they're terrible. So it
was perfect timing for us and it was the perfect team. We were a very,
very good club, but we really played with a lot of gusto and everybody
got dirty—a Pete Rose–type team that appealed to fans."

"That '86 team seemed to enter that season with a lot more
swagger than the previous year," I told Mex. "What was the difference from the year before, and why was the team, as it turned out
justifiably, so confident?"

"Well, we were determined, that's why," Keith shot back. "We
won ninety-eight games in '85 and went home, so we were *determined* coming into the next year. We were ready. We were hungry.
We were ready to go! We came very close to winning the division in
'84 and '85, but came away with nothing. Then when we came to
spring training, Davey made the big, bold prediction that we were
going to win the National League pennant and the World Series. I
remember when he said that, I went, 'Holy cow.' But I think Davey
knew what the hell he was doing. He threw the challenge out to us,
and fortunately we did it."

"Comparing the personalities of the '86 team to the '85 team, it
seemed like the '86 version was more vibrant," I offered to Mex.

"I'm wondering if that was because of all the young players becoming more comfortable in their surroundings. Guys like Roger McDowell, Lenny Dykstra, HoJo, and Kevin Mitchell were coming into their own, and then you had some of the older guys, like Rusty Staub, who had retired, and then during the '86 season, veteran George Foster was traded away. Could those have been some of the primary reasons why the club seemed more loose and alive in '86 compared to the previous year, or was it something else?"

Mex somewhat disagreed with my analysis, and then gave me his assessment on the chief differences between the two years.

"I always thought we were loose and alive," he exclaimed. "We just became more confident. Because all the young players, like Dykstra, Mitchell, and then Wally Backman coming back from the grave to become a quality player, McDowell, Darling, Doc, Sid Fernandez, and Darryl, of course—you can't forget him—they had mostly now had a couple of good seasons. They knew they belonged. So they were no longer young kids. They were no longer scratching and clawing and not knowing if they were going to make it or not. They *knew* they belonged in the big leagues. Therefore, we were *ready* in '86."

"How about the off-the-field persona of the team?" I began. "The Mets' hard-partying ways were well documented in the book *The Bad Guys Won*."

Hernandez jumped in right away, sounding slightly agitated by the topic.

"Everybody makes a lot of to-do about the Mets being this party team," Mex began. "I played on some St. Louis teams that didn't do anything differently. There are always players who aren't going to take care of themselves, but most of the players do. I knew that we played mostly night games, and I knew that I couldn't stay out until three or four o'clock in the morning if I wanted to perform. But certainly on the road, getting back to the hotel at eleven o'clock, I could not go back up to my room after I was all geared up from the game and go to bed and watch TV. I just couldn't do that. I had to go out. And what better way than with your teammates. It was a fraternity. It really was like a college frat. Meet the guys downstairs, talk about the game, and have a couple of beers and yuck it up and have a good time. That was *normal*. It's a long season, a lot of frustrations, a lot of stuff gets inside and needs to come out. And, boy, if you sit and bottle it up, sooner or later you're going to get a nervous breakdown."

I backtracked a bit, telling Keith that I had heard again and again from some of his '86 teammates that, no matter how late some of the guys stayed out, the team was ready for battle the next day.

"Well, that '86 team, everybody wanted to play," Mex said. "And we're leaving Ray Knight out of the equation, too—another fiery player that was healthy and had a comeback year."

For as great a season as it was, it could easily have been stymied in the NLCS had the series gone to a seventh and deciding game, with Astros ace Mike Scott, the winning pitcher in both Games One and Four, looming. However, Mex didn't completely see it that way.

"I always felt that we would have found a way to beat Mike Scott," Hernandez said. "Our pitcher would have matched him in that game. I just felt we would have found a way to win. Now we'll never know. The only two games we lost in that playoff series were against him, and he dominated us. He particularly frazzled Gary Carter more than anybody. He was just a good pitcher. He had a great year, a dominating year. And for a right-hander to dominate us, it speaks volumes for the kind of stuff Scott had that year. And whether he cheated or not, we don't know, and whether he cut the ball up, I wasn't going to get all caught up in that. You still have to throw the ball over the plate. See the ball and hit it.

"Anyway," Hernandez continued, "we went into Game Six knowing that, yes, we had to beat [Bob] Knepper, too, so we really had our hands full with Houston. We were hoping the Giants would have won the damned [NL West] division! We knew we were going to have to go up against Scott, [Nolan] Ryan, and Knepper [in the Houston series]. They weren't going to pitch a fourth guy against us. And that was as good a starting three as you were going to see. So [Game Six] was just a remarkable game, the greatest game I have ever played in my life. Sixteen innings. And to go out there from the ninth inning on where if they take the lead, we lose. So we're out there on defense, on point for seven innings. That game right there for me was so pressure-packed. And the fact that we had the best record in baseball, why the hell did we have to open up in Houston and play Games Six and [a potential] Seven in Houston? It should have been Games One and Two, Six and Seven in New York. So we had to do it on the road and in the Dome, and that's a whole different ball of wax."

Mex agreed with me when I said the NLCS was really the first test the Mets had encountered the entire season to that point.

"Once we went into St. Louis in late April and swept the four-game series, we never looked back," Keith said. "We were never tested all year. We just cruised into the postseason, and [the NLCS] showed the character of our team because we were behind in every game except Game Two."

With the emotional series and the sixteen-inning Game Six behind them, I brought up how it seemed like there was a hangover effect entering the World Series against the Boston Red Sox. While Keith didn't seem to disagree, he didn't use it as an excuse for the Mets dropping the first two games.

"Boston had the same [issue]," Mex said. "Boston had equally as difficult a playoff series. They came back and won in Anaheim [in

Game Five], got on an airplane, and won the final two. We had the long flight home after the sixteen-inning game and didn't get in until like five in the morning from Houston. Day off, then the World Series. Both teams from both those playoffs were emotionally exhausted. Whichever team would win that first game was going to have a leg up. So we lost 1–0 on the error by [Tim] Teufel, and it elevated them and sunk us. Then we got killed in the second game. But then, lo and behold, we go to Boston and did what we had to do. We certainly had to win Game Three. And Lenny hit that leadoff home run that ignited us. There was a big determination in that dugout. It was all business. And I think Davey did the right thing by not having us work out the previous day. He told us, 'Stay away, go out and have dinner and relax. I don't want you at the ballpark answering the press and all the negativity. I'll be there. I'll answer to it.'"

The Mets, of course, rallied back and took the World Series in seven. It was an incredibly riveting postseason, maybe the greatest October baseball has ever seen.

Hernandez gave a great anecdote about how the resiliency of the Mets was still being talked about well after the season ended.

"I was having dinner one night in New York after we won the World Series," Mex said, "and the Hilton family was in the next room. They called me over and asked if I wanted to go as their guest to stay at their hotel in Las Vegas and accept two ringside seats to the Tyson-Berbick fight. I said, 'Sure!' So I went to that fight with my brother and in the pre-fight and post-fight cocktail schmooze, we ran into George Allen, the former Redskins head coach, who's a huge baseball fan. My brother and I talked with him about football and baseball for around an hour, and it was the most fascinating thing. Allen said, and I [up to that point] didn't really think of this, 'Your team in the playoffs showed the guts and the personality and the character that we didn't see during the season. But when the chips were down, when the pennant was on the line and then when the World Series was on the line, your team had remarkable comebacks and remarkable resiliency. It just showed the character of your team.' And that meant a lot coming from George Allen."

| | | | | | |

Still, for as great and gritty as the mid-eighties Mets were, for them to walk away with just the one world championship was a disappointment for the franchise. There are many different factors that can be pointed to as reasons for the perceived underachievement of the team, but the one that is referenced most is the drug problems encountered by Dwight Gooden during the 1986 season and beyond. I thought Keith's perspective, as both team captain and as someone who had once used drugs and was able to walk away from their grip, would be valuable in determining if anything could have been done to set the young Met superstar straight.

"Doc was a once-in-a-generation kind of pitcher," I began. "He was still very good in '86, though clearly something wasn't the same after the dominating season he had in '85. Were there any red flags you could see or efforts made by management or the players just to sit down and ask him what was going on and if everything was okay?"

Mex didn't hesitate.

"Well, I remember Frank Cashen didn't want to have him up in '84," Hernandez said. "He felt Doc was too young to put into the spotlight, particularly in New York. He wanted him to have another year—at least a half a year—in Triple-A, but Davey Johnson managed him the year before and was adamant that Doc was ready and that he come up. That was a big bone of contention between Davey and Frank. I've had dinners with Frank and he always regretted not having Doc in Triple-A in '84."

Still, as Mex continued, he said he could hardly blame Davey for wanting to bring Doc up as soon as possible.

"Doc was ready," Keith said. "You can't hold someone's hand and watch them twenty-four hours a day. Some of Doc's associations were a little suspect—one female, in particular, who I won't get into, that I felt was 'trouble up River City,' and I found out that she was. So you're a man, you live your own life. Doc was on top of the world—like Michael Jordan—and young. He had his billboard up in Manhattan painted on a building. A lot of people want to hang around that, and it's hard to filter out the bad element that's just there to suck off of you and take what they can take. There are not-really-good influences and then there are those that really care about you. It's in your heart to find those that really care about you, and that basically starts with your family. So I really don't know if there's anything that we could have done."

There was more Keith wanted to say and, after a pregnant pause, perhaps some quick introspection, and then a sigh, he continued.

"I've had my share of troubles, too," Hernandez lamented. "I mean, I made my share of mistakes. I was doing things detrimental to my career prior to being a Met. Fortunately, I was strong enough to pull out. But, you know, you make mistakes in life and you always hope you learn from them. Some guys are strong enough to nip it in the bud, and some guys . . . I've seen careers ruined. So it's a fine line."

Keith then got back to the "Doc conundrum," which has plagued the veterans from that '86 Mets team for nearly three decades.

"What could management possibly have done?" Mex asked rhetorically. "[Doc] was a grown man. He's going to go home after a game in New York and hang out with his friends. What are you going to do, tell him *No, you can't go out with this guy or that girl?* You can't do that. There are limits. Drugs are very seductive and they get ahold of you and you're in a whole lot of trouble. There's nothing good to be said about narcotics. There's only so much you can do. I've had the right people around me in my career. I feel like I've had a guardian angel over my shoulder my whole life.

"You can't nursemaid the guy," Hernandez continued. "It's just really tragic what happened to Doc and what could have been. His accomplishments were incredible anyway if you look at his body of work. But you can always sit there and go, *Well, Doc could have been spoken in the same breath as Dizzy Dean, Walter Johnson, Sandy Koufax, Bob Gibson, and Warren Spahn. He could have been on a level with them.* It's too bad."

Of course, there were other reasons besides Doc why the Mets didn't win another championship with the star-studded group they had. I brought up some theories for Keith to consider.

"The team had all this young talent," I began. "Most Mets feel as if the team should have won a couple more championships with that core group that they had. Davey made so many of the right calls with that team. He let them be men. He let them do what they needed to do, like canceling the workout prior to Game Three of the '86 World Series, which, by all accounts, was a brilliant move. But it did, along with seemingly setting so few boundaries for the team, cast Davey as a 'players' manager.' Taking nothing away from Davey, especially the job he did leading up to and during the '86 season, but did his leniency hurt the team moving forward or was it more the trades and non-signings of key players that kept the Mets from winning another World Series?"

"We could have had a little more discipline on the team," Mex said without hesitation. "The most disappointing season for me with the Mets was '87. We should have won the division two years in a row. We won ninety-two games. But we opened the season with Doc in the drug tank, and the last week of spring training McDowell gets operated on for appendicitis and he misses the first month of the season. That year, we lost all of our starting pitchers at [some point]. Frank brought up young pitchers that weren't ready because he had the confidence in our offense that it would carry us through. Doc was out for a long time, Ojeda was down for a bit, and Sid [Fernandez] had knee problems and we lost him. Then Ron Darling, our best pitcher [that year], red hot down the stretch, gold glove fielder—while pitching a gem, he fields a swinging bunt down the third base line in September, bends over to grab the ball, and he tears a ligament in his throwing thumb. We lost Ron for the last three weeks of the season, losing four of his starts. And we lose in the last week of the season to the Cardinals. If we had Doc all year and we didn't lose all of our starting five at different parts of the season, we would have won that division. Injuries are part of the game, but that season is the one that sticks in my craw."

While Keith clearly believed missing the playoffs in '87 was primarily because of key players going on the disabled list, he noted a different, more negative dynamic at work the following year, despite the fact the Mets won the division title and one hundred games that season.

"In '88, we started falling apart," Mex said. "We were getting destroyed from within, pulling apart. Lenny was becoming more unhappy with his platoon role. As a team, we weren't getting along as good. I felt we were tearing apart. I thought we were ready to get upset by the Dodgers in '88 [in the NLCS]. I didn't go into that playoff series confident *at all*."

"Really?" I asked, recalling how truly mediocre the Dodger lineup was compared to the Mets. "That really surprises me to hear you say that, particularly with how the Mets were far superior over-all and had added David Cone to the staff."

"Well, they had good pitching," Mex said. "We had the better offense, but pitching is the name of the game, and they beat us with their pitching. And if [Mike] Scioscia doesn't hit the home run in Game Four, we go up three games to one, ball game over. But tip your hat to the Dodgers. I just felt we weren't the same. We won a hundred games, for Chrissake! But that's when we started seeing some friction. I guess that's just the nature of human beings. We had been together for a while. And in '89, it all fell apart."

There was a pause and then Keith reverted back to the subject of the Mets' failure to repeat in '87—obviously still, after all these years, disappointed and at least a little peeved about it.

"You know, it's hard to repeat," Hernandez said. "But we were ready to win again in '87, and *dammit*, there would never be this talk about this underachieving team. I don't think we underachieved. There were just some damned good teams that played against us. The '85 and '87 Cardinals were good. It was very competitive—that's for sure."

"And a great era for baseball," I said.

"It was," Keith answered.

| | | | | | |

Today, Hernandez, a twice-divorced father of three daughters, is a moving target between the three locales of his homes in Juno Beach, Florida, and Sag Harbor, Long Island, and his regular appearances in New York City—otherwise referred to by Jerry Seinfeld's character on a *Seinfeld* episode as the "Bermuda Triangle."

And *Seinfeld* is a good segue, because shortly after Keith's playing days were over, he made a downright historic guest appearance on arguably the iconic sitcom's best-known episode, "The Boyfriend," during the height of the show's popularity. A story line that played on his "bromance" with Jerry and how it became complicated once he started dating the Elaine character, played by actress Julia Louis-Dreyfus, was so clever and well received that *TV Guide* ranked it the fourth best television episode of *all time*.

Mex would also make a cameo appearance in the final episode of *Seinfeld*, and the comedian, a huge Mets fan and owner of a luxury box at Citi Field, makes occasional appearances in the Mets' broadcast booth during ball games.

While Hernandez continued to get small roles in movies and commercials, he eventually discovered a second career as an Emmy Award–winning baseball analyst, first on MSG, and currently with SNY's Mets telecasts. He's been at it for well over a decade and is tremendously popular with viewers for his honest, no-holds-barred observations of the game.

The triumvirate of Gary Cohen, Ron Darling, and Hernandez in the current Mets' broadcast booth is one of the very best listens in baseball. I have long believed that a kid learning the game will pick up more useful information and hear more critical thinking in a handful of Mets telecasts than in a year of listening to some of the other major-league broadcast teams out there—they're that good. Naturally, they are pulling for the Mets to win, though they are anything but the "homers" you hear with some other clubs.

A broadcast with Keith is never dull and often colorful, filled with similes. A personal favorite was when an umpire called a very low strike and Mex observed, "That ball was knee-high to a grasshopper!"

Keith once said in an interview that he is kind of like "the Phil Rizzuto of the Mets' broadcasting team." But while "The Scooter" was beloved and became everybody's favorite Italian uncle with his entertaining commentary, cannolis, and birthday greetings during Yankee telecasts, there really is no comparison. When it comes to baseball broadcasting, Hernandez is more a mix of Tony Kubek's analytical skills and Joe Garagiola's gift of gab.

As should be expected with any broadcaster who never shies away from controversy, some of his comments over the years have made headlines. There was the time he questioned why a female massage therapist should be allowed in the San Diego Padres dugout (which he later apologized for). Then another when he came down on Gary Carter for promoting himself to replace then Mets manager Willie Randolph. And in demonstrating he is not averse to sometimes being critical of the Mets, Mex was blasted by a just-fired Mets hitting coach Dave Hudgens for his observations of the club's passive hitting approach in taking too many pitches.

As a member of the media now, Hernandez naturally has a different perspective from the days he wore a uniform. I wondered if he saw any significant difference between today's ballplayer and the typical ones from his playing days, particularly in the clubhouse environment.

"Keith, I get the sense things were different in the eighties, that maybe it was more fun," I said. "How is being a baseball player today different from when you played?"

"I don't sense the camaraderie that we had when we played," Keith began. "We didn't have televisions throughout the clubhouse to watch the MLB Network, baseball games, movies, or whatever. There were headphones, but we didn't have music in our ears, we didn't tune out, and we didn't stick our heads in our lockers and disappear for an hour without interacting with each other. There was *constant* interaction. Now there's just too much going on. Now the clubhouses are like country clubs. They have pinball machines, pool tables, and there's so much use of computers going over what this or that pitcher does—it's just too scientific, there's too much information, as opposed to twenty-five guys coming together and interacting throughout a very long and grueling season. I mean, it's hardly even worth going into the clubhouse today before a game because they're just not there. [At Citi Field] they have a room almost as big as the clubhouse where the press can't go and, okay, that's fine. We just had a little, tiny room in the back [at Shea] where maybe only six guys could hang out at one time. It's just a whole different ball of wax. That's the difference I see."

We talked a bit about the future of his broadcasting career, and Keith told me he would like to stay in the booth until he is at least seventy years old, which would give Mets fans at least another eight or nine years of listening to the outspoken, unpredictable, and baseball-savvy color analyst.

"How about an autobiography?" I asked. "You have a great story to tell."

Hernandez, no stranger to the literary world with two highly acclaimed books he's written with coauthor Mike Bryan—*If At First: A Season with the Mets* and *Pure Baseball*—and a third—*Shea Good-bye*—written with Matthew Silverman, seemed delighted by the question.

"Well, that's flattering," Keith said, a smile coming through in his voice. "But right now I have my hands full with my commitment in the booth."

So, for now, fans will have to settle for the entertaining and spot-on commentary of a New York icon who helped turn the club's fortunes around and ushered in the greatest era in Mets history.

· 7 ·

THE UNSUNG SHORTSTOP

Every time you see one of your guys going up to the big leagues, you can say, "I was part of the development of that guy." And that really makes you feel like you're doing something special.

—RAFAEL SANTANA
WHO HAS HELPED COUNTLESS DOMINICAN PROSPECTS
MAKE IT TO THE MAJOR LEAGUES
(METS SHORTSTOP, 1984—87)

When Rafael Santana returned my call to discuss a time and place for us to meet, he did so in a most formal manner. Until I asked him to please call me Erik, he referred to me as "Mr. Sherman" or "sir." He has a stellar reputation in baseball circles as one of the game's true gentlemen. And of all the Mets, he seemed the most eager to accommodate my interview request, relishing the opportunity to discuss his career and how thrilled he is to continue putting his stamp on the game of baseball.

Over a seven-year major-league career, his offensive numbers don't jump out at you. But as the starting shortstop for the Mets during their glory days from 1984 through 1987, without much acclaim, he played steadily at the most important defensive position on the field and was indispensable. In fact, a statistical case can be made that during his time with the Mets, only the great Ozzie

Smith himself was his superior defensively at shortstop in the National League. And because the mid-eighties Mets were built around outstanding young pitching and timely hitting, Santana's role as a defensive stalwart was deemed just as important to their success as that of another shortstop from the club's only other world championship, in 1969—Buddy Harrelson.

I caught up with Rafael following a card show event at Hofstra University in Hempstead, New York, which he had flown up from his home in Miami earlier in the day to attend. Santana is still in terrific shape for a man now in his late fifties. His face and chest have filled out since his playing days, though he is still lean and would probably dominate any old-timers' game or fantasy camp he played in. Along with a few of his '86 Mets teammates, he had just finished two solid hours of signing autographs for fans and, despite battling a terrible cold, still managed to keep his sunny disposition.

"Let me tell you something," he started out, with still a hint of a Dominican accent. "This show is just another example of why New York is probably the best baseball town in the world. Because if you do something good in New York, people will remember you *forever.*"

Santana then chuckled, adding, "And everybody tells me that because the Mets haven't won again since '86, we're still on top!"

We talked for a bit about how New York has had so many other world championship teams since his Mets won it all—not just in baseball in the Bronx, but in football and hockey, as well. But there was something special about his '86 Mets and the effect they had on their fans. I brought up the talent and characters the ball club had. He preferred to talk about the mutual love affair his team had with the throngs that filled Shea Stadium on a regular basis.

"We were attached to those fans," Raffy said. "Every day we went out and signed autographs for them because we knew that they were there for us. And they knew that we were there for them. So when we won, that's why the fans went crazy. So when you put together the great support, the winning situation, and the character of our team, that's what made that ball club so much fun."

I mentioned how, despite the diversity and the different walks of life the '86 Mets came from, they still seem like a family all these years later.

Raffy agreed.

"A lot of our guys, we get together almost every year. I don't think we have let more than two years go by over the last ten or twelve without seeing each other. There's always some Mets thing on TV or some autograph signings or something else in New York that brings most of the guys together."

I brought up the perception that Raffy was one of the more reserved players on a team with larger-than-life personalities like Dykstra and Strawberry, and he clarified for me how the chemistry of the club made the team a joy to be a part of.

"I think I was a good fit for that group and we *all* got along well," Santana told me. "The other guys hit the media more than I did. So maybe that was the reason people thought I was quiet. I hit .218 in '86. Everybody thought I hit .300, but I only hit .218, though I was second in the National League in defense, so I did my part. Still, I wasn't the guy that would often get the key hit or the most hits in a game, so maybe that was the reason I didn't talk much [to the media]. As for my teammates, Hernandez and I were close, as we had played together in St. Louis [in 1983]. I was also especially close with Mookie. And Wally [Backman] and I knew each other since we played against each other in Rookie Ball, so we got along as well. Plus, I was the only Latin player on the ball club, so everybody seemed to want to hang out with me."

New York is certainly a long way both in distance and energy from La Romana, the small city of Santana's youth in the Dominican Republic. Rafael, the son of a farmer and one of six Santana children—three boys and three girls—grew up with a baseball glove on his left hand, while enjoying the backdrop of some of the Caribbean's most beautiful beaches. And unlike most Dominican towns, as a thriving tourist and resort mecca La Romana has long been a place of near full employment for its residents.

It was, in a word, paradise for young Rafael.

But while it didn't have the dirt, grime, and grit of 1980s-era New York, it didn't have its excitement, either. And La Romana was also far from Santana's favorite team, the Yankees. So imagine the thrill when, as an eighteen-year-old, the Bombers signed him as an amateur free agent in 1976. The Yankees, at the time, were in full "Bronx Zoo" mode. Raffy gave me one example of the reach and grip controversial Yankees owner George Steinbrenner had on the entire organization, at times assuming roles normally reserved for the general manager or skipper of a club.

"I came right up from the Dominican to the Yankees' minor-league system," Santana told me. "During spring training, Steinbrenner used to call players into his office and tell them stuff like, *You're going down to Double-A or Triple-A or wherever. We think a lot about you. Just go out there and bust your ass.* So George did that with me."

Unfortunately for Raffy, he was shipped off to the St. Louis Cardinals organization in 1981, his dreams of wearing the pinstripes denied. But the trade would present an opportunity for Santana. The Yankees were traditionally big spenders, always on the lookout for the top free agents on the market, lacking the patience to nurture and promote young prospects to the big-league roster. That was not the St. Louis way and it wasn't long before Raffy would make his major-league debut with the Cardinals on Opening Day 1983, entering the game at third base as part of a double switch in the eighth inning.

Still, with Ozzie Smith playing Raffy's natural position of shortstop, there wasn't much of a future for him with the Cardinals, and he was released the following January. The Mets, seeing the opportunity to pick up the talented Santana without giving up any players, signed him later *that same day*.

At the start of the 1984 season, the Mets auditioned a parade of shortstops, with Santana in the mix along with the versatile José Oquendo, Ron Gardenhire, and their primary third baseman, Hubie Brooks. Raffy had his best offensive season, hitting .276, while Oquendo and Gardenhire generally floundered.

Following the season, the Mets shipped Brooks off to the Montreal Expos as part of the Gary Carter deal, and traded Oquendo to the Cardinals. Gardenhire would split his time between Triple-A Tidewater and the major-league club, leaving Raffy as the last man standing at shortstop entering the 1985 campaign.

For Raffy, the years have dimmed the disappointment and memories of coming up short in 1985, a season he told me he believed the Mets had the talent to run the table and win a world championship. For him, it was all about 1986 and how the team rallied when they had to in what may have been the greatest and most dramatic National League Championship Series of all-time.

"We won a hundred and eight regular season games, but Houston had a good team," Raffy recalled about the NLCS. "Pitching kind of dominated a little bit, and we were lucky we came up with some timely hitting. But we never gave up hope, never quit. And when we get together, even today, that's something we always talk about. We had good chemistry and knew how to fight and go out there and win ball games. And when the game was over, whether we won or lost, we were never in a rush to get home. We stayed in the clubhouse, talked about why we won or why we lost and got ready mentally for the next day."

Raffy had a huge series in the field, establishing NLCS records for most putouts (thirteen), assists (eighteen), and chances at shortstop (thirty-one) in a six-game series. He played flawless defense and was a part of four double plays. Not too shabby for a player often overlooked on a team of superstars.

Santana would also go on to start all seven World Series games against Boston, despite looking over his shoulder at a young Kevin Elster, who was being touted as the Mets' next big star and future shortstop.

However, for as fine a prospect as Elster was, he was still the greenest of rookies in his only appearance of the 1986 World Series. Barely twenty-two years old, he entered Game Six as Santana's replacement after Raffy was pinch-hit for by Danny Heep in the bottom of the fifth, with the Mets down 2–1 against Roger Clemens but rallying. While Heep's double-play grounder allowed the tying run to score, the Mets now didn't have the coolness and veteran leadership of Santana in the pressure cooker that was Game Six.

Perhaps, in part, due to nerves brought on by the enormity of the game, Elster committed a throwing error in the seventh inning that helped Boston take a 3–2 lead later in the frame. The fact that Santana was pulled so early in the game surprised many, including Raffy himself.

"Did that surprise you?" I asked.

"I was really surprised because it was *only* the bottom of the fifth," Santana said, implying that if he were pinch-hit for, it usually came much later in games. "But that was Davey's decision, and he was one of the greatest managers in the game. We almost got hurt, but he was looking [for the big inning]."

Of course, it all worked out in the most mystical of ways in the tenth inning and then two nights later with a Game Seven victory.

Like most of his teammates, Santana was surprised the Mets didn't repeat as at least division champions in 1987, when considering how his club had thoroughly dominated the year before. Still, he considered the ninety-two wins the Mets had as an accomplishment when recalling how badly their pitching staff was decimated throughout much of the season. And for Santana personally, it was perhaps his finest all-around season as a big leaguer.

Still, the Mets were seduced by the pop in Elster's bat, and the young shortstop appeared ready to take over the reins for Raffy, making him both expendable and the answer to a trivia question. In getting traded to the Yankees following the 1987 season, he was part of the first transaction made between the crosstown rivals that included major-league players.

"So Rafael," I said. "It must have been like night and day leaving the Mets to play for the Yankees in 1988. Going from an electric environment with attendance topping three million at Shea in '87, with the nucleus of a very good young team still creating buzz, to a Yankees team in constant turmoil. It must have been so different."

"It was *completely* different," Raffy said with conviction. "With the Yankees, we had a good team, but there was no chemistry. We started out with Billy [Martin], who got fired near the middle of the season. Then we had some of the front office guys that wanted Piniella, who was the general manager, to come in to manage, which he did, taking over for Billy. The lack of stability was a big difference from the Mets. The Mets stayed together and we played together."

Raffy then talked about all the leaders the Mets had, and how the Yankees didn't have anyone that wanted to step up into that role.

"When I joined the Yankees, I forget which reporter came over and told me, but he said that I could be the leader on that team because it didn't have one. And he said they needed one. I said, 'No, I'm not that guy. What happened with Mattingly, or Willie Randolph, or Dave Winfield, or Rickey Henderson? All those guys have been here for a long time. Why can't any of them be a leader of this team? And so now you want *me* to face George? No, I just joined the bunch.'"

Raffy continued, saying how incredible he thought it was that none of the great Yankee veteran players wanted to lead.

"I didn't know the reason why none of those guys wanted to be the leader, especially Willie, who had played for the Yankees for twelve or thirteen years. 'Winnie' could have been the leader also, but I remember his mother was very sick that year, and at some point he had to leave the ball club to be with her. But the rest of the guys didn't want that role, either."

Perhaps upon some quick reflection, Santana paused, and concluded that it was a tough situation.

"Let me tell you, the front office was a zoo," he said. "George fired a manager and then would move the guy he fired up to the front office and would then bring someone from upstairs to run the team. And George was hearing from guys questioning every move the manager on the field was making."

Raffy also contended that The Boss was getting poor advice.

"At some point [in '88], we needed pitching," Raffy said. "But then the guys helping out George went out and got another infielder instead of getting a pitcher. I remember at some point Baltimore was shopping Mike Boddicker. Do you remember him?"

"Sure," I said. "Good pitcher."

"Right, so anyway, I thought, *Hey, that's what we need*. Baltimore was asking for either Hensley Meulens, Roberto Kelly, or Jay Buhner. So we didn't want to get rid of any of those guys. So Boston got Boddicker and he went out and won seven games for them down the stretch. Getting Boddicker gave Boston the title. If Boddicker had won those games for us instead of the Red Sox, we would have won the division."

As it turned out, the Red Sox traded plenty to get Boddicker, but wouldn't realize it for several years. The two prospects they dealt to the Orioles included a then light-hitting center fielder named Brady Anderson, who would go on to hit as many as fifty home runs in a season and have a fabulous career. The other was Curt Schilling, who would become one of the dominant starting pitchers of his era and actually return to Boston years later to help end the notorious "Curse of the Bambino," Boston's eighty-six-year drought without winning a World Series.

"The trade we ended up making," Santana said, his voice elevated with some disdain, "was getting Ken Phelps from Seattle for Jay Buhner! It didn't make any sense because Jack Clark was our DH and was leading the club in home runs and RBIs at the time. And Mattingly was playing first, Phelps's other position."

"Ugh," I said. "One of the worst trades ever."

And it truly was, helping to set the Yankee franchise back years and giving the Mariners a cornerstone player for the next thirteen seasons.

But despite Raffy playing for his favorite childhood team in a state of disarray, he got along well with Steinbrenner. In fact, knowing that Santana played most of 1988 with painful bone chips, the usually harsh Boss back in those days said late that season, "I'd love to have him on my *football* team."

I reminded Raffy of the quote, and he smiled, saying, "From the day I came over to the Yankees from the Mets, when George came over to me and told me how nice it was to see me again, until the end of the season, he was great to me. And he must have known the reason I hurt my arm was because I didn't want to stop playing to heal it because we were in the middle of the pennant race and I didn't want to leave the ball club. I just wanted to go out and win. So that's why the arm got aggravated. I ended up getting surgery on it and missed the following season."

"So I have to ask you," I said. "At that time, did you wish you had still been with the Mets?"

"Well, I made my career with the Mets," Santana said. "I thought I was going to be part of the Mets for a while, but they had Elster coming up and they had to get rid of me. I was thirty years old and Elster was only twenty-three. They wanted to take advantage of his youth. And the year before they traded me, he had a good year in Triple-A, so there was no reason to keep me."

"The business of baseball?" I asked.

"Right," Santana replied. "The business of baseball."

It was clear he longed for his former Mets teammates when, on an off day for the Yankees that September of '88, he visited them in the Shea Stadium clubhouse. It happened to be the same night the Mets clinched the division title. The fact he made the effort to visit the Mets on his first real night off in weeks spoke volumes.

"Why was it so important for you to go over and visit the guys?" I asked him.

"Well, that was probably the only opportunity I had to go over and say hello to my friends, the ones I had left behind from when I played for the Mets. I thought, *I've got to go back there again and say hello to Hernandez and Mookie—all those guys.*"

An article about Raffy's visit appeared in the next day's *New York Times*. While he made it clear in the piece that he was now a Yankee, the lightheartedness and good-natured ribbing he shared with many of the Mets players that night, as reported in the article, made it appear that he understandably missed his former teammates and playing at Shea.

I began to ask him what the Yankees thought of his visit to their rivals in Queens, and before I could even finish my question, Raffy, knowing where I was going with it, jumped in, saying, "I think I told them, 'This is my day off, I do whatever I want.'"

I found it interesting that in less than a one-year span, Raffy had played for three of the highest profile managers in the history of the game—Davey Johnson, Billy Martin, and Lou Piniella. I wondered aloud how their individual styles may have helped Raffy later in his post-baseball career as a minor-league manager and coach.

"They all had an influence," Raffy told me. "Davey was a great manager because he studied the game. Billy always wanted to push and push and push! He was always picky about something to get the most out of his players, which was sometimes negative. But Billy challenged you to be better. He wanted to know what you were going to do and then told you to go out there and do it. And if you could back up what you told Billy you were going to do, then he knew you could play for him. Billy's style was completely different from Davey's, who was also more mellow. As for Piniella, he was just starting out as a manager when I played for him, still learning. But I think he had a good experience managing the Yankees at that time, because it helped him become one of the greatest managers of his time."

Raffy's final big-league stop was with the Cleveland Indians after they signed him as a free agent for the 1990 season. It was a dreadful place. Cleveland's Municipal Stadium, known as the "The Mistake by the Lake," was an often cold and windy cavernous ballpark, which rarely attracted big crowds. In 1990, they were last in league attendance, drawing an average of around fifteen thousand fans a game. And they were managed by John McNamara, a curmudgeonly man not exactly known for his people skills in guiding players.

Perhaps the only positive for Santana was that he was rejoining Hernandez and Jesse Orosco, also acquired by the Indians as free agents.

"Cleveland must have been a pretty drab place after the thrill of playing in New York," I said to Raffy. "What was it like for the three of you to be in Cleveland after playing for those great Mets teams before those millions of adoring fans?"

"Well, it made us feel good because we were around guys that we knew," Santana answered. "So we didn't feel strange in Cleveland because Jesse, Hernandez, and I felt like, *Hey, we have a little Mets team here.* That made it easier to make the adjustment of coming to a new team. We had to get to know the other guys, but that was easy for us.

"The problem was that in New York, we were always a contending team," Raffy continued. "We got to Cleveland and we were horseshit. We couldn't do anything—it was a completely different environment. I didn't see any togetherness on the team. Everybody was in their own corner and all that. It was *different* from the Mets in every way. I remember during that spring training when we broke camp and I was asked by one of the front office people about what I thought about the ball club and I said, 'Hey, I think we've got a chance in this division.' But the answer that I got from him was 'I just don't want to finish in last place.' I thought, *Oh shit, this is going to be interesting this year.* I went to Hernandez and told him what the front office guy said, and Mex told me, "Hey, get ready for a long year."

"Somebody in the *front office* said that?!" I asked incredulously.

"Yep," Raffy confirmed.

As it turned out, it was a disastrous year, but at least a short one for Raffy. He was released a month and a half into the season. It wasn't much better for Mex and Jesse. Mex had a bad back, and hit just .200 in only forty-three games. And Orosco was Doug Jones's backup reliever, saving just two games that year. Cleveland finished in fourth place, with a very un-Mets-like eight games under .500 record. The three Mets clearly weren't in Flushing anymore.

"So were you ready to retire at that point?" I asked.

"No," Raffy answered. "In fact, I reached out to the Mets mid-season because they needed a backup guy. I knew my arm was not one hundred percent, but it was good enough. Plus, I still had my condo in Bayside, Queens. Buddy Harrelson, who I knew really well, was managing the team then, and I said to him, 'Buddy, I don't care if I start or not. I can stay here with the team and I'll be the backup to Elster just in case something happens.' So Buddy talked to the front office about it and told them, 'I need Raffy. Raffy can be a backup shortstop for us.' But they told him they had something in the works with the Seattle Mariners to get Mario Díaz, whom they eventually got in a trade for Brian Givens. After that, I was out of the picture."

Santana's playing career may have been over, but a second life in baseball was just beginning. Raffy made a near seamless transition from player to coach, working in three major-league organizations, first with the Kansas City Royals, then with the Boston Red Sox, and finally in his current and longtime affiliation with the Chicago White Sox.

It cannot be overstated the significant role Santana has played in the development and surging numbers of Dominican players in major-league baseball for the last two decades. He is currently the

Dominican Republic supervisor of player development and administration for the White Sox, a role in which he practically splits the year evenly between Miami and the island nation, averaging eight trips annually.

I asked him to what he attributed the growing trend of Dominican players in the game today.

"Well, the Dominican has always been like a baseball country," Raffy said. "But now we have a type of draft all our own every July. [Dominican] organizations prepare players and do a showcase so the big-league scouts can evaluate them. Right now, every major-league organization has a baseball academy in the Dominican Republic. So you have thirty organizations each carrying two teams. I'm telling you, it's getting bigger and bigger every year."

The academies for promising Dominican prospects that Santana speaks about are impressive. Not only have they become incubators for the major leagues, but they also educate the players in learning to speak English and prepare them for life during and after their playing days are over, as well as giving back to their local communities through club-sponsored projects. The training facilities are state-of-the-art.

"Right now," Raffy continued, "I'm handling the Dominican situation for Chicago, which I've been doing for the last eight years or so. I move from Florida to the Dominican all the time. I don't have to go anywhere else except when I go to spring training in Arizona in March. In Arizona, I work with the infielders and attend meetings where we make decisions on players, as well as discuss the Dominican program, what we have down there, what we need and what we don't need."

"Developing so many young players must be very rewarding for you," I said. "What do you consider the best part of your job every day?"

"Every time you work with the guys," Santana said with much pride and sincerity, "you're hoping they're going to make it to the big leagues. It makes you understand that you're doing something for the game. And that makes you love the game even more."

"Those kids and the White Sox are lucky to have you," I told Rafael. "But I must say it just doesn't seem right to not see you working for the Mets. Have you ever approached them about getting a job in their organization?"

"Yes, I did," Raffy told me. "And it's a very good story. A few years ago, when Omar Minaya was their general manager, he had just come out in the papers saying that I was one of the candidates to be first base coach for the Mets. I called Fred Wilpon on his cell and then at his office and left a message with his secretary. Fred returned my call right away and told me, 'Raffy, I have given Omar all the power to make all the moves. I'm going to talk to him, but I want you to call him directly and speak with him.'

"So, I called [Minaya] a couple of times on his cell phone, but he never returned my calls or anything. So I just let it go by and, of course, he went out and hired someone else."

I couldn't help but think it was strange that Minaya, a fellow Dominican with a track record of recruiting some of the best Latin talent in baseball, would throw Raffy's name in the mix for the Mets' first base coaching job and then not even bother to return his calls.

"That's so bizarre," I said.

"Yeah, it is," Santana replied. "But that's life. I've been with the White Sox since 1998, so you never know. You can't burn any bridges."

Santana's other baseball passion besides developing young Dominican players revolves around development closer to home— with his two sons.

"How are your boys doing in baseball?" I asked.

"Alexander was drafted in the second round of the 2011 major-league draft by the Dodgers," Santana said proudly and with much conviction. "He's a kid with the greatest talent in the world. He was a third baseman, but they just moved him to the outfield. He's got a chance to develop into a five-tool type of player. He's only twenty-one, so who knows what can happen?

"And I've got the other one, Audry, who's a year older than Alexander. He plays second base and we [the White Sox] drafted him last year."

"That's fantastic," I said. "With all your travel and time away from home, how did you help get them involved in baseball to the point where they are both professionals now?"

"Since they were little kids," Raffy explained, "we moved to Florida and got them started in T-Ball and they went up from there. They really got into baseball and then saw an opportunity to get drafted, which they both did."

And with that, the gracious Santana hurriedly left Hofstra to catch a flight back to Miami and prepare for yet another trip down to the Dominican Republic the next morning.

Rafael Francisco Santana, the boy from La Romana, has truly come full circle in a long and rewarding baseball life.

· 8 ·

ONE WAS TORMENTED

Things got so bad that some "fan" sent me a Rexall Drugs prescription for cyanide. The directions said "take until termination."

—DOUG SISK
(METS RELIEF PITCHER, 1982–87)

It was a Saturday afternoon on September 8, 1984, at a packed and boisterous Shea Stadium, the crowd roaring to every single pitch. The first-place Chicago Cubs were in town, and the Mets had thoroughly dominated them in the opening game of the series the evening before, with a 10–0 victory behind Doc Gooden's complete-game one-hitter. Banners screaming "Cub Busters!" a rallying cry in homage to the adopted Mets theme song and that summer's hit movie *Ghostbusters*, were being waved by fans and hung from the railings throughout the ballpark.

The fans smelled blood.

A win on this overcast day would pull the Mets to within five games of Chicago in the National League East. A loss would all but end their hopes of winning the title in a division in which they had spent sixty-five days in first place during their unexpected, magical summer run.

Chicago led 2–0 when Davey Johnson summoned Doug Sisk to pitch the top half of the seventh inning to keep things close against Cubs starter Rick Sutcliffe, the would-be Cy Young Award winner for the National League that year.

Sisk had followed up a brilliant first full season with the club in 1983—a year he finished third in the Rookie of the Year balloting—with an even better 1984 campaign to that point, entering the game with an astounding 1.95 ERA to go along with fifteen saves. He was one of the building blocks the Mets had relied on during this turnaround season, and his nasty sinker ball had more movement than any other in baseball.

But on this day, Sisk picked the wrong time to not have his best stuff. The Cubs connected against him for four hits in plating two more runs, to give themselves a seemingly insurmountable 4–0 lead with their ace Sutcliffe on the mound.

As Sisk walked toward the Mets' dugout after the final out of the frame was made, the boos rained down on him hard. *Very hard.* Watching the game on television, I was in near shock at how the Shea faithful could be so extraordinarily harsh on one of their own, particularly a relief pitcher who had been so remarkable up until that fateful game.

The Cubs, of course, would hold on to win the game, effectively sealing the Mets' demise.

As for Sisk, he would remain with the Mets through the '87 season and would even help them win a world championship, but would never be as effective a pitcher as he was over much of his first two seasons with the Mets.

And worse yet, many fans would never let him forget that early September day in 1984.

| | | | | | |

"You like oysters?" Sisk asked me over the phone as we set up our meeting together. "We have the best out here. We can go to a bar I know. Don't worry. You'll be okay. The other Scum Bunchers won't be there!"

The bar would be inside the That's-A-Some Italian Ristorante in Poulsbo, Washington. And true to his word, but to my great disappointment, his fellow Scum Bunch pals Jesse Orosco and Danny Heep would not be joining us.

For much of the eighty-mile loop around the Puget Sound to Poulsbo from the Seattle-Tacoma Airport, tall pine trees that led into the vast forestry of the beautiful Pacific Northwest lined the sides of the highway. Doug, a large and friendly man, was kind enough to meet me halfway, at a gas station just after I crossed the Tacoma Narrows Bridge, and I followed him for the remainder of the trip into Poulsbo. In just that one-hour-and-fifteen-minute drive, typically for the region, the weather went from bright sunshine, to heavy clouds, to rain, and then back to clear, brilliant blue skies.

Located on Liberty Bay, Poulsbo is a charming town which, on this early December day, resembled a Christmas village, with festive decorations of the holiday season throughout. The architecture has a Northern European flavor to it, the origin of which is the many immigrants from Finland and Norway that inhabited the town in the late 1800s. Flower boxes adorn many of the windows, and a church with a tall steeple can be seen at the highest point in town.

We walked into the bar and were seated at a table near the back.

Our section was dimly lit, even in early afternoon, though Christmas lights gave it a warm feeling. There was literally a wall of wine bottles to our left. An army-navy football game was playing on the television. Italian crooners could be heard over the speakers when Tommy, the owner of the place for twenty-five years, stopped over to say hello to us.

"This guy could have been a great pitcher," Doug said tongue-in-cheek of Tommy. "I just couldn't room with the son of a bitch!"

"Nobody can," Tommy said, chuckling. "That's why I'm a loner with a boner."

I would discover later, when Tommy's very pretty and charming wife introduced herself to me, that he likely was anything but a lonely man.

It would be the start of a long discussion into the early evening when a bottle of Pinot Grigio was brought to our table. Doug has become somewhat of an expert in wines, as he currently works as a salesman for a small Washington State distributor called Unique Wines.

"We have some really good wines. You're not drinking one right now—this is from a *different* distributor," Doug said with a hearty laugh.

The culture of drinking throughout baseball history has been well documented. And while I promised Doug, at his request, not to ask too many questions about the hard-partying ways of the Mets and focus, instead, more on the baseball intellect of the championship team, Sisk couldn't resist opening up our discussion with stories about how his beloved Scum Bunch operated.

"In front of the plane were the reporters," Doug began. "They didn't drink anything. But every time they went to the back of the plane the Scum Bunch wouldn't let them through. We charged them a 'guzzle' to go to the bathroom. It was like paying their dues, a toll. We did it with the players, too. We didn't mess with Mookie, because he was there in the lean years and we knew he didn't drink at all. I've never seen him drink a beer or glass of wine or even chew tobacco. He kept himself in the absolute best shape and had the best body fat on the team—three percent in the dunk tank, which is the most accurate you can get. Anyway, we didn't mess much with George Foster, either. But we *really* messed with Rusty Staub when he was on the team, more than anybody else. I know he really liked it, but I'm sure there were times when he was pretty perturbed with us as well."

Doug then segued into a story about an alcohol-induced incident on one of those plane rides.

"Probably the worst we ever had was during the '84 season," Sisk said. "Walt Terrell was in the back with us and started calling Darryl names."

"Calling *Darryl* names?" I asked. "Strawberry was built like a Greek god. Terrell had guts."

"Yeah, he did," Doug said. "And to make matters worse, everybody got up on the plane and there was some pushing and shoving going on. After it finally settled down and a few of us are in the back, just sitting there and having a few cocktails, a steward comes to us and says, 'I don't know what you guys did to him, but he's totally upset up there.' I asked, 'Who?' And he said, 'Strawberry. He said that he'll remember this.' I asked what he meant, and the steward answered, 'Because he said you guys back here don't know what it's like to be a superstar.'

"So Walt gets on the megaphone they used to talk throughout the plane and just starts screaming at Darryl, saying some terrible things, before going, 'Anytime, if your wife wants to know what it's like to be with a real man, send her over to my house!'

"That was it," Sisk continued. "All hell broke loose. So the plane lands in New York, and Davey gets on the loudspeaker and addresses the twenty-five or so beat writers, saying, 'None of this will leave this plane. *None* of this! If I see one thing in the newspaper, or anything like that, you guys will be banned from our flights.'

"So I would say about two weeks later, the *Sporting News* had a piece on how the Mets were doing, stories about their minor-league system and players to look out for, and then there was this little general information section that noted how all hard liquor had been banned from all Mets charter flights. And that was basically the only thing written about that day."

"Do you think that incident was what led to Terrell getting traded after the season?" I asked.

"Yep, I *know* it was," answered Doug. "No doubt. And it ended up being a very good trade for both the Mets and Tigers. They got Walt over there, a real workhorse. And, of course, we got Howard Johnson."

I told Doug that Darryl was the next Met that I was going to visit, and he had nothing but glowing things to say about him.

"I enjoyed Darryl as a teammate," Sisk said. "Of course, I played with him from Rookie Ball all the way up."

"I heard he was pretty tough on guys like [Tim] Teufel," I said.

"I never saw it," Doug said. "Darryl was always fun, and he loved the Scum Bunch, *loved* us guys. He tried to hang with us a couple of times, but we took him down."

"You took *Straw* down?" I asked incredulously.

"Yep, we took him and [Kevin] Mitchell down," he said. "We called them the *Knucksie Brothers* because they had muscle faces, like knuckles. So one night in Pittsburgh, Straw said to me, 'We want to take the Scum Bunch out for dinner.'

"So they took us to some bars that were *absolutely not* for the Scum Bunch."

"You mean places popular with the 'brothers'?" I asked with a grin.

Doug laughed and said, "You bet they were. So they kept up with us for a while, but I don't remember what happened to them the rest of the evening."

Listening to Doug reminisce about his days with the Mets, it's clear that, despite the treatment he often endured from Mets fans, he positively loved the baseball life. And playing for a team laden with superstars from the '86 team likely made everything that much better.

"In '86, our team was on auto-ship," Sisk enthusiastically went on. "Davey's job was to keep everybody in line. The coaches were like babysitters by that point. The talent was there regardless if you were sick or tired or anything. I mean, Darryl Strawberry at fifty percent was better than most outfielders at one hundred percent. There was no weakness on that club. And any one of those players could have a beer, a glass of milk, or whatever, and fit in with any crowd [on our team], and that's what was so cool about it. I think what you're trying to accomplish with this book of yours, showing people what we're doing now, is going to be a surprise to a lot of people. A *huge* surprise. They probably assume now that all the Scum Bunch wives would be gone, their kids would be in nuthouses, and they would all have liver issues. But I'll tell you what, *we* were the *most* stable of all of these people!"

"Well, sure," I said. "And how about this for irony? The only '86 Mets player to have passed away is Gary Carter, and he was one of the handful of clean-cut players on the team. What kind of odds could you have gotten on Kid being the first to go? Think about it.

Lenny's still around. Darryl's still around. Doc's still around. The Scum Bunch is still around. And you're still married to your wife, right, Doug?"

"Yes, still married to Lisa for thirty years now," Sisk replied. "And we have three children. My son Brady—named after my old Orioles teammate Brady Anderson because my wife loved that name—is down in California doing stand-in commercials and modeling as much as he can. And we have two daughters. Lindsay was an '86 baby like Teufel's, Jesse's, and Rick Anderson's kids. And Katelin, the 'Katelinator,' got a scholarship to pitch fast-pitch soft-ball at Florida. She's now finishing up at Washington State getting her nursing degree. So it's all good."

Doug would go on to tell me how much they enjoy living in Tacoma and that they get a great deal of tranquility from a cabin they own in Belfair. It's a life that's a long way from those wild days on the road with the Mets.

| | | | | | | |

To truly understand the hurt that Doug felt from the ire of the fans at Shea Stadium, some background is important. The first point would be that, despite being raised in Tacoma, Sisk actually grew up a Mets fan and it was always his dream to play for them.

"I can recall the '69 World Series," he told me, "and I could always name every player on that team. And then I could always recall the '73 National League playoffs when Willie Mays was on the club. I mean, how many kids from the Seattle area back then could name the rosters from those two teams? I might have been the only one."

Then Sisk recalls when he first met Tom Seaver.

"I get signed as a free agent with the Mets in 1980," Doug said.

Dwight Gooden at his Long Island home with son Dwight Jr. "Doc" was on his way to a surefire Hall of Fame career before drugs short-circuited his quest for superstardom. Today he spends much of his time giving his testimony to young people on the dangers of drug use.

Ed Hearn with his son, Cody, and wife, Tricia, at their Kansas home. Ed has endured nearly thirty years of daunting health challenges while his son, Cody, has battled lymphoma. Ed has used his life experiences to help countless others in his work as a motivational speaker.

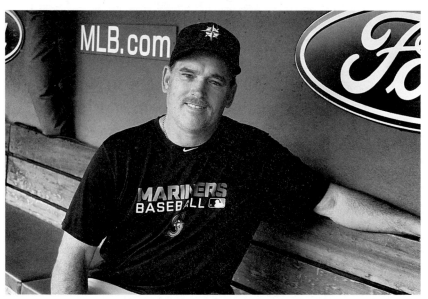

Howard Johnson in the Fenway Park dugout as hitting coach for the Seattle Mariners. Once given the chance to play regularly, "HoJo" would become one of the most prolific sluggers in club history.

Kevin Mitchell at a poolside café in San Diego. "Mitch" was mistakenly believed by the front office to be a bad influence on Gooden and Strawberry and was traded shortly after the '86 World Series. He went on to have a sparkling career, which included an MVP season in 1989. Mitchell, who has endured several heart-wrenching family tragedies, dedicates much of his time giving free baseball instruction to children.

Lenny Dykstra in a hotel lounge in Los Angeles. "Nails" made a fortune in business following his baseball career before losing it all, landing in jail, and allegedly getting his teeth knocked out by a prison guard. Dykstra, as determined as ever, is working hard to get his life back on track.

Keith Hernandez at an event on Long Island. The trade for Hernandez in 1983, which followed his admitted recreational drug use while a Cardinal, was the best in Mets' history, delivering the team a bona fide superstar, leader, and veteran presence who helped turn around a perennially losing franchise. "Mex," the greatest defensive first baseman of all time and who should be in the Baseball Hall of Fame, is now the colorful, unfiltered, award-winning analyst for Mets' games on SNY.

Rafael Santana at Hofstra University. The Mets' solid championship shortstop has played a significant role in the surge in Dominican players in the Major Leagues over the last twenty years.

Darryl Strawberry with his wife, Tracy, in their living room in St. Peters, Missouri. The couple, recovering drug addicts, met at a Narcotics Anonymous convention and are now both ordained ministers. "Straw," the eight-time All Star and four-time World Series champion, has completely turned his life around, conquering both drug and alcohol dependency as well as two bouts with cancer. He is now an evangelical preacher who gives sermons around the country and has been cancer-free for over fifteen years.

Doug Sisk at a restaurant in Poulsbo, Washington. On a team worshipped by its fans, "Dougie" was much maligned by them. Despite pitching through pain and injuries, Mets' fans never seemed to give their once-stellar relief pitcher a break.

Bobby Ojeda at an event in White Plains, New York. Ojeda was the ace of the Mets' heralded pitching staff in '86 and epitomized the team's take no prisoners swagger that season. After leaving the Mets, "Bobby O" miraculously survived a fatal boating accident that took the lives of two of his Cleveland teammates. A contract dispute last year with SNY ended his run as the popular, outspoken studio host of Mets' pregame and postgame shows.

Danny Heep with his Incarnate Word players in the background at the San Antonio university. The ultimate team player and leader of the Scum Bunch, Heep was a member of five different teams to make the postseason. He is now one of the most successful coaches in the country, having elevated the Incarnate Word baseball program to great heights during his eighteen-year run there.

Mookie Wilson with wife, Rosa, at their home near Columbia, South Carolina. Mookie played the entire decade of the eighties with the Mets and is generally regarded as the most beloved player in the team's history. Wilson recently became an ordained minister, though he still works for the Mets as a team ambassador and roving instructor.

Wally Backman in Las Vegas as manager of the 51s, the Mets' Triple-A club. The onetime scrappy second baseman has played a major role in the development of many of the Mets' young stars today, but a promotion to manage in the big leagues has been suppressed by alleged off-field transgressions from nearly fifteen years ago. With six first-place finishes and two Minor League Manager of the Year awards, Wally may very well be the greatest manager to have never managed in the Major Leagues.

Gary Carter's widow, Sandy, and their two daughters, Christy, left, and Kimmy, right. The acquisition of Carter from Montreal following the '84 season gave the Mets the power-hitting right-handed bat they needed and the veteran catching presence their young pitching staff craved. The clean-living "Kid" was not exactly popular in the hard-partying culture of the Mets' clubhouse, but became revered by many of those same teammates later in life.

"Then I made the team in '83 and am pitching on Opening Day in relief of *Tom Seaver*! It just blew me away to go into a game after him."

Then the other part of the equation is how Sisk said he gave his heart, body, and soul to the Mets his first couple of years with the organization, which led to arm issues around the time he began to struggle.

"In '82, I was the ERA leader in the Texas League, which is extremely tough because you had all those little band boxes in places like El Paso and Midland," Sisk said. "I pitched over a hundred innings there that season. Then immediately afterwards, I pitched in the big leagues, then the instructional league, then winter ball, and then finally the Caribbean World Series. I stayed home for two weeks and then went straight to spring training and broke a Mets record for most pitching appearances in the '83 season."

Sisk then talked about how relief appearances back then were much different than in today's game.

"These guys today are pitching in seventy games with just sixty innings," Doug began. "That to me is crazy."

"The save has really been cheapened," I said.

"Oh yeah," Sisk agreed. "I always thought if a guy struggled for an inning or two or his pitch count got up, but he's still on course and doing the job, give him a chance to win the damned ball game. It's so specialized now that they're taking the 'balls' out of you. I can recall games that I went out there and wasn't feeling good—the flu, a hangover once or twice, whatever—but there were never any excuses. You went out there and went after the opponent. Now they're counting pitches in the *bullpen*!"

"Doug, when I was a kid, the first time I went to Yankee Stadium in 1976, I saw a game between the Red Sox and Yankees," I said. "Catfish Hunter pitched all eleven innings in a 1–0 Yankee win. Time of game was just two hours, thirteen minutes."

"Unbelievable," Doug said incredulously.

"You'll never see that again," I added.

"I can recall games in '83 and '84 when I pitched the first game of a double-header and got the save in the second game," Sisk countered. "And it was never discussed. You did what you had to do because if you didn't, there was somebody else that was waiting to take your spot.

"I once pitched in six games in a row in '84," Sisk continued, "and Davey came over to me after the last of those games and said, 'Doug, you're not pitching tomorrow.' So Jess [Jesse Orosco] and I went out until the sun came up the next day. Jesse shouldn't have been with me, but whatever. So before the next game, I'm out shagging [fly balls] and I'm still hammered. I did my running, and the sweat was stinging my eyes because of the Schnapps and everything else we were drinking. I had no cup on, no spikes, because I wasn't playing that day. Then we got to the fifth inning, I'm lying in the cart, and all of a sudden the phone rings. I pick it up, and Davey says, 'Hey Doug, can you get an out?' I said, 'Sure, no problem.' So I grabbed my spikes, threw three or four warm-up pitches in the bullpen, went to the drinking fountain I don't know how many times, and they bring me in and I get the out. Davey asked me to stay in the game, and the rest is a blur to me until the ninth. I get the final out, get into the clubhouse, and a reporter comes up to me, shakes my hand, and says, 'That was a great save you got.' I went, 'Save?' And he said, 'Yeah, that was a save.' I said, 'Wait a minute. I came in in the fifth.' But he was right. It was the official scorer's discretion."

We discussed whether that might have been the longest save in baseball history, but, in fact, that distinction belongs to Joaquín Benoit, who pitched a seven-inning save in a 2002 game while with the Texas Rangers. Nevertheless, Sisk's performance is all the more impressive considering how he was feeling that day. But most importantly, it shows how Doug did whatever was requested of him for the betterment of the team.

Now Doug was on a roll, giving another example of the pride he took in his role as a Mets workhorse relief pitcher who finished what he started.

"One more story about wanting the ball," Doug said. "Back in '84, Bruce Berenyi had pitched six strong innings and was ahead 1–0. Bruce was once unbelievable with the Reds, but we got him after his arm had gone bad. So I enter the game in the seventh and pitch into the ninth, when lightning began to strike. Back in the day they didn't stop games because of lightning. So I didn't even do warm-ups. I was like, 'Let's go. Let's get it going.' I get the first two guys out and *Boom!* The rain hits. Everybody runs off the field. So we're in the clubhouse, and after a forty-minute rain delay, Davey comes out and says to me, 'Hey, if we resume play, you're not going back out there. So give me the ball.' And I said, 'No. I'm not giving up the ball.' He walks away, and then about ten minutes later, he comes back and goes, 'All right, give me the ball. Here's a beer. Take the beer, give me the ball.' I said, 'Davey, no. I'll tell you what, I'll drink the beer, *and* I want the ball.' While this exchange is going on, I notice Jesse was just licking his chops about coming in for the one-out save. Anyway, the game got canceled and I ended up getting the save."

Tommy walked over to our table with a glass containing a strange-looking concoction. He asked Doug if he wanted to try it.

"No, thank you," Doug said. "And don't give Erik one, either."

"What is that?" I asked. "A rum and coke?"

"No, I think it's a whiskey," Tommy said.

"Oh, you *think* it's a whiskey," I said, to laughs.

As Tommy left the table, talk turned to Doug's disastrous '85 season, the only truly poor one of his career, and how ruthless the fans were to him.

"I was very fortunate to have Mel Stottlemyre as my pitching coach," Sisk began. "Mel was a sinker baller, too. He knew I had to be in a lot of games because to throw the sinker ball, you've got to pitch tired. But I think after several years of all those innings, I ran out of bullets. There was a point in '85 where things were just not right."

"When did you feel a difference?" I asked.

"It was during a game in Montreal," Sisk said. "I'm thinking everything's coming back. I blow the first two guys out and then I walk the third guy. The ball was going different ways on me. Davey comes to take me out of the ball game and brings in Jesse. I put my arm in my jacket, and afterwards, when I went to take it out, I couldn't. Bone chips had locked into my elbow. In the clubhouse, they gave me some anti-inflammatories and told me to get some ice, but I said, 'No, not this time, guys. Not this time.' So we went back to New York and I went for X-rays. I found out I had about twenty bone chips in there.

"So, I'm having a beer in the back room at Shea before that night's game, and Davey comes in and looks at me and asks, 'So how long has this been going on?' I said, 'Davey, man, I swear to God . . .' 'Well, it's over,' he said. 'Everything's going to be good. This is a relief. We knew something had to be wrong.'

"After my elbow surgery, the Mets did something that I always respected them for," Sisk continued. "They flew me back to New York and had a press conference at the ballpark. Dr. James Parkes was there and said the bone chips that I went through was definitely something that screwed up my season and that I was going to be *just fine*. It was done in an attempt to get the fans off my ass. It didn't work. And they still harass me."

"I can see you're getting a little emotional," I said. "Who was the one that orchestrated that press conference?"

"I think it was Frank Cashen," Sisk said. "I don't know how others felt about him, but he was a class act to me."

"How tough was it to do your job, injured as it turned out, with the fans on you like they were?" I asked.

"It never really bothered me too much," Doug said. "I guess what generally bothers me more than anything now is to read all the stuff about me being the player most hated in the big leagues for the Mets. *C'mon!* I guess it's a privilege to have that [label] when you look at it indirectly, because I would have had to have done something really good to have something bad enough happen to earn that distinction.

"But there were times I didn't like it for my wife, Lisa. I told her not to come to games sometimes. And there were times when the Mets told me not to go down and sign autographs before a game because who knows what kind of information they were getting. There were times people would follow me home and I'd duck into a bar and have those guys have the living snot beaten out of them."

"You would fight them?" I asked.

"I wouldn't, no," Sisk said. "I had some guys follow me one night, and instead of going home and having them find out where I lived, I went to a bar in Port Washington on Long Island. I went in and the owner goes, 'Hey, Dougie, nice to see you.' I told him, 'I've got a couple of guys following me.' And he said, 'We'll take care of it.' The guys came in and were told, 'We're closed.' The guys said,

'Looks like you're open now.' And they were told, 'It's closed to *you*.' Then the guys were taken to the back and smacked around a little bit and told not to bother anybody. That was the end of that.

"But there were letters," Doug continued. "*A lot* of letters. And there were times when fans would scream and yell to our bullpen stuff like '*Roger, stay away from him! He's the devil! Stay away from him!*' And Roger [McDowell] would just wave them off and say, 'Grow up.'"

"And then wasn't there another time when you were pulling your car out of the Shea Stadium players' parking area with Jesse when a gun was pulled on you?" I asked.

"Yeah, a fake gun," Sisk said. "The guy stood right in front of the car. Jesse went down in his seat. Scared the hell out of me."

"How did you know the gun was a fake?" I asked.

"Oh, we didn't at first," Doug said. "But eventually we got closer and could see it was a fake gun. He did just like this with his finger." Sisk made a pulling-the-trigger motion.

"After a while of this nonsense, Davey stopped pitching you at home games," I said. "Did you discuss that decision with him at all?"

"No, he did that on his own," Doug said.

"After he made that decision, did you ever go to him and say something like, *Hey, Davey, I'll pitch wherever you want me to?*" I asked.

"I was just happy he still had confidence in me," Sisk said. "Remember, he was my manager in Jackson, as well. My struggling was hard on him, too. There was never any animosity between me and Davey. I always liked him. He was a player, too. And I think he was a real player's manager because he had played as much as we did. There was not too much you could tell him.

"There were times," Doug continued, "when he'd come out to

the mound to see me and the fans were just screaming. *Screaming!* And booing. One time I said, 'Well, Davey, you might want to put a little distance between you and me. That way they won't get us both in one shot!'"

We laughed a bit at his self-deprecating story before I asked him if any specific game other than the aforementioned one against the Cubs in '84 stuck out in terms of fan contempt?

Sisk didn't hesitate.

"There was a game against the Padres at Shea where I had already pitched an inning, got out of it, and was coming up to hit," Sisk recalled. "When I got up to the on-deck circle, the fans started booing big-time. Just crazy. As I came up to bat and my name was announced, the San Diego catcher Terry Kennedy says, 'What the *fuck* did you do to these people, Doug?' And I said, 'Hey, just throw a few pitches down the middle and let's get it over with.' So there's a pitch down the middle and I get a base hit. I get to first base and there's Steve Garvey, and *he* says to me, 'What did you do to these fans?' I said, 'I don't know, Steve.' And Garvey goes, 'You don't deserve this. If you would have hit a home run, they still would have booed you!'"

For the most part, Sisk seemingly took the abuse from the fans in stride, aside from what it did to his family. But he finally fessed up to one specific thing about it that bothered him personally.

"I love Keith [Hernandez], one of the best first basemen to ever play the game of baseball," Sisk began, "but to read his book, *If At First: A Season with the Mets,* and see how he ripped me—I'm cool with it, because it was that kind of year. But that same year, in 1985, he goes back to testify on his own behalf [at the Pittsburgh drug trials] and was granted immunity. He was guilty [of cocaine use] along with Dale Berra, Rod Scurry, Dave Parker, and the rest of them. And you know who sold it to them? It was the Pittsburgh Pirates' mascot who got it to them. And here I am getting my ass totally booed at Shea Stadium for something I didn't really know if I had much control over, and then Keith comes back after being gone two days for testifying in court and they give him a standing ovation."

For the first time all afternoon, Sisk's voice rose a few decibels when he said, "I had an *issue* with *that*! Now, *that's* real!"

"Were you ever able to understand the fans' logic in this regard?" I asked.

"No, I never did," Doug said. "I think the fans in New York are very critical and they're very educated. I think it's the greatest place to play baseball. But it can also be the worst."

"I don't want to put words in your mouth," I said. "But if you say they're the most educated, shouldn't they have known better in how they treated you?"

"I think the true fans already know that," Doug said after a pause to ponder the question. "But it does bother me."

"So at any point in your Mets career did you ask for a trade?" I asked.

"Yeah," Doug said. "I did it in a closed office situation with Frank Cashen [in '87]. [Mets' assistant general manager] Joe McIlvaine asked if he could join the meeting as well. I said, 'Sure, Joe.' I always enjoyed Joe as well. I sat down and gave them my reasons. I was not disrespectful. I was totally appreciative to the organization, thanking them for taking a chance on a guy like me. I said, 'Frank, it's time.' He said, 'Well, I can't. I can't do anything right now.' I said, 'Okay, well, you do it when it's appropriate for you guys. If it's the off-season, that's cool. I'm going to miss you guys. And I'm never going to say anything to the press. I'm never going to get weird.' Frank replied, 'I'm just telling you. Sid's [Fernandez] not been pitching well. He's hurting. We've got some things going on and you're not going anywhere right now.'"

Cashen would grant Sisk his wish and deal him to the Orioles following the season.

"The Orioles were probably the farthest team away from any type of conflict [with the Mets' interests]," Sisk said.

To this day, Doug has great affection for Cashen, who passed away in 2014. Sisk shared one of his fondest memories of the former Mets general manager.

"What really got me," Sisk began, "was when the Mets had that 'Shea Goodbye' event. We had a press conference and some of us were sitting at a table with our names in front of us so the media could ask us questions. I was sitting directly next to Frank and he put his arm around me and goes, 'Dougie, Dougie, it's so good to see you. You know I was always fond of you. I just want to let you know that you played a more important role on the '86 team than you truly believe.' I said, 'Well, I appreciate that, Frank. But how?' And he goes, 'Because you enabled me in 1983 to trade Neil Allen for Keith Hernandez.'"

"Ohhh, yeah, that's true!" I said, after a brief moment to figure out what he was insinuating.

"*That*," Sisk began with a dramatic pause, "sent the hair up on the back of my neck. Think about what he said. Neil Allen was expendable because you had Jesse and me. And Jesse had always been a starter, but they decided at that point that his deal was as a relief pitcher. So Neil went over to the Cardinals with Rick Ownbey, and that's what *got me* more than anything from Frank."

"And getting Keith changed everything for the Mets," I said.

"Totally," Doug said. "But he was not happy about the trade at the time."

"Right," I said. "He asked his agent if he had enough money to retire and was told he didn't."

"That's right," Sisk said. "I had the same agent, Jack Childers. Plus, Keith was in the middle of a divorce at that point and it was ugly.

"But it was kind of funny that, in '85, the same summer Keith had to go to Pittsburgh for the drug trials, we're in St. Louis and Keith tells some of us, 'You guys, I've got a bar that a good friend of mine owns. If you guys are going out, you should go there. You'll be safe. They'll take care of you.' Well, we weren't in there for a half hour before there was a police sting raid for drugs."

At this point, Doug is almost falling off his chair from laughing so hard telling the story.

"So we're walking out of this place saying to one another stuff like 'Nice job, Keith! We could have done that!'

"Then the next year, in '86, when Teufel and all those guys got into a fight at Cooter's in Houston," Sisk continued, "they asked me if I was going to go out with them because Timmy's son was born and they were going to celebrate. I said, 'No, my cousins are in town from Del Rio. Where are you guys going?' One of them said, 'We're going to Cooter's.' I said, 'Don't go to Cooter's.' They asked why and I repeated, '*Don't* go to Cooter's. I'll tell ya later.'

"I got on the bus the next day and found out that they got into a brawl there. Well, I had gotten into a fight in there in 1983 with some off-duty police officers. I was very fortunate the Mets never found out about it. That was not good."

Doug leaned back in his chair, reflected for a moment, and then came up with yet another Cooter's story.

"Also in '86, the Seattle Supersonics were in town playing the

Houston Rockets and two of the Sonics players got into a scuffle at Cooter's as well," he said. "The bouncers said that they didn't think they were athletes. Six-ten black guys in a redneck bar? *C'mon!* They asked a white girl to dance and that's what did it. So there was more than met the eye at that 'quality' place in Houston."

| | | | | | |

I got the sense from our lengthy, mostly liquid lunch that the experiences Doug went through in New York made him stronger. We talked about some of the coaching he did as the athletic director of the Boys & Girls' Club in Tacoma, and he gave me the impression his travails were a benefit to the kids.

"I was the worst pitcher in baseball and also the best pitcher in baseball," Sisk said. "And all that stuff in the middle of it—being hurt, being down, people booing you—that's all information that helps people. It all helps kids develop in the sport. There is *nothing* I haven't seen. Not a damn thing. I've played this game sober. I've played this game with a hangover. I've played this game when I was hurt. I've played this game when people were booing me. And I've played it when I was at the top of my game."

Sisk added that he never wanted to seriously get into coaching at the professional level because of the travel involved and the time away from his family. Still, he wonders if he would have ever been given a real chance to make a difference in the corporate environment of major-league baseball today. He cites the Mets as an example.

"Look at Mook, man," Doug begins. "Great player. 'Hood ornament' for the Mets. Exactly what it is. Goddamn hood ornament! And it drives me nuts. And Gary Carter. Kid called me one day and he says, 'Hey Dougie, I've got an opportunity. I'm here in

Port St. Lucie and I'm going to be the coach for the Port St. Lucie Mets. But here's the deal. The front office tells me what I can put on the field.' I said, 'Kid, man, you're a Hall of Fame catcher. Why would they hire you then? They should hire you for your knowledge of the game. What are they worried about with the handling of your players, that you're not going to put their number one picks on the field because they're not producing?'

"You have to let the guys do what they do, let them teach the game the way they were taught. Because ninety percent of the time it's going to be good."

Later in the discussion, Doug gave his take on the current Mets management team.

"What about Wally [Backman]?" Sisk asked. "I kind of wonder if he's even going to get the opportunity to stick through it because of his past. I don't like the guy they have in there now [Terry Collins]. And I don't like the general manager [Sandy Alderson]. I don't like any of them. It's not a difficult game, especially when you know what's at stake in New York. You've got the opportunity and the money's there. The people will come to the games and the excitement could be there. But it's just not happening."

"Working against Wally," I said, "is the fact there has never been a brighter spotlight on domestic issues as there is today, even if Wally's alleged one occurred many years ago."

"But if they want somebody that can win," Sisk said, "Wally will win for them. He's a baseball guy. Here's the deal. These clubs fuck up, they take their regime and leave. And then they get re-hired with someone else. You've got to surround yourself with some baseball people, bottom line. It will work, but it's just that the front office people don't want to deal with the baseball guys. It's true.

And Fred Wilpon and his son, they've been around long enough. They know. They've had baseball people involved in this organization. Are they making any money as a club? I don't know."

There's a pattern with many of the '86 Mets, and Sisk is no exception to it. If some of them seem overly critical of the current organization, it's because they care and believe things could be better. Some say it more diplomatically while others are more direct, but they all have a vested interest in the team doing well, and their passion is not unlike that of the fans you hear on talk radio. The only difference between them and the fans is that they are the ones that actually won big, and won big in New York.

"[In the early eighties] the Mets did an outstanding job in the draft, with picking free agents, and with their scouting," Sisk told me. "The only time I had ever seen anything turn around quicker than that was the Atlanta Braves when they went worst to first in the early nineties. And to see that transformation happen was absolutely incredible.

"The Mets were very patient with their players," Sisk continued. "And the people that were running the team knew what they were doing, had done it before, and there were a lot of them that were ex-players. You don't see that anymore. These guys are businessmen. And it's a shame when we're trying to go out there and compete and tell them what we think about kids, and they've got a stopwatch showing them who runs a four-four and saying they should be a prospect. It doesn't work."

Another bottle of Pinot Grigio arrived at the table and Doug came back to my book project.

"It's amazing that you have the opportunity to travel around and sit down and listen to all the bullshit that [the '86 Mets] got to tell," Sisk said. "Here's a question you should ask all of these guys. Ask if they still dream every once in a while of that season in '86 playing for the New York Mets. I guarantee you, each and every one of those players will say 'once or twice a week.' Because I do. And I think part of the problem is—my wife thinks I'm sick—is because I felt like I was unfulfilled. I get those dreams when I'm on my way to the ballpark but I can't get there. I run out of gas. I can't find my glove. My shrink could probably tell you more about it. But to me, those are the kind of guys I want on my club. Because those are the kind of guys that still want to do it more."

I'm not a psychiatrist, but it was clear as day to me that Sisk's dreams likely have a good deal to do with how much he misses the life he had with his old Mets teammates and how his own career, which started like a shooting star, left him wanting more. Later in our talk, Doug practically said as much.

"This may sound weird," Sisk said, "but that last year in '87 when we all got in the showers at the very end [of the season], we kind of looked at each other and I said to Jesse, 'Well, here's your last chance of looking at this.' We all knew. And it was sad. I think we had another year in us."

Sisk, a little choked up, then said, "I would have loved one more shot with those sons of bitches."

After a sip from his glass, Doug said to me, "It's just great that you've come all this way to see me. It really is. Thirty years later. What we did was important."

After more than five hours of discussion, Doug and I said our goodbyes to the people he knew from the restaurant. The plan was for me to follow him to Bainbridge Island, where I would drive my car onto a ferry to take me back to Seattle.

"I'm pretty excited for you getting on the ferry," Sisk said.

"I think you're going to enjoy that. It'll take about thirty minutes to go across. You can go upstairs and have a glass of wine, some clam chowder, and take in a great view as you go across the Puget Sound."

As one of the '86 world champions, Doug Sisk, despite all the heat he took, is a nice guy who finished first.

·9·

STRAW FINDS HIS WAY

My life has been multiplied in such a different way compared to what my baseball career was—hitting home runs and winning championships. Now I'm winning souls.

—DARRYL STRAWBERRY
ON HIS WORK AS AN EVANGELICAL PREACHER
(METS RIGHT FIELDER, 1983–90)

I retrieved a voicemail from my office phone relatively late one December evening. I was on the road in Arizona at the time, and making a return call to the recipient back east at the advanced hour was a question of common courtesy. I decided to call home first and, while on speaker phone, told my family who had left me a message.

"It's probably too late to call him tonight," I said. "I'll call in the morning."

My teenage daughter, Sabrina, agreed.

My wife, Habiba, however, saw it differently.

"You've been sending emails to him for two months," she said with conviction in her voice. "You should call him back while you're still on his mind."

So I did. I called back Darryl Strawberry, the eight-time all-star, four-time World Series champion, and the Mets' reigning all-time home run leader. I apologized for calling at the late hour, sheepishly adding that my wife thought it would be okay.

Straw, chuckling in his deep baritone voice, said, "Well, wives are usually right."

He then apologized for not getting back to me sooner, telling me he didn't do many interviews, but that after much thought and prayer, he'd decided to grant my request to visit him at his home in St. Peters, Missouri. Our conversation continued for another twenty minutes, with Darryl telling me a little bit about how his life had changed since his wild days and nights during his baseball career and how committed he was to spreading the gospel as an evangelical preacher through his Strawberry Ministries.

Darryl seemed at peace with himself, and I hung up the phone wondering if I was a bit naïve to be as thoroughly convinced as I was that a man who had endured five stints in rehab for alcohol and drug abuse, had spent eleven months in jail, had been involved in domestic disputes, and had been in and out of crack houses, could have completely turned his life around and become so committed to his faith. And after all, weren't there still the skeptics I had spoken with who remembered all too well the fast-lane life Straw led and how the superstar could be self-centered and even, at times, condescending and belittling of some of his teammates during his playing career?

Had he truly changed?

Although I personally had no reason to doubt Strawberry's transformation, I was anxious to see it for myself.

| | | | | | |

St. Peters, Missouri, is a sprawling St. Louis area suburb that boasts a population of over fifty-two thousand residents. Most of the five-mile drive from my hotel to Straw's house was on a single road with strip malls interspersed between open grassy fields and housing developments on what used to be farmland. There were also schools and churches along the way, some mega-sized and others quite small. It was America's heartland, about as far away as Darryl could get from the temptations of his old life.

I was thinking how glad I was that I left New York a day before my meeting with Straw, as rain had been relentless from the time I landed and there was now flooding in the area. Flights coming into St. Louis faced major delays or were canceled altogether.

I pulled up to Straw's house—still decked out with Christmas lights and a seven-foot decorative candy cane on each side of the front door—on what was a quiet, lazy, early January afternoon.

Darryl, still a towering figure at six-foot-six, greeted me warmly as I entered the house and walked with him into his living room, a great open space and immaculately clean. The barking of two Italian miniature greyhounds could be heard from the kitchen, a college football game was on the television. But there were no signs anywhere—no plaques, trophies, bats, balls, or the requisite encased uniform jersey—that I was in the home of one of the most feared power hitters in baseball history. Instead, the sight that jumped out at me was the placards with inspirational messages that were displayed prominently on one of the walls.

We exchanged some small talk as Straw shut the game off and brought two glasses of water over to the sofas, where we sat down. I noticed how Straw was struggling a bit to get comfortable, perhaps going through some of the physical pain so common with the former players I have met with. Still, he was pleasant and was anxious to hear about some of the other '86 Mets I had interviewed.

"What's Doc up to these days?" he asked, about the former teammate he was always linked with during his days with the Mets.

"He spends much of his time giving talks to kids about the perils of drug use," I said.

"Oh really?" Darryl said. "I didn't know that."

"And Lenny's been out of jail for over a year and is working hard at trying to put his life back together in the business world."

"Oh is he? Okay."

"HoJo—he's the hitting coach of the Mariners. And Raffy, he's doing scouting work in the Dominican Republic, a great source of young players for the major leagues now. So a lot of interesting stories on what the guys are all doing today."

Darryl, with a gleam in his eyes, perhaps remembering the good times, said, "Well, that's good. I'm glad they're doing well. I don't really keep up with baseball and a lot of former teammates anymore."

"Why is that?" I asked, wondering how, despite all the troubles in his past, he could shelve the glory of the world championships he shared with some of them.

"It's nothing personal, you know?" Strawberry explained. "I'm just in a different setting, a different time of life. My whole life has changed for the better. I married a wonderful girl and we've both come to a greater place and purpose with everything we're doing."

"I can really see that," I said. "I've read your latest book you wrote with your wife, *The Imperfect Marriage*, seen a couple of interviews you've done, and it seems like you're in a completely different place from the 'bright lights, big city' that you—"

Straw, laughing, cuts me off and interjects enthusiastically.

"*Oh yeah! Oh yeah!* Totally different!" he said. "And I'm truly glad that I am away from those 'bright lights, big city.' That was a career, but I basically always knew there was something much greater for me than that in my life. Even through playing baseball and the trials and tribulations I dealt with, deep down inside I always knew there was some greater calling I was meant to answer. I was just afraid to step into it because I never felt qualified."

We spent a good deal of time talking about his life's journey, from where it began to where it is today. Darryl credited his mother for introducing him to Christianity.

"My mother was a strong woman of faith," Straw began. "She always believed that all of her children would be saved. And we are all now following God in life, so her wish did come true. But she didn't get a chance to see it when she was alive. But we found notes she had written for each one of us where she prayed we would overcome the struggles and difficulties in our lives. It was incredible for us to find them after her passing."

His relationship with his father, he would tell me, was far different.

"It was broken because of the physical abuse, beatings, and everything I endured from him," Darryl said. "There was real hatred there. A lot of young men grow up with the same struggles and broken relationships with their father that I had, but they never get healed. I was able to heal mine."

Darryl would tell me he didn't speak to his father for thirty years, until a preaching engagement took him back to California one Saturday morning in April of 2012.

"The Lord spoke to me that Friday night," Straw explained. "I knew my father was in a hospital in San Diego and He told me to drive down there. The Lord told me to repent to my father and not him repent to me. He said to not say anything about what my father did to me, so I just went down in obedience to what the Lord said to me and asked my father to forgive me for being wrong in keeping him out of my life. I cried so hard. But it was a healing process, and I was able to lead my father to the Lord because he knew my life had changed. God used me and spoke clearly to me to understand that it wasn't about me, it was about a broken person and that two wrongs don't make a right. You learn about those kinds of things when you've really changed inside. And I've been changed inside for a very long time. I'm just being used for His greatness, not my greatness."

"So holding a grudge and not reconciling a relationship is kind of like a poison, right?" I asked.

"Well, you're only hurting yourself," Straw said. "I don't think a lot of us understand, and I certainly didn't, but God forgives us, so who are we to hold grudges for things against someone else? The grace is there for all of us and He gave it to me. So I needed to give it to my father."

"So your relationship with him is much better now?" I asked.

"Yeah, it's free," Straw replied. "I mean, we don't talk or anything, and it's not because I don't care, it's just that I was ordered by God to go and do what I needed to do. Because basically what that does, Erik, is that it releases me from my part that I played. The bondage that was on my life from that relationship was broken off and it was healed."

Still, the cruelty Darryl had to endure from his father had a profound effect on much of his youth and adult life, clearly leading to a path of self-destruction. Straw, as he alluded to earlier in our talk, was a product of the father figure–less culture that permeated his South Central LA environment.

"It plays a tremendous role in young people's self-esteem," Straw began. "You usually are led into some type of wrong activity like gang or street crimes when there's not a male figure in the house to bring you wisdom. It's a real struggle. That's why so many young men end up with the wrong identity, which is that everything they are told—success, riches, fame—are what should be strived for, and that's not true. It's not just the boys, but the girls, too. You look at Hollywood and so many people get lost in the shuffle. You look at how many people have lost their lives in the drug addiction world in that industry because they just don't get it. That's because no one ever tells them no. Everything is *Yes, you can do whatever you want.* So you end up with troubled teens because no one's ever led them to who they should be."

If not for the love of his mother and baseball as an outlet in his youth, Straw might very well have become just another statistic of urban life.

"Baseball was tremendous for me," Straw said. "I had different coaches come into my life and push me, which made all the difference. They made me get up and go to practice and believe in myself as a player. That's why I could *play.* I was never too shy of confidence in playing ball. I was more shy of confidence in living life. When I took the uniform off, I didn't know what life was all about at that time."

But with the uniform on, of course, Strawberry was a special player. In the 1980 amateur draft, no high school baseball player was more coveted than Darryl. The Mets would make Straw the number one pick in the country.

When the Mets began the 1983 season 6–15, manager George Bamberger begged general manager Frank Cashen to promote Strawberry, who was tearing it up at Triple-A Tidewater, to the big-league club. In his autobiography, *Winning in Both Leagues*, Cashen wrote how he believed an extra year in the minors would have helped Darryl from a maturity standpoint. I asked Straw if he agreed with Cashen in that regard.

"I do agree with Frank," Darryl said. "Frank Cashen was a very smart man, highly regarded and well respected in the baseball world. He was also well educated on young talent. He never wanted to push the level of or destroy the mind of a younger player. I loved that about Frank. He wasn't as concerned about the ability of a player as much as whether they could handle a different place. New York is a place that will swallow you up. I think Frank always wanted to protect me as a young player instead of throwing me out there to the wolves, because he knew they could eat you alive."

"How hard was it to be a young superstar in New York City in the eighties?" I asked.

"It was very difficult for me because, at the time, I was only twenty-one when I was Rookie of the Year, and I was supposed to be the savior [of the team] now. The media and fans would say things like, *Here he is. This guy is going to be our real face, our real savior.* It was a very hard place to be. Had I gone to Minnesota or Seattle, I would never have been so much of a recognizable face. But do I regret playing in New York? No, not at all. I'm glad it happened the way it happened."

"You bring up a good point," I said. "As the number one pick in the nation, you faced enormous expectations. You were being touted as the next Ted Williams. Like him, you were a tall, skinny guy with a lot of power, natural talent, and limitless potential. But it always seemed to me like when you would hit thirty home runs in a season, the media and even some of your teammates expected you to hit forty. And if you hit thirty-nine like you did one year, they thought you should hit fifty. How did you deal with those expectations that always seemed to be higher than the really good numbers you put up?"

"*How* did I deal with it?" Darryl asked rhetorically. "I *didn't.* I went out and drank alcohol and chased women. That was my escape to deal with the expectations. That's the reality of it. Then I got into drugs and that was an even bigger escape. I always looked at myself as *I am who I am regardless of other opinions*. But there were many opinions about me in that Mets clubhouse and in the media that portrayed me as having more talent than you could ever understand. They couldn't understand how a guy could have so much ability to play baseball and make it look so easy. Then there were the comments that I wasn't trying hard enough. But it was just my natural ability that I played with. My production in those years was better than anybody else's, but it was never enough. So, again, I didn't deal with it. I drank and chased women and did all those things."

"Some of your teammates admitted to me to having 'Straw envy' back in those days, that they would have given anything to have your body and raw talent," I said.

"Well, my stardom playing in New York was bigger than any of them," Darryl said with conviction. "And they wanted that and I didn't want it. That's the whole thing about it. I didn't care about the stardom. All I cared about was winning. And I think a lot of times people look at me—even today—and I still have the same buzz walking through New York. People love me in New York. They think, *This guy, we love. We don't care what he's been through. He always performed in the clutch, he always showed up, and yet people harp on what he didn't do, forgetting what he did do.* And that's been a blessing to have from my New York days."

Another blessing from his days in the Big Apple was to be the rare ballplayer to have starred for both of the city's teams—and to win world championships with both.

"You played for the '86 Mets and the '98 Yankees, the majors' best team from the eighties and the best team from the nineties," I said. "What were the similarities and differences between those two great ball clubs?"

"Well, the toughness of those two teams stands out," Straw said.

"We brought the same kind of guts to the ballpark—wanting to win and understanding what it's like to play in New York and win. That's what those two teams had inside. The difference was that with the Mets, we were a wild bunch. You'd catch us in a bar, we were into fights. The Yankees were more calm—we would go home, we drank milk, and we'd go play baseball."

"And playing in San Francisco and Los Angeles must have been very different than playing in New York, wasn't it?" I asked.

"Yeah, I signed a big contract to go to LA and it was real different," Darryl said. "It wasn't exciting like New York. The fans in New York come early and they stay all night. The fans come late in LA and leave early. It's a big difference. The New York fans ain't leaving. They're standing over the dugout and they're going to tell you '*You suck!*'"

We had a good laugh about the sometimes *colorful* nature of New York fans. I then asked him seriously if when looking back at his life in baseball he thought a more peaceful and less wild environment like the West Coast would have been better for his well-being and his career.

"No, I'm glad it was so wild," he said without pause. "I'm glad everything happened the way it did because it made me who I am today. I wouldn't be the man of God that I am now had I not gone through what I had to go through. I think a lot of times people look back and think, *Well, I wish I could have done this, done that*. But those same people who reached the pinnacle of life, became successful and very famous, are many times still looking for the praise after their career is over. I don't. I look for Jesus and I love what He has done in my life. I love being a minister of the Gospel, and I would have never been one had I still excelled and still had everything—the money, the house, the car, and the other stuff after my career. I would not be preaching today. The material things would have been my God.

"And then there's that life of being famous and people coming to see you," Straw continued. "You're jumping out of cars and you've got five bodyguards around you. That's a fantasy to me. I did all that and it's a fantasy. But like I said, I'm glad it all happened to me because it's made me a man of true character and that's what's really important. Not the character of a man of *what* he has, but the character of a man of *who* he is."

The part Darryl said about *what* he has, I felt, was a good segue for me to ask him about whether not displaying the many trophies and mementos from his playing days in his house was by design.

"Yeah, because that's not who I am," Straw said. "I mean, that's over. I think too many of us dwell on careers and what we accomplished. And while it's great we were able to accomplish all those things as athletes, there's more to life. I think a lot of athletes don't move forward because they don't know anything else. I wanted to know more about my purpose in life than being 'Darryl Strawberry, the home run hitter for the Mets, Yankees, Dodgers, and Giants, and the eight-time all-star and four-time World Series champ.' I wanted to know more about what life is really about. And I've been able to find that through the principles in living according to the way I live and what I speak about. I don't hold any grudges towards anyone. Do I hold memories? The memories will always be there. They'll never leave me because I accomplished them. But I don't hold on to trophies. I don't hold on to things because they're 'just stuff.' They have no sentimental value to me."

"Okay, now I understand," I tell Straw. "Because I was really curious about why you would completely put aside a part of your life that had so many thrilling moments. It's a rare thing to do, but I understand now—you've moved on."

"I've *completely* moved on and I've moved on for a long time," Straw confirmed. "I have a wonderful wife who is very faithful, who lives in the principles just like I do, and we love helping and encouraging people. We want to have not just a natural impact, but a supernatural impact, on them to let them know that their lives can be changed. I think sometimes athletes have a platform where they can go speak to people, but are they really living what they're speaking about? Are they really living it themselves and having a tremendous impact on other people's lives and not just having a lot of smoke coming out? And saying how well they're doing and really not [doing well at all]? Erik, I just don't want to be a hypocrite."

Strawberry certainly has his opportunities to preach. He told me that he averages between forty to forty-five events around the country each year, with the congregations ranging in attendance from one thousand to five thousand.

"It's a whole bigger stage than I could have ever imagined in my wildest dreams when God called me six years ago," Darryl said. "Back then, I was in ministry, but not full-time. I was in New York and had just started a restaurant and God told me to close it. I knew God well by then and trusted Him, so I obeyed Him when he told me to close it down. I ended up moving forward into the ministry capacity when He called me to preach. He made me go into deep study. I isolated myself from everybody and He revealed the Bible to me in scriptures, and the spirits taught me how to preach. I never went to school. It was just supernatural, a supernatural gift that He gave me just like how He gave me the gift and talent to play baseball.

"I go and speak at a lot of events that have to do with addiction, too, to help people understand that Christ can change their life. Look what He's done for me."

Aside from his preaching, Straw talked about how he is helping people afflicted with drug and alcohol addiction through the Darryl Strawberry Recovery Center, with rehabilitation centers in St. Cloud, Florida, and Longview, Texas, which is funded by Oglethorpe, a corporation based in Tampa.

"Is that a twelve-step treatment center?" I asked.

"It is," Darryl said, his body language and upbeat voice clearly showing how proud he is of his involvement in the project. "It's a twenty-eight-day, single-bed, in-house facility. If [the patients] need longer, we have a longer time for them to get [additional] treatment and get well. And we have a Christ Center if a person wants it, but it's not forced. The Center is to help a person become whole inside. A lot of times people will go through a recovery process and they recover, but they're still not well inside. They need to go deeper. Again, we don't force it, but we give them the opportunity to go deeper."

And as if all of this didn't keep Darryl busy enough, he and his wife Tracy created a foundation for children battling autism. The genesis of their involvement was being inspired by the work of Tracy's sister, who runs a program for families that deal with autism.

"We started that back in '06," Straw said. "We were so grateful. That was the first ministry God gave us. Ministry is all about *helping* people that are hurting in their life. We started raising money for children here in St. Louis that were affected by autism. I started having celebrity golf tournaments in New York with some of my celebrity friends."

Tracy joined us in the living room. She is very pretty, but the thing that strikes you most about her immediately is her warm smile and how happy and kind she is. Tracy has that rare ability to light up a room with her presence. Like Darryl, she is also an ordained minister.

"Welcome to our home," she said to me. "Thank you for coming. We don't have many people come by, as our house is a sacred place to us. But we're glad you made the trip."

To understand the reinvention of Darryl Strawberry, you have to understand the significance his wife played in his recovery. Against all conventional wisdom, Darryl and Tracy met and began their relationship at a Narcotics Anonymous gathering in 2002. Tracy had been hooked on crack and crystal meth and had lost custody of her three sons, but when she met Straw for the first time, she had just celebrated one year of sobriety and had gotten "saved" two days earlier.

Tracy joined the conversation, and we started right in on the day she first met Darryl and the state he was in.

"Oh boy, he was very quiet, very lost," Tracy began. "You could tell in his heart he was desperately struggling for a place in life. He was a lost and empty soul that was literally on his way to physical death. He was not the big, strong slugger that you once saw before you. That person was gone. This was a very frail, thin, tall man who could barely hold up his own frame."

Darryl's drug and alcohol addiction wasn't the only thing that made him appear so weak. He had battled colon cancer and then a second bout of cancer that spread to his lymph nodes by the time he was thirty-eight years old. He also had surgery to remove a tumor and a kidney.

By 2000, he had reached a point where he elected to stop going to chemotherapy treatments.

"Why exactly did you stop the treatments back then?" I asked him.

"I just didn't want to move forward with life," Straw said solemnly. "And this from a man who once had everything. But then I had nothing, and to be diagnosed and having to deal with cancer twice and then losing my mother at such an early age, I struggled very hard with all of that. I struggled with the fact that, well, *Why should I live? What's the reason for continuing to be here?* But now today, I understand why. And I've been cancer-free for over fifteen years."

Still, Tracy would add how people at the NA convention would still come over to him, asking him for his autograph.

"Nobody else could see the same person I could see," she said. "I felt like I was the only person in the room that could see him, and it frustrated me to where I thought, *What is wrong with us as a society?* Still, there was such a kindheartedness about Darryl. He was always gracious to people. Still is. But I saw these crowds of people around this very lost man; they weren't going to let him off the hook from his stardom status and kept pulling at this star baseball player that no longer existed."

As for Tracy, while she was still on the road to recovery herself, she seemed to gain some strength in wanting to help Straw.

"I was clean and sober," she explained, "but I did not have a sound mind. And I didn't have a changed heart or a changed life. I was still the same lost person, struggling, without any relief, without any release, without any break, wondering how I was going to live this life on life's terms. So when I met Darryl, we were very relational. It was almost like a breath of fresh air because we didn't talk about baseball or anything like that. We started talking about life, and there was such a relief when you're speaking with someone where there's no judgment, because that person is just like you. I just felt as if I could save him. I could see greatness in him."

Incredibly, Tracy would go on to say how "saving" Darryl meant that she—while still a recovering crack addict—would have to pull him from crack houses.

"Now, wait a second," I said. "Wasn't this absolutely the worst possible relationship you could have at that point in your life?"

Tracy nodded in agreement.

"I was putting myself in a very dangerous situation," she said, "until one day I 'woke up' and banged down the last crack house door and pulled him out for the very last time. Something made me stop because I just hit that dangerous point when I walked in and looked at that display on the coffee table just a little bit too long. And that desire not to save him and pull him out—*maybe I'll just stay*—hit me and I was very well aware of that the very last time that I picked him up. The reality of what everyone was telling me—but I was too hardheaded to listen—became real to me."

"Was that the last time Darryl was in a crack house?" I asked.

"No," Tracy said, "but it was the last time I went and got him."

"And you had the strength and wherewithal to walk away?"

"I did, but only by the grace of God. I got in and got out. But I knew at that very moment I could never go again."

Having known Tracy for about an hour by this point, it was almost impossible to believe how this well-spoken, strong, and intelligent woman who exuded so much joy and confidence in nearly every word she spoke could have ever had such a deep and profound issue with drug addiction.

"How did someone like you get hooked so badly on drugs?" I asked.

"I came from a safe, secure, and loving home with opportunities and great parents," she said. "But I just started hanging around the wrong people and tried to satisfy a hunger for excitement. In your mind, you think you're just going out to have fun, to experience more of that excitement, and you wake up one day and you are in the midst of this lifestyle of addiction that now has you. It can happen to anyone."

Tracy also leads a busy life serving others. Aside from her many ministry duties, she works with those in recovery.

"My wife holds coffeehouse meetings in O'Fallon," Straw said. "She preaches and empowers people that come to the meetings. She's starting up a new one this year at the same place, but it's going to be more for celebrating recovery. And it's not just about addiction, it's about whatever issues you have. We'll have leaders there to empower people's lives in areas that they're struggling in."

Darryl then volunteered to me the difference between his and Tracy's ministries.

"I basically travel all the time because I'm in travel ministry," he said. "God has called me for the multitude. My wife has been more stable here in St. Louis in helping to build up young people. A couple of years ago, she had a 'Friday Night Freedom' event where she would have forty kids here on a Friday night and feed them, empower them, teach them, and help them. Even though they were involved in the church, they were struggling. And they would really open up to her. She's very strong with young people."

"You mentioned before about the frequency and the size of the congregations you preach to," I said to Darryl. "Do you think the fact that you were a larger-than-life ballplayer brings out the big crowds to hear you speak?"

"Well, God uses people that say, 'yes,'" Straw answered. "He calls all of us, but not everyone is going to answer. He uses the fullness of Darryl Strawberry's life to glorify Him in such a way and as a draw for people to come. They don't know why they're coming—they just know that *this is Darryl Strawberry*. They find out that God has changed him. And then when they see that it's real transformation, and they know I didn't go to school, they know I played baseball for eighteen years, then they know it's God. They just know it.

"Some of them might think, *Well, I'll come to see him because he was a great baseball player, but I heard he's a preacher now. How did this happen? I want to hear what he's got to say.* And then they hear a whole different terminology that comes out of me. But it *doesn't* come from me. It comes from the Kingdom of God. It comes from down in my belly and my spirit. It's a revelation that He has given me and taught me to speak and understand. When people can really get a clarification of themselves, they understand that God will use you no matter what has happened or where you've come from. He will use you for *His* purpose. And that's what's been the difference in my life today. I know it's not *my* purpose, Erik. My life is for *His* purpose."

I brought up to Straw my observation that he is not alone in his beliefs among a good number of his '86 Mets teammates.

"You're a pastor now," I began. "Mookie recently became an ordained minister, and many of your other teammates have referenced their belief in God in the interviews I've had with them. Do you think there is any correlation to how some of the '86 Mets may have lived and how they now have God playing such a significant role in their lives?"

"Well, we lived it at the highest level playing in the greatest of cities in New York," Straw began. "We had the chance to see it all, do it all, and live it all. But life gets real once you take off the uniform and you enter into real life. It's a matter of finding out who you are and what it's all about. We just can't *talk* about God. We have to live it and be an example of who He is.

"I hope these guys know that God is nothing to play with," he continued, seemingly offering caution to his old teammates. "I think sometimes we say His name because His name's God, but do we really know Him? Do we really do the work that He calls us to from all of our lives of playing baseball, to become Godly men? Because when I look back on all our lives, there were only a couple that were stable—Mookie Wilson and Gary Carter. That's it. The rest, we all lived according to what the standard was—being wild. Hopefully, over the years, their lives, through their trials and tribulations, have come to a resting place and are finding peace with God. Because when you can find peace with God, it's not about anybody else's fault. It's more like *I created this mess of my life, and nobody can help me clean it up but God.*"

One of Darryl's nephews walked into the kitchen for a drink. The boy and three of his siblings are now Straw's responsibility, the sad result of Darryl's sister recently succumbing to cancer. They joined the six children that Straw is the father to, as well as Tracy's three adult sons. Although they don't all live in the Strawberry home, it keeps him and Tracy on their toes.

"I only have two children to worry about," I said. "But you two now have thirteen! I can't imagine—"

Straw cuts me off and says with a laugh, "They keep us *very* busy."

"Considering everything you went through, how is your relationship with your children?" I asked.

"The relationship is great," Darryl said. "There are some battles, which I expect. But they love me and I love them. The thing about my life is that it has been healed. And my kids have been healed because I'm healed. Because I'm the head. If we live by the principles, God ordains the men to be the head, not the *knuckle*head. I was a knucklehead once upon a time when I played baseball. I was a *real* knucklehead, Erik. But I got in order, my life changed, and my kids' lives changed."

"And is it safe to assume that their childhoods, in spite of all of your issues, were different from yours in that they were somewhat privileged," I said. "After all, you were making a ton of money for a long time."

"Well, yeah, they never had to struggle," Straw said. "To this day, they don't know what it's like living in a home and having one bedroom with three beds in it. They're like, 'Dad, you lived like that?' And I'm like, 'Yeah.' They don't know what that is like. So they've had it pretty good. They've been pretty blessed and fortunate. My youngest ones—Jordan, Jade, and Jewel—those three never went to public school. They went to private school their whole lives. Very different from me."

Still, despite having parented children of privilege, Straw shares the same concerns of many parents today.

"Kids today don't communicate," Darryl said. "It's unfortunate that the lifestyle that has come along for them is through social media. I think a lot of kids—not only ours—are missing what it's like to sit down and have a conversation."

We then talked a little bit about how social media networking has allowed for people to congregate quickly to protest and cause violence, such as was the case close to home for the Strawberrys.

"We're sitting now in the shadow of Ferguson," I said, "not far from where the police shooting of an unarmed black teen caused days of rioting and unrest throughout the country. This is just one of the many terrible headlines we see every day now. I'd be interested to get your perspective on why things seem to be getting worse in the world instead of more civilized as we evolve."

"We've come to a point," Straw said, "where we have taken God out of everything. I think that's the real struggle. There are no Godly principles—there are only worldly principles. And that's why we're all sitting in the chaos that is here. The Bible clearly tells us that this time would come. We've gotten to a place where we've got it all wrong and I don't think most people understand it. I think people only come to God when there are tragedies. When something big happens, everybody wants to run to church for that week."

"Like after 9/11," I said.

"*Yeah!*" he exclaimed.

"The churches were packed," I said.

"*Packed!*" Straw said excitedly. "People thought the world was coming to an end. But it's going to be too late in America. [The end] is going to happen because the Bible says it will in the book of Revelation. It talks about end times and what's going to happen. Kingdoms against kingdoms. That's already happening. You're going to have all these different kinds of tragedies. You look at planes falling out of the sky. It's already taking place, but people aren't paying attention. They're on the news like, *Oh, it's such a tragedy. Why this and why that?*"

After spending the better part of the afternoon with Straw, I was convinced that he was very much a changed man from the days when he roamed the bars and clubs of New York as often as right field at Shea Stadium. I share this with Darryl and say how the most difficult thing for his legion of fans to comprehend would be how his commitment to his faith and helping others has become infinitely more important to him than his legacy as an all-time great Met.

"So what would you say to those fans to help them understand?" I asked.

Straw smiled and said, "A lot of people look at an athlete's or celebrity's life and say they have everything. But you know what, Erik? I had everything, but I had nothing. Today, I have a beautiful wife, a beautiful family, and I have the joy of the Lord. I'm free. I'm living an abundant life, which is the wholeness inside of you. I don't have any emptiness. I have a joy."

We wrapped up our most enlightening conversation, and Darryl and Tracy wished me well on the book project as they walked me to the front door. The rain had stopped, at least for a brief time, and Darryl walked with me outside to my car.

"So what do you have going on the rest of the weekend, Erik?" Darryl asked.

"I've got the first flight out early tomorrow morning," I said. "It's my son Alex's sixteenth birthday, and we play football with his friends every year. When we started, they were half my size. Now they're mostly taller than I am."

"Football, huh," Darryl said with a look of concern for me. "Well, be careful. And wish your son a happy birthday from us."

I got in my car and drove off believing I had just spent an afternoon with a man who had conquered his demons and was now a man of God and of peace, secure with his place and identity in this world and beyond.

· 10 ·

THE SQUARE PEG

I've never been on another team like that '86 club that wanted to cut your throat. We didn't just want to beat you, we
wanted to burn down your village. We were that type of
people, with that type of mob mentality to win at all costs. It
was wonderful. I'm not talking about literally burning down
a village, I'm talking about competing on the field where the
only quantifying thing if you're worth a shit is wins and losses. And all of us who got to experience that I'm sure feel the
same way. It was just a tremendous experience.

—BOBBY OJEDA
(METS PITCHER, 1986–90)

It was the dead of winter and, "somewhere out West," Bobby Ojeda
sounded like he was having the time of his life.

"Right now, I'm driving on a snow-covered, ice-covered road,
but it's *fantastic!*" exclaimed a joyous-sounding Ojeda by cell phone.
"There's four feet of snow all around and I'm heading fishing. So I'm
in a happy place here—I'll tell you that!"

Adventurous travel is as much a part of who Ojeda is as practically anything else in his life. Whether it's hiking in the Himalayas
or hunting trips in the wilderness of Montana, "Bobby O" lives life
to the fullest. If this all sounds like a man who makes each day
count and treats it like a gift from above, you would be correct.

To put it frankly, Ojeda is lucky to be alive.

Ojeda's life changed forever on March 22, 1993, an off day during spring training while with the Cleveland Indians. A teammate, Tim Crews, took Bobby and pitcher Steve Olin for a boat ride on Little Lake Nellie in Clermont, Florida. There was drinking on the boat—though according to Ojeda not in excess—during the twilight period of the early evening. The Skeeter bass boat they were on would slam into a dock, killing Crews and Olin, leaving them both virtually decapitated. Slumped in the boat at the time of impact, Bobby suffered a severe laceration to his scalp, losing two quarts of blood, but miraculously survived.

Ojeda would recover physically, but then had to deal with the guilt of surviving such a tragedy. After a time at the Sheppard and Enoch Pratt Hospital, where he received help coping with the post-traumatic stress of the accident, he returned to the mound in a game against the Orioles at Baltimore's Camden Yards that August, to a standing ovation.

The following season, he signed with the Yankees, but retired from the game after just two starts. He was thirty-six years old, age-appropriate for a pitcher—particularly one like Ojeda who lived with pain in his left arm most of his life—to call it a career.

But it was Bobby's ability to come back from the tragedy and pitch again that exemplified the character and courage of a man Mets fans came to know all too well after the trade that brought him to Queens prior to the 1986 season.

The importance of the trade the Mets made by dealing Calvin Schiraldi to the Red Sox for Bobby Ojeda cannot be overstated in terms of how it helped them capture the world championship in 1986. On a pitching staff of young and talented arms, Ojeda brought a veteran presence, his own brand of swagger, and a second left-handed starter to join Sid Fernandez. Despite an unremarkable career with the

Red Sox to that point, the Mets' front office, and many of their veteran players, knew Ojeda could be a potentially great pitcher on their club.

And they were right.

Ojeda would win more games and have the lowest ERA on the Mets' superb pitching staff in '86. And perhaps even more impressive, he was the starting pitcher in the three most pivotal and thrilling games of the postseason—Game Six in the NLCS and Games Three and Six in the World Series, which were all won by the Mets.

The trade for Ojeda, one of the best in team history, truly was the final piece in making the Mets a dominant force in the National League.

Like Keith Hernandez, Bobby Ojeda was also a great source to me when researching some of the behind-the-scenes aspects of the '86 Mets for Mookie's autobiography. And like Mex, once you got him started talking baseball, the talk went into many different directions—in Ojeda's case, from his time in Boston through his years with the Mets.

There were two Bobby Ojedas I discovered in my conversation with him. There was the brash Bobby that was still full of swagger. And then there was the sentimental version, particularly when he reflected back on his career. Other than Lenny Dykstra, Ojeda was the most outspoken, entertaining, opinionated, and filter-less of all the mostly loquacious '86 Mets I spoke with. I didn't get too many words in edgewise, and that was fine with me.

Ojeda, understandably, has rarely spoken publicly about his boating accident and, on this day, true to form, was more eager to just talk about baseball.

| | | | | | |

"I tend to talk straight," Bobby said to start off our conversation, an understatement if there ever was one. Perhaps it was his way of telling me to fasten my seat belt for a roller coaster of an interview.

Ojeda dove right in with talk about '86 and how he went from being somewhat miserable with the Red Sox to finding a home with the Mets.

"Frank Cashen, who I loved, amassed a cast of characters that were pretty much all out there," Bobby began. "But in Boston—you know the saying, 'square pegs in round holes'?—well, I was a square peg with a bunch of round holes. That team was okay, but it wasn't very good. It was a lot of angry, old guys whose careers were winding down. They really didn't care about the young guys, whatsoever. The reality was a lot of guys were on their way out and they weren't real happy with the young guys—they didn't want them around. You talk about pulling against you, oh *absolutely*! This is where I learned this little life's lesson of mine: that guys hope you fail so they won't lose their job. No question about it. No doubt. Any of those guys can deny it—I can give two shits. That's the reality."

Ojeda was on a roll now, but was careful to point out that this is the nature of the business throughout baseball and wasn't limited to Boston.

"One of the things that is fantasy is that veteran players are great mentors for others," Bobby said. "Quite frankly, at the major-league level, no one gives a shit what you do. The reality is that [individual players] want to do well. They're like, *This is a business, I'm a pro, this is my job. I've got a family to feed and a short life span in this career. So if I'm going to spend my time worrying about you, what about me?*

"That's why it's a lot of bullshit. Look, guys want a teammate to hit .300—that would be great. They want a teammate to make diving catches in the outfield, or to win twenty games. They're not rooting against you, but honestly they don't give a shit if you do.

They're like, *I want me to do well*. It's an individual game; you're pulling for each other because you're teammates, but that's where it ends. So when I hear managers say, 'Everybody's pulling for him,' that may be true, but quite frankly, at the end of the day, players really don't care."

"Was there *anything* good about the Red Sox?" I asked.

"There was a core of young guys coming up—me, Bruce Hurst, and John Tudor—that *legitimately* cared about each other, and that's what made the difference so striking," Ojeda said. "I cared if John won. I cared if Bruce won. I wanted to win, but I was a square peg in a round hole over there."

"So how were the Mets different?" I asked.

"When I got over to the Mets, I sat and watched these guys and I'm like, *I just found a bunch of square pegs*," Ojeda said with a snicker. "I just fit right in. We were a very, very good ball club. Hands down a better club than that Red Sox team—no question about it. We had superb defense, an *outstanding* bullpen—with Jesse and Roger out there closing things out. Those things make a difference to your starting pitcher because if they can hold those leads for you when you've got to get out of the game, it makes a difference."

"Well, when you came over from the Red Sox to the Mets, a couple of things happened," I noted. "One, you went from being a decent pitcher with the Red Sox to an outstanding pitcher with the Mets. Your ERA dropped a run and a half from '85 with Boston to '86 with the Mets. And with Doc still very good, but not dominating like the previous year, you became the ace of that staff and gave them a much-needed veteran presence."

"I caught a bunch of Ws with the Mets that I didn't with the Red Sox—I think I maxed out with twelve wins there—because they were just a weak team," Ojeda explained. "The '86 Mets were an *exceptionally strong* team—young and vibrant. There was a vibe going on with that team. No other team has had it since. Our '88 team [with one hundred wins] couldn't even compete against the '86 team. The '86 team would have brushed them aside like it was nothing. That '86 team was a unique, once-in-a-lifetime experience with everything factored in like the age, the talent, the manager, the general manager—just a plethora of raw talent with a diverse leadership, and the guy leading the show was Davey. Davey managed to keep it all together. There was a legitimate honor amongst thieves, a biker club mentality there—no question. And I've never felt it since."

Ojeda was clearly making valid points, though I still couldn't completely reconcile in my mind how he went from being the pedestrian pitcher he was in Boston over a good sample size of six big-league seasons to finishing fourth in the Cy Young Award balloting and even getting some MVP votes in his first season with the Mets. I believed win totals could surely go up by pitching for a better team, but could earned run averages suddenly drop through the floor primarily with just better defense?

I had another theory, and brought it up for debate.

"You mentioned how you and John Tudor used to pull for one another," I began. "Well, do you think there is any irony that when you left Boston to go to the Mets you became their ace in '86, and when John Tudor left the Red Sox to go to the Cardinals in '85, he was runner-up for the Cy Young Award? Could it be possible that being a couple of southpaws leaving the Green Monster behind contributed to your successes, or was it more leaving that 'cancer' that you allude to within the Red Sox organization?"

Ojeda stuck to his story.

"Well, it was all about going to *better* ball clubs," he insisted.

"[Tudor] went to a *very* good ball club in St. Louis. I wish there was some ulterior thing I could say, but it just wouldn't be true. The reality was we both went to better ball clubs and, therefore, had better success.

"You talk about defense," Bobby continued, "how about that *outfield* Tudor had?! That was over the top! His outfield was like a net out there. And St. Louis could manufacture runs, too."

"Let's talk about how the '86 club stacked up against other Mets teams through the end of that decade," I said. "That '88 club, for example, was very good—maybe the best the Mets ever had after '86. The team won the division easily (by fifteen games over second-place Pittsburgh), but then lost that tough NLCS in seven games to the Dodgers after being in command of the series. The Mets still remained competitive the next two seasons after that, but this great core of young players mixed with veterans never won another championship. What happened, in your view, after '86?"

"It's a great question and one that comes up a lot," Ojeda said without hesitation. "But the reality is, go back and look at the roster from '86 and then look at the one from '88. *There's* your answer. The only time that '86 team was together, intact, was '86. Because in '87, it began to change. We had injuries, players moving on. Heck, we lost Ray Knight after the '86 series. Let me tell you something, Ray Knight was a mean bastard and was a huge part of that *We're going to kick your ass* mentality.

"But again, just look at the rosters side by side and you'll see a lot of heart and soul was cut out of that '86 team. We now had guys with other interests, guys who wanted to become writers in the postseason. The '88 team during the regular season, heck, we could phone it in there was so much talent. But when it came down to crunch time, we failed. I obviously got hurt and wasn't even a part of it and that *destroyed* me. But the reality is that the '86 team was a shooting star and it was never, ever going to last. It was too volatile, just a powder keg."

"You were the starting pitcher in what is widely considered to be the greatest championship series game of all time—Game Six of the '86 NLCS against the Houston Astros," I said. "Everybody, it seemed, including many of your teammates, believed that winning that game to avoid a Game Seven with Mike Scott looming made it a do-or-die situation for the Mets. From your perspective, what was the feeling on the Mets entering Game Six?"

"Yeah, Mike Scott was Freddy Krueger and we were a bunch of girls," Bobby said, bringing us both to laughter. "He scared the shit out of everybody. And all he had to do was start his chainsaw, which meant just standing on the mound, and we all wanted to cry and hide in the closet! We knew Game Six was the end of the line. We knew that it was over [if we lost] because we weren't going to beat Mike. He was just an incredible pitcher that year—a gamer. He had our number and was intimidating. In fact, he was the only guy in 1986 that intimidated our ball club. No one, not even the *real* Freddy Krueger, could intimidate our ball club.

"Mike Scott?" Ojeda continued. "All he had to do was show up and say '*Boo*,' and we all went running. I don't know what it was. It was impressive."

But then Ojeda, like a few of his other teammates, without any justification, reversed course.

"Now, it's only hypothetical," Bobby said in a slower, more thoughtful pace, "but knowing my teammates and the mentality of that ball club, if I had to bet my house, I'd say we'd have beat them in Game Seven.

"Now we're all crying, everybody's in the closet, and under the bed, and here comes *Big Bad Mike*. But you know what, if we essentially had to play a Game Seven and were forced to come out from under the bed, I think our guys would have kicked his ass and loved doing it. Our hitting was that good, that competitive. When push came to shove, I think we would have showed up and beat them. Now, that's nothing against Mike, but I really believe our ball club was one of the best ever that year."

Talk turned to the '86 World Series against Boston and how Ojeda believed that one of the turning points in getting the Mets back in the series after falling behind 2–0 was Davey Johnson's understanding of his players and canceling the scheduled workout at Fenway before Game Three.

"There was a sense that you can take all the batting practice you want at this point of the season, but it comes down to what's in your jock and what's in the left side of your chest," Bobby exclaimed. "It's not about more swings. It's not about BP. It's not about a couple more tosses in the bullpen. This came down to who you are. Are you going to accept this? Are you going to roll over? Are you going to accept this for the rest of your life? So Davey knew that. Davey is a tremendous people person. And that's how good he felt about his ball club. He's like, *You know what? I don't give a shit about how much they hit today; they've got to hit when the bell rings tomorrow.* And that's what our ball club did. The real deal was Davey knew his ball club."

The Mets, of course, took the next two games at Fenway and finished off the Red Sox with two more wins back at Shea the following week.

"We've all got the 1986 World Series ring," Ojeda said with pride, "and we don't have the second place ring. No one cares about the second place ring except all the true Red Sox fans who—honest to God are the second best fans in the world—still have a bad taste in their mouth."

Ojeda continued, showing off his great timing and tremendous enthusiasm when discussing the irony of when the Red Sox finally did end the "Curse of the Bambino" in 2004.

"I like to beat people," Bobby began, "and I was a character on the club. I find it fascinating and somehow it warms my heart that it was eighty-six years before they won another championship. So there's that number, *eighty-six*, popping up again and rearing its ugly head. I just find it fascinating that it was *eighty-six* years. Of all the numbers and it's the one where they had that devastating loss they took in '86. So when they ask, *Well, how many years was it before you won? Oh, eighty-six.* And there it is! I *love* it!"

I couldn't help but think to myself, *My God, what did they do to this guy up in Boston?* Ojeda's ire and wrath toward them didn't seem to have diminished one bit in nearly three decades.

And Ojeda believes the feeling is mutual.

"I *still* think they're mad at me," Bobby said. "They had the hundredth year anniversary of Fenway and I didn't get invited. They later said they didn't know where to find me. Meanwhile, I get mail from them once a month. I wasn't hard to find—I lived near a big city and I did a television show! But they couldn't find me."

"Would you have gone?" I asked.

"Oh, my friends on that team, I would have loved to see them," Bobby said without hesitation. "Some actually called me the day of the thing. They were like, 'Where are you?' They think I'm in the dugout or somewhere at Fenway. But I'm watching on TV at my desk at SNY. I'm going, *Holy shit, this is cool!* But I thought they only invited certain people. But then they tell me every living member who ever wore a Red Sox uniform was invited. So I'm sitting there like, *What the fuck? Where was my invitation?*

"So I went home and go to my wife, 'Did I get an invitation?'"

"And she goes, 'Uhhh, yeah, I threw it away.'"

"And I said, 'Bullshit, you didn't throw it away.'"

"So the fact I didn't get invited for the hundredth year anniversary tells me they're still pissed off at me, which makes me happy," Ojeda said with a smile in his voice. "But I promise you one thing, Erik, if they had kicked my ass and my teammates' ass in Game Three and walked away with the big ring, they'd have invited me. They probably would have put me up on the scoreboard and probably would have had me throw out the first pitch!

"So don't invite me. I've still gotcha! I won!" Bobby continued with a big laugh.

"If you had gone, which former Red Sox teammates would you have been most interested in seeing again?" I asked.

"Well, definitely Bruce Hurst and Rich Gedman," Ojeda said. "In fact, Hurst and Gedman actually came into the locker room after we won in '86. Honest to God, and this is no bullshit, the most meaningful thing of the '86 World Series, for me, was that two of my very good friends were man enough to come in there, gracious enough to come in there, and hug me amidst our champagne celebration and chaos right after the game. To *me*, that is my number one favorite memory because when you talk about sportsmanship, when you talk about stand-up men, you can talk about those two. So, for me, there was a real sense of gratification when my friends did that."

Despite Bobby's earlier trashing over the way he was treated by some of the Red Sox veterans when he was a younger player, he changed gears and began to wax poetically about other parts of his Boston experience that he treasured.

"I loved, loved, loved my time in Boston," Ojeda said with a hint of emotion in his voice. "The first time I saw the Green Monster I loved it. It was not intimidating to us. Those three lefties we had were pretty damned good—Hurst, me, and John. We were competitors. We had that little thing in us. That wall wasn't going to beat us. We learned how to pitch with that wall and that actually made us better pitchers moving forward.

"So I loved growing up in Fenway as a pitcher and making those great friendships, getting experience, and enjoying the passionate fans. I never understood it at the time because I was too young, but it's just an awesome place to grow up."

Ojeda's love of the game is indisputable despite the pain and tragedy he has experienced in it. You can tell by the passion he exudes when talking about the good, the bad, and the evolution of the national pastime. At times during our conversation, it seemed like he was downright romantic about it.

I found the most eloquent part of that passion in how, later in our talk, Ojeda described an empty ballpark. It was a description that any kid that's ever played Little League or high school baseball can relate to.

"The beauty of sports is that it's honest, it's pure," he told me. "The game is still on the field. I happened to be with Matt Harvey at Citi Field the other day. This kid is going to be a good one for a long time. We're out there and the ballpark's empty. And while I was talking to him, I said, 'Isn't it great to be at the ballpark when it's empty?' And he goes, 'Yeah, I love it. I don't know why.' And I told him the reason you love it is because there's no one here and you look at the ball field and it's the same one we grew up on. You don't have the television. You don't have thirty thousand people. You don't have the fancy uniforms. You don't have the fancy catering. You don't have anybody kissing your ass. And you don't have anybody folding your clothes. It's just you with a gym bag, grabbing a workout, and it just takes you back to when you were fifteen years old. That's the reality of when you go to a ballpark and it's empty."

It was clear to me that neither the game nor his devotion to it has changed all that much for Bobby after all these years.

| | | | | | | |

Since his playing days, Ojeda has remained active in baseball, first as a pitching coach at both the Single-A and Double-A levels of the Mets' organization. He was considered for the Mets' big-league pitching coach position in 2004, but in keeping with a longtime pattern of acquiring talent from outside the organization, the Mets hired Rick Peterson for the job.

Ojeda then left his post in the Mets' minor-league system, but later resumed his role of pitching coach for the Worcester Tornadoes, reuniting him with old friend and Red Sox battery mate Rich Gedman, the team's manager. The club won the Can-Am championship Ojeda's first year on the job. He later left the coaching staff to join their front office.

Perhaps itching to get back on the field and seeking once again the "purity" of the game, Ojeda worked as a pitching instructor near his home for Rumson–Fair Haven Regional High School in New Jersey. It also gave him more time to be closer to his wife and children.

But it was literally back into the spotlight after many years for Bobby when, in 2009, with the bright city lights of Sixth Avenue in Manhattan as the backdrop, behind his desk at SNY's ground-floor studio, he began work as one of the Mets' pregame and postgame studio analysts. To no one's surprise, he thrived in the role, using expert analysis, outspokenness, and, yes, his signature storytelling, to become undeniably one of the best in the business in his role.

However, after six years with SNY, and with his responsibilities expanding beyond his primary analyst duties, the two sides couldn't agree on a new contract. A source of mine with some knowledge of the negotiations said the difference between the two parties may have been over as little as an eleven thousand dollar raise, making it more a matter of principle for Ojeda than the money. Perhaps never before has the departure of a studio analyst garnered such outrage from a team's fan base, and it led none other than legendary comedian and Mets fan extraordinaire Jerry Seinfeld to go on the popular WFAN *Boomer & Carton* radio show offering to organize a benefit to raise money to bring him back. Seinfeld would later backtrack a bit, offering his support to Ojeda's replacement, journeyman pitcher Nelson Figueroa.

I saw Ojeda following the release of Mookie's book at an event with other members of the '86 team in White Plains, New York, about one hour from his home in Rumson. He was tanned, with a perfect smile, with the only hint of his true age coming from the distinguished gray on the sides of his full head of otherwise jet-black hair. Wearing a dark suit, crisp white shirt, and a pocket square, he had a look that was typical of the elegant way he dressed on air and at other functions. Despite all he's been through in his life, he remains in great shape and still looks like he could throw a few innings.

At the event, I made a point of thanking him again for all the insight he provided in my interview with him for Mookie's autobiography.

"Hey, I heard it's doing very well. Congratulations," he said warmly.

We talked about Mookie and how the book was received by the public before he graciously said I could contact him if I needed anything else.

Ojeda has spent the better part of his baseball life as a part of the Mets' organization. He's been a perfect fit and anything *but* a square peg.

·11·

TOP OF THE HEEP

It was like we were just kind of messing around and, all of a sudden, the Scum Bunch [name] came up and it stuck. We had about four or five of us that were a part of this thing. Then we actually let everybody in.

—DANNY HEEP
(METS OUTFIELDER, PINCH-HITTER EXTRAORDINAIRE,
AND LEADER OF THE SCUM BUNCH 1983–86)

San Antonio is listed as the seventh most populous city in the United States, but you would be hard-pressed to compute that fact by visiting it. It's a sprawling metropolis with a relatively small downtown area that centers around the Alamo. The tallest structures are mostly hotels. Still, it has the distinction of being one of the country's fastest-growing cities of the last twenty-five years.

Sullivan Field, home to the University of the Incarnate Word Cardinals baseball team, is located just off of US-281 at roughly the midway point between San Antonio International Airport and downtown. The ballpark is modest by Division I standards, and sits in the shadows behind Benson Stadium, the school's impressive football facility. Sullivan Field has a mere sixteen rows of seats behind home plate, and just three rows along the first and third base lines. Sponsor signage on the left field wall is for a local deli advertising box lunches for schools and churches. A small, dated scoreboard, boasting "Southland Strong," is positioned beyond the right field wall. Still, the dimensions are big league–like—335 feet down the lines and 390 in the power alleys.

It's a cold February afternoon for this south-central part of Texas, with temperatures in the mid-forties under gray skies—hardly baseball weather. A steady, chilly breeze sways trees barren of leaves beyond the outfield walls. But no matter. The Cardinal players begin to stroll in for their three o'clock practice as they ready themselves for their season opener in two weeks.

"Welcome to our friendly confines," their head coach and the former Mets' world champion Danny Heep says with a grin as he approaches me along the first base side of the field.

Heep has led a charmed baseball life. He played thirteen years of major-league ball for five different teams—the Astros, the Mets, the Dodgers, the Red Sox, and the Braves—all of which made the postseason at some point while he was on their roster. He has two World Series rings, one with the '86 Mets, the other with the '88 Dodgers.

But it is his post-career success at Incarnate Word that is one of the least-publicized and best-kept secrets of all the '86 Mets. His remarkable eighteen-year head coaching career there includes more than 550 victories and nearly 200 more wins than losses. Just as impressive, under his direction, he's helped elevate the Cardinals from the lower-level collegiate NAIA to Division II and then, ultimately, to a Division I program. He has taken the Cardinals to four NCAA regional playoffs, winning two of them.

But despite his long list of accomplishments, Heep has been overshadowed by some of his former Mets teammates' more sensational back page headlines, reality show appearances, and successes in the high-profile world of the broadcast booth.

Now in his late fifties, Heep's face has a deep, everlasting tan from years of sun-splashed Texas summers on the ball field. He is still in great physical condition, the result of a daily workout regimen he has stuck to religiously since his playing days. He speaks in a steady tone with little inflection—calm by college coaching standards—yet he clearly is self-assured in how he goes about his business.

"So this field is a *long way* from the packed houses of Shea Stadium back in the eighties," I said tongue-in-cheek, after we sat down in the first row of the stands by the home dugout. "But despite the modest environs, you've truly achieved greatness in the college ranks—doing more with less. Do you have a specific managerial style that you can attribute your success to?"

"I don't know if I have a style," Heep said with only a trace of a Texas accent in his speech. "But the one thing I've learned just by coaching is that you have to evolve. Kids now are different than they were fifteen years ago. I have very few rules here other than going to class, being on time, and working here, because I understand there are time restraints on these kids; there's a lot of pressure on them in class, and there's a lot of pressure on them with our travel schedule. We have them out of here quite a bit."

Heep paused for a moment of reflection, then actually did reveal one of his blueprints for success.

"Each team has a different personality every year, and I kind of have to find out what that is," Heep said. "Some teams I can be more aggressive with, more forceful. But with some other teams, I can't really say a lot because they don't seem to respond well to it. So I don't think you can just cookie-cut one way of coaching and think you're going to be successful. All good coaches have certain rules and ways that they run things, but after that, I think we all wing it."

"Well, you did play under two of the more charismatic and

successful managers in major-league history in Davey Johnson and Tommy Lasorda," I said. "Did you take anything away from those two?"

"Yeah, actually everything I've learned I've learned through the coaches that I've had," Danny revealed. "Like with hitting, everything I've basically learned was through Bill Robinson in New York, Ben Hines in Los Angeles, and Walt Hriniak in Boston. You learn different things through their different styles. As for managing, Davey and Tommy were on the opposite ends of coaching styles. Davey was just quiet, stayed within himself, worked with the team, and that was it. Lasorda was more of a fan, more animated and a part of all the stuff that was around there in LA. I never had another coach like Tommy. But he was a part of the LA experience. He's what they want out there. It's Hollywood and he fit right in. And he liked it and enjoyed managing that way. His coaching style worked there very well."

"So Tommy was more interactive with the players than Davey was?" I asked.

"Davey would talk to us," Danny said, "but he just had a different kind of style. Tommy did a lot of stuff outside of practices. Or while we were practicing, he might have movie stars around the batting cage. And he did a lot of speaking engagements. Tommy was a part of Hollywood. He was an actor himself and was just all over the map. But I would think, *Hey, he's won world championships, so it works*. It just proves that there's not just one way of doing things."

"Staying on the New York–LA theme," I began, "you were a part of two of the very biggest moments in World Series history. So what was a bigger moment—Mookie's ground ball or Kirk Gibson's home run?"

Danny leaned back, let out an exhale, then smiled, giving some serious thought to the question.

"Well, you know Kirk's home run was in the first game and Mookie's was in our elimination game," Heep said, appearing satisfied with his analysis at that point to a very difficult question. "So I look at Mookie's play as being something that made a *complete* difference."

Still, Heep wanted to emphasize the significance of Gibson's home run and what it meant to the outcome of the 1988 World Series.

"But you know, that was Kirk's *only* at bat in that World Series," he went on. "It set a tone because, I'm telling you, the Oakland A's thought they were going to sweep us. They had their brooms out in the first game. Kirk was our best offensive player all year long until he tore his hamstring and couldn't do anything. When he came up in that game, we didn't even know if he could hit. And if he did, even he was wondering if he could make it to first base. But I guess it didn't bother him when he jogged around the bases because he was so wound up at that point to think he was hurt."

"He was probably floating," I said.

"He hit that home run one-handed and couldn't put any pressure on his back and front feet," Heep recalled incredulously. "I liked playing with Kirk Gibson. I've had the chance to play with a lot of really good players, Hall of Fame players, and he was one of the guys who was no-nonsense, focused on the game, was hard-working and tough. He was a football player playing baseball."

Heep then got back to what he ultimately considered the even bigger moment.

"But Mookie's ground ball, if that doesn't go through [Buckner's] legs, we might *still* be playing that game," Danny said, chuckling.

"In that same '88 postseason, you played the Mets in the NLCS," I brought up to Heep. "You had a lot of friends on that team, as you were on the Mets for years. I realize you came up with Houston, but you really came into your own in New York. Was it at all strange playing against the Mets, and did they seem like a different team than the one you won a world championship with just two years before?"

"There were a few guys missing—Ray Knight wasn't back, Mitch and I weren't there—but that was still an excellent club," Heep said.

"A hundred-win team," I added.

"Yeah, I thought the Mets were the best team in the National League in '88," Danny said. "For myself, it was weird being in the visiting dugout [at Shea]. It *was* a little strange. But that's baseball. It's a business. You move on. The Mets were really the first time I'd been with a team where we all kind of grew up together. We had the trades [for Hernandez, Carter, and Ojeda], but a lot of us—like the guys from the Mets' system—were all kind of the same age. We went from losing ninety-something to winning 116 games in a short period of time. Then, all of a sudden, I'm playing against them. It was kind of an uncomfortable feeling, but I was trying to win games as much as anybody else. That '88 Dodger team, we weren't tearing it up. We had lost Gibson, our best offensive guy, and we had backups in there because we were all banged up. Let's face it, the pitching really carried us, and then we kind of pieced it together with some role players that ended up getting it done with some timely hitting when we needed it—especially in that series against the Mets. It was one of those cases where it probably wasn't the best team that won. But that's why you play 'em."

Heep was acquired by the Mets in 1983 and set the club's single-season record for pinch-hit home runs at four, a mark that still stands all these years later. Two years later, when Darryl Strawberry went down with an injury for the better part of a month in the middle of the season, Heep filled in admirably. I wanted to know what it was like for him to accept the position of role player all those years in New York.

"When Straw went on the DL in '85," I began, "you hit around .300, were arguably an upgrade defensively over Straw, and the popular perception was that you hustled more than him as well. I recall you received a groundswell of support from fans and media alike for the Mets to find you a starting job somewhere or have you spell Darryl once or twice a week. But that didn't happen and you accepted your role with the Mets as their primary pinch-hitter off the bench and as a guy that would only occasionally start. At the end of the year, you decided to stay with the Mets instead of demanding a trade and becoming an everyday player for some other team."

"Yeah, I mean, I understood," Heep said. "I wanted to play, but we had an all-star team in front of us. I look back at my career, and I always wish I could have started more, wish I could have played more. But I never played for a losing team. There were always quality players ahead of me—all-stars. So did I think I was going to beat out Darryl in the outfield? I mean, Darryl had Hall of Fame potential."

"His ceiling was higher," I said.

"Exactly," Heep said. "But Davey did an excellent job of trying to keep people sharp. He understood Kevin Mitchell and the other guys could be trusted to go in and give guys days off because Davey would try to get us those six, seven, or eight at bats a week to keep us sharp in case somebody went down. And we had a very strong bench. [The reserves] could go in and compete and there wasn't a big drop-off. Maybe we weren't quite as good [as the starters], but we weren't just going to lose games. We were too deep for that. It was too good of a team."

"You were basically a .340 hitter in the minor leagues and were used to playing every day," I said. "Was it a difficult learning curve adjusting to not being an everyday player in the big leagues?"

"Well, the pinch-hitting part I learned from Rusty Staub," Heep explained. "When I first came over from Houston, Rusty helped me a lot on preparation. I never pinch-hit before. I had always played every day in college and the minor leagues, and then all of a sudden you've got to sit around and go out and hit against somebody who's probably a Hall of Fame or Cy Young reliever. It's very difficult. Rusty kind of helped me prepare mentally and physically on how to do it and that helped. I still always thought I was better when I had the chance to play on a regular basis and always thought I would have been able to put up some numbers."

I was floored by what Heep said next.

"I didn't think I was ever a really good pinch-hitter," he said surprisingly, before explaining what he really was trying to say.

"But I don't think *anybody* is a really good pinch hitter. Some do it better than others, but it's just too hard a job to only get an at bat against major-league pitching a couple of times a week and be successful at it."

"Still, you played a critical role off the bench for those great Mets teams," I said. "Plus, you never complained publicly about your playing time. Is being that kind of team player something you stress to the young men you coach here?"

"How does that equate to what I'm doing here?" Danny asked himself aloud. "Well, because I had to go through it, I kind of shuffle my lineup around a lot. I don't let people sit around. I do rotations in the infield and in the outfield. I play guys. I'm not one of those coaches that says, *This is your role. If he gets hurt, you're going to play later*. I don't like doing that because I didn't like that myself when I played. So my lineup won't be the same too often. It'll vary. Guys here, guys there, and keep them playing. I know how hard it is, and I can't ask them to do it if I wasn't able to do it very well myself."

We talked a bit about the importance of preparation and making the most of opportunities on the ball field when they present themselves. Heep knows all about those attributes. A player simply doesn't survive in the big leagues for thirteen seasons and help five teams to the postseason if he doesn't understand and live them.

But then talk turned back to 1986 and how none of his postseason experiences with his other teams compared to what he went through with the Mets.

"It's because those '86 playoffs were all-or-nothing," Danny explained. "We were so good. We won the division and made it look easy. But there was a little bit of panic mode in the late innings of Game Six [of the NLCS] when we were set to face a tough pitcher [Mike Scott] that we didn't match up very well against in a potential Game Seven. Then after coming back to win that game, we're down 2–0 in the World Series and we're like, *We didn't come to do this*. We had just beaten everybody up all year long. What were we, 108–54 in the regular season?"

"That's exactly right," I said.

"So, you look at that record and it's pretty staggering," Heep said. "We were like the number one offensive team, the number one defensive team, and the number one pitching team in all of baseball. So there was a lot of pressure on us. But you know what, we handled it pretty well. Nobody panicked. We didn't do anything different. We didn't start yelling at people or do any of that stuff. We knew the situation. We didn't have to have somebody tell us. We could all read. That's where the maturity and the leadership and the kind of guys that we had just picked it up. We just needed to play better and we did. Everybody pitched in and we got right back into the World Series, winning the next two in Boston, and put the pressure back on them a little bit."

Having played in both New York and Boston, Heep then offered a unique perspective of the two cities.

"I've had the chance to play in pretty much all the big markets—New York, LA, and Boston," Danny continued. "The environments in New York and Boston in any sport are pretty intense—but especially in New York. If you're doing well in New York, it's a great place to be. But if you're not doing well, there are ten million people on that island and they all know where you live. So it's tough. I've seen it make careers and I've seen it destroy careers. I look at guys and everybody wants to go play for the Yankees because they pay the most or whatever. But it's not always the best fit. You've got to know what you've got. Sometimes, it's better to play in a place like San Diego and finish your career there."

As Danny spoke, I began to wonder if perhaps a two-time world champion and a college coach with the skills to develop young players and win big like Heep has might have thrived on a bigger stage than the one he has had at the Incarnate Word. After all, he showed how he could mentally handle the toughest and most challenging markets in baseball.

"I realize you're a San Antonio guy and you came back home to manage," I said to Danny. "But you've been here eighteen years as the head coach—many of those years when the baseball team was in Division II. At any point, did you consider moving on to a bigger college baseball program or work for a professional team?"

Heep didn't hesitate.

"My daughter Joanna was born probably about thirty days after I quit playing [following the 1991 season]," Heep said. "At that point, I didn't want to get back on the bus and go through the minor-league systems. That wasn't the kind of coaching I wanted to do. In fact, sometimes lower-level minor-league coaches are not really able to teach. Their lineups are made depending on the draft choices. I wanted to come and work with some kids.

"I wasn't looking for a job right away, but a friend of mine was doing some bird-doggin' for the Pirates and said to me, 'Hey, they're looking for an assistant coach over at Incarnate Word. It's kind of a young program that started in 1988. If you're tired of sitting around, you might want to do it.'

"So I interviewed with Steve Heying, the head baseball coach here at the time, and he said, 'You're hired.' He let me have free rein to run things. We were kind of like co–head coaches and I enjoyed it. We could pick who we wanted and recruit who we wanted. It's not an easy job to be GM, coach, and CFO all at the same time because it's a lot of work. And you can't blame somebody else if you're not winning, because you went out and got the players."

Heep would take over as the head coach in 1998 after Heying's son graduated from Incarnate Word, and Danny has been running the team on his own ever since.

"So you've been the architect of this club for a while now," I said.

"Yeah, and it's really hard," Heep said. "You've got to evaluate talent and see if they'll fit in. Some of these kids I look at are sixteen or seventeen years old. And there's not too many people who have jobs that depend on motivating eighteen- to twenty-two-year-old guys. And now we find ourselves in Division I."

"What's the difference going from Division II to Division I?" I asked.

"It's a whole different animal," Danny began. "It's like going from A-Ball to the big leagues. I like it, though I wish I had started a little earlier in my career. It's a much more pro-style game. You're now dealing with a really good athlete, a better motivated athlete, and a more mature athlete because you can sign kids that we once never had a chance to get because we're in Division I now."

Heep laughed when he said that everybody wants to play them because they are still relatively new to Division I.

"They know we're young and getting started, so we have no problem getting teams to play us," he said. "We're now able to play teams like the University of Texas, the TCUs, the Baylors, the Texas A&Ms, and the Mississippi States of the world. It's another transition for us. We've got to figure out how to recruit a little better, how to get our name out, and how to get the mystique out that we're not a Division II team. And I've got to raise some money."

Heep then took a look out around the ballpark, cracked a smile, and added something else to his wish list.

"We've got to do something with this facility," he said. "This is a Division II facility, not a Division I. We're not ever going to be like A&M or the University of Texas—they're really professional. They basically have major-league stadiums other than they are just about thirty thousand seats short. But still, they have forty-million-dollar baseball fields. We're not going to get that, but we need to get something that is going to allow us to recruit and the facility comes with the whole package."

"What have some of the primary differences been for you, personally, since moving up to Division I?" I asked.

Heep chuckled and said, "Well, I don't necessarily have to be a grounds crew guy and do odds and ends as I did in Division II.

"But seriously," he added, "our job is to win, recruit, and graduate our kids. We can now concentrate on what our core reasons are for being at this university."

"So, any potential big leaguers on your roster this year?" I asked.

"We've got a pitcher that looks to be probably one of the top ten college pitchers in Texas," Heep said with some excitement in his voice. "His name's Geno Encina. We did a fall workout here and had about twenty major-league scouts looking at him. If he stays healthy, he's got a chance. Probably not a first-, second-, or third-round pick, but he would probably get slotted between rounds five and eight. He's an example of the baby steps we need to take. We've had a couple of kids drafted out of this program, but you've got to really stand out in the Division II level to get drafted. It's hard to sign a guy who doesn't see ninety-plus-mile-an-hour pitching all the time or doesn't face the top fifteen to twenty colleges in the country.

"Geno pitched for us last year in Division I and was 7-7 with a 2.60 ERA as a sophomore. This year he's probably going to get some starts against Texas and TCU—two College World Series teams. So the scouts are going to be able to make a fair evaluation on how he matches up, which will give him a much better chance of getting drafted."

Listening to Danny talk, it was easy to see how happy he was coaching college ball at the Division I level and why he would likely never seek employment with a major-league organization at this point. But I asked the question anyway.

"So how about you? Any chance you would consider a shot at managing in the big leagues if it presented itself?"

In answering my question, Danny explained to me how things work and the advantages of college over the pros.

"To coach in the big leagues," he said, "you've really got to pay your dues in the minors. And once you start on the college side like I did, it's kind of hard to get back into the pro side of it. Minor-league coaches don't make any more money than mid-level college coaches. And right now, I can tell you there are probably several Division I universities in the state of Texas that pay their coaches better than a lot of major-league coaches get paid."

"*Major*-league coaches?" I asked, shocked.

"Yep. Right now the UT coach makes a million dollars a year," Heep told me. "And there are a ton of coaches out there in the upper level of the Division I level that are well up into six figures. I would say the average salary in the SEC for a baseball coach is over three hundred thousand dollars."

"Okay, so I can understand some of the reasons you like coaching at the college level," I said. "But it does seem to me that somebody like yourself, someone who knows the game and worked hard his whole career at it, would have been a natural to come back and coach for the Mets at some point. Over all these years, did they ever reach out to you to work in the organization at some level?"

"No, there hasn't been much communication," Heep began. "And there have been some guys that I've played with that I thought would be *tremendous* coaches. *Tremendous* coaches! But they didn't do it. And the reason for some of that is you've got ownership and some GMs out there that really have no coaching experience. So there's going to be friction. To be a major-league coach right now you almost have to be a diplomat. You've got to appease both ends of it. And guys that were really great players want to do it their way. They want to run their own stuff.

"I think of guys like Keith Hernandez, one of the best players there was, and he ain't coaching anywhere. Dwight Evans was another one of the best players of his time and really knew the game—a student of the game—and understood everything and could tell you how things worked. He coached a little bit, but ego got in the way of his doing the things he wanted to do. I wish it was different, that owners would let [the former players] do their job and that they would just be the money guy and get out of the way. But some of them don't do it that way."

"I'm really glad you brought up Keith," I said, "because I have always believed he would have made a great major-league manager. I've talked with about half the '86 Mets' team and many of them tell me basically the same thing about him—that Keith was a great motivator, a great teammate, had excellent leadership abilities, and was a great player you could learn from. He was all those things, and it just seems like perhaps what happened with the drugs all those years ago may have held him back."

"It could have, I guess," Heep said. "But it didn't seem to bother the Texas manager Ron Washington very often. [Author's note: Washington tested positive for cocaine in 2009 while managing the Rangers, yet remained in that role late into the 2014 season.] I don't know—maybe that's some of it. But I also think some of it is his personality. Keith's a guy that says what's on his mind, and sometimes the front office doesn't want to hear that. They want a yes-man. They want somebody that's going to keep quiet and deal with what they got the best they can. I mean, there have been a lot of managers out there that were great players—like Davey. But there are also a lot of managers in the league that really don't have a lot of major-league playing experience."

"And not a lot of the GMs, either," I said.

That comment really hit a nerve with Heep.

"The GM's got *none!*" Danny said emphatically. "*None!*"

"Some of them are Ivy League guys that teams put right into front-office positions," I said.

I could see that Heep's mind was spinning now. This was clearly a topic he felt very strongly about.

"When Texas brought in Nolan Ryan [as CEO]," Danny began, "and let him run the team, look at how quickly he turned that program around. And then they split ways for whatever reason. It's just different now. I don't know. The way the Spurs do it here is by letting Gregg Popovich run the team and the owner stays out of the way. And that works! You get the right guy and let him do his thing. I understand there are times you have to make changes—something happens or it's not the right fit. I get that part. But sometimes I think ownership gets in the way and should just let the coaches do their job. They know what they're doing. *Listen* to them. But I think the way things are keeps a lot of really good ex-players from getting into the coaching and managing part of the game."

"While we're on the subject of the front office, I'm sure a month doesn't go by without you hearing about the trade then Mets GM Frank Cashen made to get you from Houston. Cashen traded pitcher Mike Scott, who, as we touched on earlier, would go on to terrorize the Mets in the '86 NLCS. What was it like for you to come over to the Mets for a pitcher who would reinvent himself to become a Cy Young Award winner?"

Heep didn't hesitate.

"Roger Craig really did a great job teaching him the *split*. The whole idea with Scott was he had great stuff but wasn't winning. He needed another pitch. And it was Roger Craig who also reinvented Nolan Ryan to a point. Ryan was a power pitcher, but understood he needed a third pitch. He always had a great curveball to go with a fastball. But once he got the third pitch the wins started coming.

"[In '86], Scott had a great season. For a while there, he was unhittable. People ask me all the time about the trade and I say,

'Well, I've got two world championship rings, so at least I've got something over him,'" Heep said with a laugh.

"All right, so you know I couldn't do an interview with you without bringing up the Scum Bunch," I said with a grin. "Siskie told me that you were the true leader of the 'Scum Bunch.'"

Heep leaned back and let out a big laugh.

"We put that thing together just trying to get the team together," Heep said. "I don't even know or remember how we came up with our title."

"The way I have heard it from your teammates, the 'Scum Bunch' started with you, Siskie, and Jesse Orosco," I said. "But then you had 'honorary' Scum Bunchers as well, right?"

"Yeah, like Gary Carter would be an honorary Scum Buncher if he got in trouble or he wanted to go out with us," Heep said, chuckling.

"Now, wait a minute," I said incredulously. "*Gary Carter* would be the *last man* I would think of as even an *honorary* Scum Buncher. What kind of trouble did he ever—"

"Never, no." Danny cut me off while smiling. "But we didn't get into any trouble, either. The whole idea about that team was—and it was really good—we'd be in the locker room and guys would go, *Hey, we're going out to dinner*, and before it was all over there would be fifteen, sixteen guys going. There weren't any cliques. There weren't any groups that did their own thing. It was *very* close-knit. And I will say this—and you don't find this very often in teams— we *honestly* rooted for each other. And that's hard to say. Because in this dog-eat-dog world of professional sports, when you've got a guy playing in front of you, there's always a little thing in the back of your head that you don't want him to be too successful because you want to play. And if you're not playing, you're not going to make a whole lot of money. So it's often hard to distinguish between your own agenda and winning championships. But we put all that aside."

"I get the sense from meeting with you and your Mets teammates that the special camaraderie that you all shared still exists today," I said.

"Yeah, it's weird that we can still call the guys—with only Gary Carter and [coach] Bill Robinson gone—and say to each other, *Let's hook up in New York*, and *everybody* will show up," Heep said with a sparkle in his eyes. "We do some card shows and if you're not in jail," he laughs, "I mean that's the only reason that keeps them from not being there—they're going to all show. We just did something where Mookie and Rafael and Doug and Mitch and I all met. I don't do these shows to sign cards. I do it because it gives us all a chance to get back together and catch up.

"You know, it seems like we're all doing the same thing, like it's just never stopped. We're just not playing baseball anymore. Everybody still gets along. We still laugh and think about the stupid stuff we did. We thought we were terrible. We thought we were some sort of problem child. But we were actually choir kids compared to what they're doing now. But it's great to spend time together, sit in a room, talk about our families and what's going on now. It's kind of a neat deal. I've never done that with any of the other teams I've played for. I mean, LA's done nothing [with their '88 World Series winner]. It's kind of weird."

"Are the card shows the thing that brings you guys together the most?" I asked.

"Yeah, but when Darryl opened up a restaurant a few years back around Citi Field and asked some of the guys to come in, we were *all* there," Danny said. "I'm not talking about just ten of us—I've got a picture and it was *every* guy."

Like the majority of his old Mets teammates I had met with, Heep asked me how everyone else was doing. I said they all seemed to have their lives on track, even Lenny now.

"That's good to hear," Danny said. "Lenny is still a concern to us."

With that, the onetime leader of the Scum Bunch, who as baseball coach at the Incarnate Word has made positive, lasting impressions on the lives of hundreds of young men over the last two decades, walked me over toward a gate and thanked me for making the trip to see him.

Danny Heep now had a practice to run.

THE MORAL COMPASS

Your life is pretty much the best example that you can use for anything and I've been blessed to have gone through a lot. I've seen so many things change for the better. Some not for the better. But change is always necessary.

—MOOKIE WILSON
(METS OUTFIELDER, 1980–89)

During the spring and summer of 2013, I had the privilege of working with Mookie Wilson on his autobiography, *Mookie: Life, Baseball, and the '86 Mets.* It was a book that raised more than a few eyebrows, mostly for its poignantly honest portrayal of Mookie's on-again, off-again, more than three-decades-old association with the Mets organization. It would have been one thing had some of his comments come from his more outspoken or unfiltered teammates—of which there are many—but it was all the more revealing and even a bit shocking to see the words written by the player with the thousand-watt smile who outwardly always appeared happy and content. The book revealed a side of Mookie that millions of his fans, who thought they knew the man, hadn't realized existed.

Of all the Mets on their fabled '86 championship team, no one was more highly looked upon than Mookie. So when Mookie's autobiography was finally released, it was taken as gospel of what really has gone on with the Mets over the last thirty years and was supported almost universally by his colleagues, the media, and scores of fans that lit up the talk radio airwaves.

The tabloids and blogosphere blared headlines like MOOKIE WITH AN EDGE, MOOKIE THROWS BOOK AT METS, and finally the redemptive MOOKIE'S NOT ALONE, a *New York Post* article that quoted unnamed '86 Mets who, like Mookie, felt their entire championship team had been largely marginalized by the organization.

At the time when Mookie and I began work together on the book project, he was employed by the Mets as one of their team ambassadors and roving instructors. He had already written a rough draft of around a hundred pages, providing more than enough "clay" to jump-start the project. I was initially taken aback by some of the content regarding his treatment by the Mets first as a player and then as a coach, where—using a metaphor that comes from his love of cars and trucks—he famously described his current role in the organization as nothing more than a "hood ornament." It wasn't that I was completely surprised by any of it, but more that he, as a current employee of the club, would want it published.

Wouldn't he be fearful about losing his job? I thought.

I have been coauthor of three autobiographies, and I can say without any hesitation that the trio of subjects couldn't have been any more different from one another if they tried. But there is one constant with all of them. When you cowrite an autobiography with someone, you have to go deep; deeper than most subjects often go with even their own spouse, clergy, psychiatrist, or best friend. And when those intimate thoughts and personal experiences are shared over many months, a strong bond and friendship inevitably develops.

Mookie was no different.

With this in mind, I was torn. On the one hand, I knew that controversy sells and that some of his comments would certainly be like filet mignon to the media and give book sales a boost. But on the other hand, I wanted to protect a friend and New York icon from putting his job in jeopardy.

So one afternoon, during a break from our writing, I offered to role play with him for when he would, I felt certain, be called to the carpet by the front office about some of the more inflammatory remarks in the book. I asked the tough questions, including why, if he was so unhappy, would he want to stay with the organization?

His answers were spot-on, clearly well thought out, and with complete respect toward the organization. He told me he wanted to remain a Met, though he believed fully that his talent as an evaluator and experience as a player and coach were being vastly underutilized by the club, and as someone who cared deeply about the organization, he wanted to be a part of the effort to pull the club out of their abyss at the time.

Mookie was adamant that he *wanted* that meeting with Sandy Alderson or Fred Wilpon or anyone high enough up in the front office or the owner's box to give him answers.

He *wanted* the explanation he never received for being fired from his first base coaching duties after just one season following the 2011 campaign.

He knew the book would make waves, but he wanted the Mets to know of his disappointment and desire to have a position of authority with a bigger say in player development.

A man of dignity, he was willing to accept the consequences for his honesty and convictions.

To this day, he still hasn't been granted a meeting to clear the air or received an explanation for getting fired as first base coach.

His autobiography—a *New York Times* bestseller—and his comments within it, have yet to be even acknowledged by Mets management. But in hindsight, it's all right by Mookie, as his primary goal wasn't necessarily to change their opinion of him, but rather something he needed to do for himself—to let people know how he felt.

He remains employed by the club, and he is treated as if nothing was ever written.

| | | | | | | |

I flew into Columbia, South Carolina, on a sunny, early spring day to meet with Mookie and his wife Rosa at their home in nearby Eastover. The Columbia airport is the kind of place that displays Southern hospitality at its finest. While at the baggage claim, I was offered a free bottled water and fresh popcorn while I waited. Everyone I came across in the airport, from a security guard to the Hertz rental car agent, greeted me with a warm smile and was eager to please. When I got to my rental car, I was reminded that even the South Carolina license plates are friendly, with the state's motto, "Smiling Faces, Beautiful Places," emblazoned along the top.

Once I was inside the car, the satellite radio was set to an oldies station that was broadcasting the late disc jockey Casey Kasem's old *American Top 40 Countdown* show. At this particular time—most appropriately and ever so ironically—the station was counting down the top hits of *1986*. It was a moment of serendipity and, considering my mission on this trip with the man who is sometimes referred to as "Mookie '86," seemed like a cross between entering *The Twilight Zone* and some sort of time machine.

I was soon in Eastover, South Carolina, a small town that covers an area of just one square mile and is situated about twenty miles southeast of Columbia. According to the latest census, of its just over eight hundred residents, African-Americans make up over 92 percent. The usually tall green trees of Eastover were still mostly gray or brown—unusual for this time of year—partially the result of a rare cold and long winter in these parts.

As I exited off of US 378, I began to have some doubts that I was headed in the right direction. Other than a few older, modest homes on the left side of a long road with large swaths of forestry in all directions, there were few signs of life. But then my trusty GPS—one of mankind's greatest inventions—instructed me to take a left into what appeared to be either a driveway or private road.

It was both.

Mookie basically has his own road leading up to his house or, to better describe it, his *compound*. He calls it a country house, but that would be putting it modestly. The single-level five-thousand-five-hundred-square-foot home sits on fifty secluded acres of property that includes a guesthouse, his own private lake, and enough land to run the summer camp the Wilsons have each summer.

In other words, it's a residence fit for the world champion who inhabits it.

I was greeted by the barks of two German shepherds behind a fenced-in area as I pulled my car in alongside the main house. And then Mookie appeared—now nearly sixty years old but still in playing shape—beaming with a perfect smile and sparkling eyes. If not for the gray in his chin beard, he wouldn't look a whole lot different than he did in the eighties.

I couldn't resist and asked him what his secret is to staying in such good shape when many former players his age are overweight and hobbling around.

"They don't have fifty acres to keep up!" Mookie said with a hearty laugh and a classic Southern accent. "There is a lot of ground

here, and during the summer and winter Rosa and I do all the man-
icuring ourselves. It keeps us busy and keeps us moving."

The inside of his home is spacious and open, with high ceilings
above and a stone wall with a fireplace encased within—roaring on
this day as there was still a chill in the air outside—on one side of
the family room, at the forefront of the house. There was a copy of
his autobiography proudly displayed on a book stand in the foyer
and a warm family feeling of school and Little League photos of
their now grown children on one of the walls. There are signs that a
major leaguer lives in the house, with a few bobble heads and signed
baseballs sitting on shelves, but nothing overboard.

We sat on a comfortable semicircular couch to catch up on life, as
friends would normally do. I was a bit somber, as my stepfather was
stable after suffering a stroke a couple of days before, and Mookie
expressed his concern for my family. There was perhaps no better cure
for a heavy heart than seeing Mookie again, whose wit, expressions,
and infectious laugh could even bring a smile to one of the Queen of
England's royal guards.

Mookie and I stay in regular contact with one another, as our
lives have become intertwined with various projects that sprang
from the success of the book we worked on together. His autobiography brought about a greater awareness to the masses of some of
his strengths and talents away from the baseball field, and has
resulted in some interesting opportunities for him.

One of those came from his first alma mater.

"So what's going on with Spartanburg Methodist College?" I
asked. "Did they make you an offer to come on to their board?"

"Yes, they've invited me to be a member of their board of trust-
ees," Mookie said with a hint of pride. "The term will last three
years and then we'll decide about coming back again. I'm excited

about it. And they're excited about my involvement with the school and being a part of their staff."

Wilson then talked for a while about how Spartanburg was the genesis of his becoming the dynamic speaker he is today.

"In my first year at Spartanburg, the one thing I really had to get over was shyness because I didn't like being in front of people," Mookie said. "So one of my first courses there was public speaking. I didn't choose the course to become a public speaker, but more because my shyness was something I needed to get over. And the course at Spartanburg helped me a lot."

From there, Mookie relied on his own experiences and humor to enhance his speech-making after he joined the Mets.

"When I got to New York," Mookie said with a grin, "they would ask me to speak at *every* Welcome Home Dinner. I did that for *years!*"

The conversation then moved to discussion about a charity that Mookie actually got me involved with—one that helps raise money for the Long Island–based Henry Viscardi School. Viscardi is a private, New York State–supported 4201 school that offers children with severe physical disabilities an academic setting instead of one they might receive in their homes or a hospital. Speaking from personal experience, the school is a slice of heaven on this earth for the care they give to these children.

Mookie is a regular at their Sports Night dinner, joining the likes of Joe Namath, Darryl Strawberry, Doc Gooden, and other major sports stars.

"It's all about raising money for them," Mookie said in a serious tone. "I'm always involved with whatever I can do. I've been involved in skits at their dinners and whatever they ask of me."

"Since I've known you, you've always been a man in motion," I said. "You're now an ordained minister, author, speaker, licensed securities trader, occasional truck driver, fisherman, chef, roving instructor, team ambassador, and philanthropist, among other things. Which do you enjoy and get the most out of personally?"

Mookie smiled as I rattled off the many roles he plays in life, but didn't hesitate in giving an answer.

"I enjoy preaching the most," he said. "And I've had this conversation with my bishop—I don't consider myself a preacher as much as I do a speaker. And where they may be one and the same, I just look at it differently because I think preaching is a little more formal and scripted. With public speaking, I can kind of inject my experiences and relate it to biblical scripture and stories that have really, really helped me over the years. And I enjoy it tremendously."

Wilson continued.

"The truck driving part is fun, too," he said. "It's what I do part-time. It's relaxing and a skill I want to keep up. And that's really why I do it. So those are the two things I enjoy the most right now."

"I've got to ask the question," I said with a grin. "You're pulling up an eighteen-wheeler into a truck stop, and Mookie Wilson gets out to buy a cup of coffee. How often has someone said, *Hey, you look very familiar?*

Laughing, Mookie said almost never.

"It's unbelievable," Wilson said incredulously. "Since 1992, when I began driving a truck on and off, I think I've only met one person that actually asked me that question. Now, that doesn't mean that others probably didn't look and wonder. But only one person actually asked, which is very refreshing and the way I like it. He just said, 'Aren't you Mookie Wilson?' And normally I would say something like *Nah, he just looks like me.* But on this occasion I said I was, and he said, 'I thought so!' And the conversation ended there and he went about his business."

"Now, there is another thing you do from time to time, and that's teaming up with your good friend Bill Buckner at card shows to sign countless photos of the grounder you hit through his legs to win Game Six of the '86 World Series," I said. "You had a good thirteen-year career, but let's face it, it has been overshadowed by that one play. How do you reconcile in your mind between making a nice supplemental income from the autograph signings with Bill and how the play is the only thing that many people will remember about your long career? That may seem like an odd question, but are there times when you wished the play had never occurred or had happened differently?"

Mookie paused for a moment, and then gave a thoughtful response.

"There are never times when I wish it never happened," Mookie said. "If it weren't for that play, I probably would have still been well known in New York, but because of it I can also go into almost any city in the country or even the world and people know who I am. It wasn't a regional thing. When you're talking about the World Series, it's a *world* event. So while I don't wish it never happened, I just wish that people would keep it in context for what it was—an event—that didn't define me *or* Bill Buckner. And that's a conversation that Bill and I have had on numerous occasions. But it's something that we cannot get away from, and we're not even going to try to make it go away now. It's such a big part of our lives and we're joined at the hip for life. If not for that play, I don't think that we would have become the friends that we are today."

| | | | | | | |

Rosa enters the room and gives me a warm embrace. She is looking particularly pretty on this day, fresh off a trip to the beauty parlor to get her black hair straightened and curled at the ends, just below shoulder length.

Throughout the project and on Mookie's subsequent book tour, we grew close, and Rosa would tell me that I had become like one of their family. Rosa, like Mookie an ordained minister, is a strong and intelligent woman with a lifetime of pretty much having seen it all. She speaks her mind and has strong opinions on most every issue. And like many baseball wives, she is ardently protective of her husband, always trying to make sure Mookie doesn't get taken advantage of. By her own admission, she is willing to say some of the things that Mookie won't—telling it the way it is. Mookie once told me how this balance between them is one aspect where they complement one another and has helped their marriage of nearly forty years thrive.

The timing of Rosa's arrival was perfect, as the topic I wanted to talk about next concerned how many of Mookie's old teammates had the commonality of having sons reach the ranks of professional baseball. Rosa's son, Preston, who became Mookie's stepson at the tender age of four years old, would by far have the best career of them all— once driving in a *Ruth-ian* 141 runs in a single season with the Colorado Rockies five years after being the key player the Mets traded in obtaining Mike Piazza from the Florida Marlins. I asked Mookie what role he played in helping Preston become such a terrific ballplayer, and he gave an answer, I believe, that all parents should take heed of.

"I think the role that I played with Preston was pretty much the role my father had with me," Mookie said in a steady tone. "My father was hands-off when he was around my coaches. And I believe that once a person decides to play any sport, you have to let the coaches do their jobs. It's okay for you to have discussions when your information is asked for. But I think my hands-off approach had a lot to do with Preston excelling."

Mookie had a couple of other theories.

"Preston was always around the game," Mookie continued. "And when he was around the game and the players, he was able to draw information from them. And I gave him the freedom to do that. I also gave him the freedom to choose what he wanted to do. I never suggested at any point that he play baseball. But when he did decide to play baseball, he came to us. I never wanted to say to him you *need* to play baseball. I never did that."

I felt at that point Mookie was not giving himself enough credit for Preston's development and choice of pursuing a baseball career, and I said as much.

"You took him *everywhere* with you," I countered. "Through the minors. Through the majors. You allowed him to live that professional baseball life—he was in the clubhouses, around the players. You once told me that baseball players are the best babysitters."

"The *best* babysitters in the world!" Mookie said emphatically.

"So he was exposed to all that," I said. "Wasn't that encouraging him to become a baseball player?"

"I think deep down I was hoping that he would play," Mookie said, before laughing and adding, "but I think Rosa may have wanted something different for him."

We both turned to Rosa, looking for a reaction, but all we got was a knowing smile without elaboration, leaving me to wonder what profession she may have wanted for her son.

"But even when he wasn't with us on the road," Mookie continued, "he played on a sandlot team at home that I had played on. I think he was just prepared mentally for baseball. It was built into him to be able to play baseball and understand the ups and downs and the scrutiny and stuff of that nature. And he also got to see the upside of it because even when I went on appearances and speaking engagements, I took him with me. So he got to see that part of the life, too, so nothing came as a surprise to him."

"And now he's in broadcasting," I said. "Those experiences must have helped him."

"I'll tell you what," Mookie said, turning serious. "There is nothing in the world that would have prepared him better for what he's doing now than being around the game like he was growing up. He's the *perfect* person for what he's doing now. He understands the game and he's very intelligent—almost to a fault. I mean, he is sharp. He could go to any Ivy League school. And I listen to him all the time on television when he's talking, and as good a ballplayer as he was, he's just as good announcing."

"And Preston blessed your family with a granddaughter," I said, just adding to the pride that Mookie and Rosa show when their son's name is brought into the conversation.

"Taya," said the proud grandfather, smiling. "She's a typical twelve-year-old girl—*very* energetic. We spend as much time as we can with her because we go to Florida quite often. She also spends weeks at a time with us here. I think Preston makes sure she gets to spend ample time with us. It's really been a joy. I don't think we ever spend as much time with her as we'd like to because we're so far away, but the time we do spend is much more enjoyable because we always have a lot to catch up on. And she calls us often—whenever she feels like it. And when Preston reads her a bedtime story, we're on the phone, so in a way we're also there. We're part of the raising of her even though we're not always with her."

I asked how their two daughters, who both currently live in the Myrtle Beach area, were doing.

"They're doing well," Mookie said. "Adesina just made the dean's list and is working on her teacher's certificate. And Ernestine made the dean's list, too. She is finishing her studies up in alternative medicine."

I shifted gears and inquired about Mookie's love of writing.

"You've always enjoyed writing," I said. "You once told me that one of your goals with writing your autobiography was to touch people's lives with the story of your personal journey. So now that that's out of the way, are there other topics you now look to write about in an effort to make a difference in people's lives?"

"I am determined to complete a four-book series," Mookie said. "Now that the autobiography is out there, and people really know who I am and where I came from, I want to go further and discuss another important part of my life—religion. So in my next book I plan on going into my relationship with baseball and religion and how the two have merged to help me overcome and become the person that I am right now. And then there's another one that I'm going to do which I got the idea from you, really, which is based on my messages over a year."

"*Fifty-Two Sundays*," I said.

"Yes, *Fifty-Two Sundays*," Mookie confirmed. "I would do a book on that.

"And then the last part, the fourth book that I want to do, is just like the afterword from the autobiography," Mookie continued. "I want to write about how people responded from book to book to book, and how doing those three books has really impacted my life. So I have it mapped out."

"So how high is your mountain of scrap paper with all those ideas?" I asked jokingly, knowing that Mookie and I share the same habit of jotting down our ideas at all hours on whatever we can find to write things down on.

"*Oh man!*" Mookie exclaimed, letting out a big laugh. "I've got little pieces of paper *everywhere*! But I've got a notebook now that I use because it looks more *professional*," he continued, smiling. "So when I'm driving a truck, I have it with me. When I take a break, I put my notes down. But I don't need to put much down—maybe just two words to bring it back. It's the same thing in the middle of the night— I put my thoughts down so I can go back to sleep. I find that your best thoughts come when your mind is at ease. Because sometimes you sit down and ask yourself, *How do I do this?* And it just won't come. But when you relax, all of a sudden, it's like *boom, boom, boom*."

"You were recently honored at the prestigious Hudson Valley Writers' Center Gala in New York along with scholars, poets, and novelists," I said. "It was also announced that you would be co-curator at the Center's World Series of Sports Writing. Did you get a sense of coming full circle with your interest in writing all these years at a night like that?"

"I don't know if it was a sense of coming full circle," Mookie began, speaking slower and softer, "but I had a sense of accomplishment in that regardless of what the book does or what I do from here on—it's that I accomplished *that*. It was very satisfying and I felt like I belonged. It's just like when I was playing baseball: It took me a couple of years to get to the point where I felt I belonged. I was kind of treading in uncharted waters because I had never done a book before, but there I was with other people that had accomplished that. It gave me the chance to sit down and talk with them about how they felt when doing a book and everything that went along with the process. Because I could relate to the conversation, it was very rewarding."

"So you wrote a touching autobiography, describing your early challenges living in poverty, dealing with racism, then talking about your triumphs in baseball and where you are today with your ministry, yet it seemed like the media—particularly in New York—focused instead on the few controversial remarks you made in the book," I said. "Did that bother you at all?"

"No, because I kind of expected it," Mookie began. "But I think to be perfectly honest, no one's life is all glamour and roses. There's adversity you have to face, and I wanted people to understand that you have to face up to it. When everything seemed like it was all fun and games, as my life *appeared* to have been to everybody, there were things that I had to deal with. I wanted people to understand that you can be successful and happy, but there are things you are going to have to deal with. Everybody doesn't have to know your troubles."

"Just prior to the book tour," I said, "I called you on a Saturday afternoon, a little flustered, because SNY had pulled Mex away from his vacation the evening before to comment on the air by phone about the old news mentioned in your autobiography of Gary having an issue with Keith being named captain of the team, because of his previous involvement with drugs."

"Common knowledge," Mookie interjected.

"Exactly," I agreed. "*Common.* The story has been out there for over twenty years. In fact, when you mentioned it to me while we were working on the book project, I told you that I had heard about the story years ago. Yet SNY pulls Keith into their pregame show to comment on it. So from the entire autobiography of one of the Mets' most popular players in the team's history, that was all the network seemed to focus on. So when I called you about it, again a little flustered because I know Mex is a great friend of yours, you started laughing at me in a comforting way, saying, 'Erik, I've been doing this for over thirty years. This is how the media in New York works. Relax, I'm fine.' So it seems like you're used to how the media sometimes needs to make a story out of, in this case, very old news."

"Understand two things," Mookie began. "The Mets have not been relevant for a few years now. And SNY is a Mets station. This [Keith and Gary story] gave them something to talk about. And it's about Mets that people love and adore. You're talking about Keith Hernandez, Gary Carter, and Mookie Wilson. Those were the three people involved in this whole little story in the book. So they were like, *Let's see what we can get out of this*. And even though it was common knowledge, it wasn't common for *me* to write about the story. And I talked about it in the book to just explain *how* their relationship evolved.

"Gary was not welcomed when he first got there," Mookie continued. "Anyone that denies that is just lying. That's just the way it was. They won't say it now because they feel like it's not doing justice to Gary's legacy. But it has nothing to do with that. It's about how Gary evolved from 'Gary the Expo' to Gary being a Met who became a pretty good friend to most all of the guys. But, initially, Gary was not welcomed. They just didn't like Gary. And you can go to any other clubhouse [back then] in the league and they would have told you the same thing—nobody liked Gary.

"But I was not surprised by SNY," Mookie went on. "And Keith being Keith, he wasn't going to get drawn into this controversial thing, because there was nothing to be controversial about. Keith quickly put an end to it [by denying knowledge of what Gary said about Hernandez's captaincy] and then they let it go."

"One of the great things about your autobiography was the transparency and how you spelled out what was going on with the current Mets' regime while other former players from the championship years have been generally unnamed sources," I said. "The *New York Post*'s Mike Puma, a real straight shooter and respected journalist, used some of those sources to back up your comments, writing about how irked they are with the Mets' front office in an article printed just prior to the book release."

I showed Mookie a copy of the article I was referencing.

"I didn't read this," Mookie said as he glanced at the story. "But I don't read the New York papers. I really don't."

Mookie read the part of the article where it said that Paul De-Podesta, the Mets' vice president of player development and amateur scouting, allegedly once said in a staff meeting, "I'm tired of hearing about the '86 Mets."

Wilson chuckled as he read the article, then looked up and said to me, "DePodesta denied saying it. He had to."

Mookie finished reading the article, shook his head, and grinned.

| | | | | | | |

"So next week, you head down to Florida for Mets spring training in your role as roving instructor," I said. "You've been going to these spring trainings for the last thirty-five years, starting at the end of your minor-league career, all through your years in the majors, and continuing on throughout your time as a coach and instructor. Does it ever get old?"

"It *does* get old!" Mookie said with a laugh. "It gets old if you're there for a length of time because of the redundancy. But over the years my role at spring training has changed, so now I'm limited in the days I'm there, so it's actually a lot of fun. I get to see fresh faces for about a week and a half and then I'm done. I'm outta there! But it's the same thing. Repetition. I think what wears players out is the redundancy. Every day starting at six o'clock in the morning, it's the *same* thing. And it gets to be a boring, boring, boring thing."

"I've heard just that adjective from other players, too—that it's *boring*. Is it too long, too?" I asked.

"Actually, it's not too long because you really *need* that time," Mookie said with conviction. "Pitchers need that time. Hitters need that time to get in what we call 'playing shape,' because you can run all winter, but until you're out there standing on your feet for hours and hours at a time, getting that routine together, evaluating yourself, making changes and experimenting with some things, you aren't ready [for the season]. So you really need that time—as boring as it is—because it's time really well spent."

"So let's talk a little bit about your current role with the club as a roving instructor," I began. "It's a somewhat limited role in that you spend a week or so at spring training and then travel to the Mets' various minor-league teams for a few days here and there throughout the season to help them out. One of the things that I recall from early on, after we first began working on your book, is how astute you were in judging young, raw baseball talent. You have an eye for it, often going against the flow and conventional wisdom.

"Like when the Mets were so high on Ike Davis," I continued, "you were all over their *other* young first baseman, Lucas Duda, but told me that the team would need to allow Duda to hit to all fields and be more aggressive. Well, Duda eventually did those things, won the first base job, and is now one of the premier sluggers in the game, while Davis has become a journeyman.

"Another example was when the Mets weren't as high on Juan Lagares as they are now, you said he was going to be a special player with some pop and an outstanding glove in center field, though it was important that the Mets let him play. But soon after your assessment, they traded for an aging Bobby Abreu who took away critical playing time from Lagares. There was even talk of trading Lagares back then. But you said he was a keeper, and he ended up winning a gold glove and having a solid year at the plate the next season.

"And then there was the case of Travis d'Arnaud who, despite struggling mightily at the start of his career in 2013, you correctly predicted would grow into his role as the Mets' starting catcher. The following season he flourished and finished seventh in the Rookie of the Year balloting.

"Does it still bother you that the Mets don't seem to hear your voice in judging personnel?" I asked.

Mookie paused and began to speak at a slow, deliberate pace.

"It doesn't bother me," he said. "I've learned to accept certain things. You can only offer your assistance, but people really have to ask for it. And right now, they're not in a position, or don't feel they're in a position, to ask anybody for judgments from the outside. Although I don't consider myself to be an outsider, the bottom line is it doesn't bother me anymore."

Mookie then began to talk about how the Mets aren't alone in not tapping into former players as a resource as much as they should.

"I do feel that more clubs need to involve more former players in how they run their organizations," he said. "Those are the players that have gone through it. They *know* how players think. Because half the GMs out there now—they *don't* know. They may have played in Little League, but they really don't know. What they do know are numbers. So I'll think, *Okay, so you handle the numbers, you let me handle the talent.* But they're not going to do that.

"That bothers me more than the fact that they don't ask me personally for evaluations," Mookie continued. "I think that all of baseball is kind of reluctant to bring in former players to get their advice on players. Oh, they'll tell you to go scout some guys, but they're not going to listen to you. That's just the way it is. I wish that baseball would take advantage of the talent and resources that they have right at their front door, but they don't."

"And you're now seeing Ivy League guys becoming general managers," I said. "Teams have gotten away from the traditional family-run organizations to a more corporate structure."

"And it's all over baseball," Mookie said. "That's why you see less ballplayers being involved in the game."

"Regarding your situation, you weren't just fired once as a first base coach with the Mets, but *twice*," I said. "And that just enrages guys like Sisk, Heep, Lenny, Straw, Mitch, and Doc. They all told me, without my prompting, that they just don't understand it, bringing up such traits as your baseball intelligence, communication skills, and how you're one of the game's good guys. In other words, *Why would they do it?*

"But I do recall you once telling me how you were in the dugout prior to a game at Citi Field in 2011," I continued, "and the public address announcer was giving the starting lineups and coaches for each team. When he got around to you, and announced, 'Coaching first base for the Mets, Mookie Wilson,' you received the loudest ovation. That caused some issues, didn't it?"

Mookie began to chuckle, before saying, "I think some of the coaches didn't appreciate it and were making little sly remarks. One of them said the only time we get any cheering is when I step on the field. So I knew there was a little resentment there from some of the coaches."

"So the issue was more with the coaches than with any of the players?" I asked.

"Oh, I had no problems with the players," Mookie was quick to say. "They were great. I never heard a negative thing from them. Players are always curious about what we did and how we did things—that's what they always wanted to talk to me about. They're generally curious about how we survived, how was this player and how was that player, and what it felt like to be in the World Series back when I played, because none of those guys had experienced that."

"So you have a wealth of experience, strong evaluation skills, and had a good rapport with the players," I recapped. "Mookie, your getting fired just doesn't add up."

"It really doesn't," Wilson said. "And that's why I just asked for an explanation. And to this day, I haven't gotten one. I don't know if there is an explanation. I think they gave me the coaching job the second time because I was convenient until they could get the people they wanted."

"The new front office regime, right?" I asked.

"That's the only logical explanation," Mookie said.

At this point Rosa chimed in by alluding to a confidant of Mookie's in baseball who delivered a fateful, almost cryptic message to him just after he was let go from his coaching position.

"Somebody told you that what happened was just what he was afraid was going to happen," Rosa began. "But he just left it hanging there like that. That's the only thing he ever told Mookie about it. I mean, that's a broad statement. You're left wondering what's what."

"So he had a sense of what was coming and then it actually happened?" I asked.

"Yeah," Mookie said. "So what happened? I don't know what happened."

Mookie then paused, clearly befuddled by the whole subject, and then once again spoke at a soft and deliberate pace.

"I do know that Terry [Collins] wasn't too happy a lot of times, thinking the team was abusing me because every time they wanted something done, they would come and get me. So I had to do my job on the field and then go do this other promotional stuff, too. And Terry thought that was abuse. But it still doesn't explain what that guy's comment meant. I don't know, because he won't say anything else about it.

"But even after all this time," Mookie continued, "you would think that one of them in management would say, *Well, look, this is what we felt about you.* But nothing."

Rosa then added, "If the team is going bad, but you've got players coming out to talk to you to try to improve, does that not help the club? And if you've got people who cheer when you're standing on the field, isn't that just an acknowledgment for what you *have* done? I think what you've got is a team that wants *their* name, *their* seal on it, and they *don't* want to be associated with the past."

"There are just so many things that it could be," Mookie concluded. "But their lack of effort to explain anything leads people to draw their own conclusions."

"Of course, there is a chance the Mets might finally tap into their past glory and give Wally Backman a shot at manager should the team struggle again this coming season," I said.

Mookie's eyes lit up at the thought.

"I spoke to Wally about it, and it's going to be interesting to see what happens based on what has already transpired between him and the Mets," Wilson said. "Now, I don't talk to these front office people—they don't talk—but I don't see it happening. I just don't see them bringing Wally up. Wally is Wally. He is a tad bit tamer now than he was. I've worked with Wally now for quite a few years. He's a *good* manager. He relates to the players as well as anybody I've ever seen. The players *love* him. He can be hard on them, but some players like that—they want to be pushed. Wally's not afraid to push the envelope. He will go against the grain. He will go against upper management. He's already been reprimanded for that a couple of times. But he is *so good* they can't fire him, because then people would ask why. You're talking about a Minor League Manager of the Year several times. Of course, you heard the rumors that he was supposed to be the third base coach of the Mets in 2015. I'll let Wally tell you about that because I got it secondhand so I won't go into all of that. But it's very weird."

"I did hear about the rumor," I said. "They were going to move Tim Teufel from third base coach to hitting coach."

"I heard that's what was going to happen," Wilson said. "They actually called Wally, and then all of a sudden something happened overnight. And that's when they brought in this other hitting coach."

"Kevin Long," I said. "The guy the Yankees had just fired."

Shaking his head, Mookie said, "I just don't get it. I *don't* get it."

| | | | | | | |

With the topic of the mystery surrounding Mookie's firing exhausted, we moved on to discuss a subject more near and dear to Mookie's heart.

"As you know, I have met with many of the key players from the '86 championship team," I said. "Generally speaking, they are very different individuals in 2015 than they were in 1986. Straw is an evangelist. Doc seems to have found his way through faith. Ed Hearn's a religious guy. Doug Sisk, who probably enjoys Communion, and Kevin Mitchell talked religion with me. Danny Heep has coached for years at a Jesuit university. The faith of Rick Aguilera, Rafael Santana, Ray Knight, and Tim Teufel is well documented. So you have a lot of your old teammates that kind of walked a little bit on the wild side in the eighties who say they have found God. In fact, I could probably count on one hand the '86 Mets that *haven't* professed their faith by now. I asked Straw the same question, but am interested to hear your comments on the matter. Do you think there's a cause and effect with how the Mets partied hard in the eighties and how it may have led them to finding a higher purpose later in their lives?"

Mookie glanced at me with a straight face, saying, "Erik, I'm afraid if I answer this you are going to mess up a chapter I'm writing on that," before letting out a big laugh.

"It's called 'Two Worlds,'" Mookie said of his chapter. "Most people, specifically professional athletes, have to live in multiple worlds. You have a world that involves your career, one that involves your family, and another that involves your religion. And you have to learn how to manage those three worlds, because there's always going to be conflict between them. The ultimate goal is to be happy. But there's the old consensus that the worlds don't mix—that you can have one, but you can't have them all. And most players that feel the risk of being criticized or deemed hypocritical won't show certain parts of their lives. It's a struggle. They think, *This is the one life they want to see and this is the one they're going to accept.* For example, no one will accept Scum Buncher Danny Heep as a Christian. *No one.* But that had nothing to do with the way Danny Heep was feeling inside. So guys got caught up with living in *that* world, or at least portraying *that* world. Then you had some that were trying to do both."

"Straw told me that being a major-league baseball player in New York is so far from reality," I said.

"It's *so far* from reality," Mookie confirmed. "Straw has found God, lost God, found God so many times, but deep down that's where he wanted to be. But it was this world here that he didn't want to let go of in the process.

"I had the pleasure of getting to know these guys on a very personal level," Wilson continued. "And there was not one of those guys that I didn't trust Preston with. *Not one.* I mean, when Preston came on the road, some of the guys would come into the room to get him. These guys were not necessarily the guys the general public perceived them to be. Rosa and I saw the good in them.

"The only person," Mookie continued with a good-natured laugh, "I probably would have questioned Preston being with was Lenny."

"But here's the funny thing, though," Rosa said. "There's some good even in the worst of us. And I say that because I've seen Lenny be a good father with his sons. Everybody is not going to walk the straight and narrow, and there are some people who lose their way. I think Lenny lost his way. Because Lenny wasn't always all the way to the left side. I did see compassion, love, and his being fatherly—it was there."

"And he is living with his ex-wife again primarily because they share two sons together," I added.

"Because she sees him in that moment where she saw him *before*," Rosa said, her voice rising with affirmation. "And you never lose hope of that. If you are a Christian, you never lose hope that somebody can always find their way back."

Mookie then pointed out how some of Lenny's influence has played a role in his son Cutter's baseball career, before adding, "I had a conversation with Cutter when I was in Brooklyn. He actually might make the big leagues this year. He's a pretty good-looking player."

As for William Hayward "Mookie" Wilson, there are no regrets. There is no longer any angst over sharing playing time with Lenny Dykstra for all those years during the prime of his career. And while he would still relish a meaningful opportunity in the major leagues, there is no longer disillusionment over not having the chance to manage there. He is comfortable in his own skin and the life he leads today.

"If I had been traded after '86 and played every day," Mookie told me, "my life probably would have been on the same path as it was. That's because my career ended in '86 with the Mets. There's nothing about me *after* '86. Nothing. I was already accomplished and established. Everything I did after '86 was like, *Oh, and by the way, he did this, too.* If I remained a starter, the only thing that would have changed would have been my lifetime numbers. But as far as the way I am now, it wouldn't have changed at all."

Mookie and I walked to the deck at the back of his house to look out at his lake, as the midday sun glistened off the water.

"What kind of fish do you catch out there?" I asked.

"Oh, some bass, bluegill, sometimes sunfish," Mookie said. "I get out there every chance I get."

"Does the lake have a name?"

"No, it doesn't have one," Mookie said.

"You should call it Wilson Lake," I said. "After all, it is *your* lake."

Mookie was chuckling at the thought when Rosa came out to get us.

It was now time for an early lunch before my flight back to New York. The Wilsons took me to a place called Doc's Barbeque in Columbia for a Southern buffet, where three friends continued conversing about the issues of family, life, and baseball.

·13·

WALLY BALL

Do I think I'm going to be a good big-league manager? I know I am. Am I prepared for it to happen? I've been prepared for a long time. But I have to focus on what's at task right now.

—WALLY BACKMAN
(METS SECOND BASEMAN, 1980–88)

It should have been one of the happiest days of Wally Backman's life.

A press conference was held on a sunny, autumn afternoon in Phoenix in 2004.

After fourteen years as a scrappy, overachieving major-league second baseman and four largely successful seasons managing in the minor leagues, Backman was going to bring his passion, experience, knowledge, and intensity to his new post as the manager of the worst team in baseball, the Arizona Diamondbacks.

"I'm here to win," Backman told the throng of reporters that afternoon. "That's what I've always been about."

But Wally would never even get the chance to fill out a lineup card.

Not even close.

The following day, in a *New York Times* article about his hiring, a list of his past legal issues—including what was termed inaccurately a "domestic dispute with his wife Sandi"—was used to help characterize his "passionate personality" both on *and* off the field.

The Diamondbacks, despite having been Wally's employer while he managed their Lancaster A-Ball team that year—a season which earned him Minor League Manager of the Year honors from the *Sporting News*—claimed ignorance and put the blame squarely on him for not disclosing his legal woes during the interview process for the major-league job.

Just three days later, Backman's dream of managing a big-league team had turned into a nightmare. He was unceremoniously fired by the organization, never to receive a dime in compensation due to him, despite passing up other possible managerial opportunities—including the Mets post that ultimately went to Willie Randolph—that same week.

Still, it was a safe bet that a manager with Backman's pedigree would get another shot as a major-league manager before too long. Managers are hired and fired every year at the big-league level, and there would be plenty of chances for someone like Wally, personal issues be damned.

And wasn't it true that some of the greatest managers in the history of the game—including a few in the Hall of Fame—had their own tussles with the law?

Wally's time surely would come.

After a couple of years away from the game, feeling reenergized, he started over again, taking a job well beneath his level of expertise with the Independent League South Georgia Peanuts, and led them to the league title. His success there put him on the fast track to managing a major-league affiliate again, and two years later the Mets came calling and hired Backman as manager of their Single-A Brooklyn Cyclones team. He rewarded their decision by leading the club to the McNamara Division title with a stunning .680 winning percentage. After promotions to Double-A Binghamton and Triple-A Buffalo, he heralded in the Triple-A Mets' affiliates' move to Las Vegas with back-to-back first place finishes in 2013 and 2014, the latter campaign earning him Pacific Coast League Manager of the Year honors.

With well over seven hundred career wins as a minor-league manager, six first-place finishes, and two Manager of the Year Awards, Wally Backman may very well be the greatest manager to have never managed a major-league game.

But still, he waits for his chance.

| | | | | | |

I first visited Las Vegas during the summer of 1992, staying at the home of my dear friend Tim Neverett, now a play-by-play announcer for the Pittsburgh Pirates. At the time, the Las Vegas metropolitan area was nothing like it is today.

The population, for one, has more than quadrupled, to over two million, since then. Caesar's Palace, once the epitome of high-class dining, shopping, and entertainment, now competes with more mega-casinos and five-star hotels than in any other city in the world. And the city has grown up from being a place almost exclusively known for gambling, drinking, and prostitution to becoming the go-to venue for business conventions and even family vacations.

I arrived at Cashman Field on a picture-perfect day under a clear blue April sky. The game that day would be the home opener for the Las Vegas 51s, and the traditional red, white, and blue bunting hung along the railings of the grandstand. Cashman Field is an older ballpark by today's standards, but it is still a great venue in which to take in a game, with mountains and palm trees serving as a backdrop beyond the outfield walls.

I was led by the Las Vegas 51s' highly competent and accommodating media relations director, Jim Gemma, to the home dugout, where I would wait for Wally to finish an on-camera interview with an exceptionally attractive full-figured blond reporter wearing a clingy pink silk dress and high heels.

Once his interview with her was complete, he lit up a Marlboro and walked over to me.

"Hey, Erik, nice to see you," he said.

"Thanks," I said. "But after her, I'm sorry you have to look at me for the rest of the afternoon."

Wally laughed at my attempt at self-deprecating humor, adding, "Yeah, she was smokin' hot."

We sat at the far corner of the dugout. Despite the gray in his mustache and a few extra pounds, Backman is still easily recognizable as the onetime sparkplug atop the Mets' '86 championship lineup. One of the things that immediately surprised me a little bit after a few minutes with him was how calm, friendly, and introspective he was, characteristics far different from the dirt-kicking, fiery manager I had seen clips of throughout the years.

"I know you would rather be managing in the majors," I said, "but how do you like it out here in Vegas? Do you get out and enjoy it or do you pretty much live here at the ballpark?"

Wally smiled and said, "Pretty much at the ballpark. I live outside the city, in Summerlin. My day consists of basically being at the ballpark, but sometimes when family or friends come in, yeah, maybe I'll spend a night out in the city with them once in a while—but not very often."

"And your wife, Sandi, does she stay at your primary home in Oregon?"

"No, she actually stays here with me. She's retired, so she gets to go back home when she wants to, like when the team's on the road."

Backman is all business and has been for the better part of the last two decades in his quest—*obsession*, really—to one day manage in the big leagues.

"Wally, you arrived at the ballpark today like I was told you always do—at noon for a seven o'clock game. Is that a trait unique to you or do most all minor-league managers do the same?" I asked.

"You know, I'm not certain about the other managers," he began in a measured, steady baritone voice, "but I think the one reason I'm always here at noon is nobody is going to out-prepare me. There are a lot of things to go over, a lot of numbers to go over—left-right stats, how we're going to play our defense. There are just so many little things that I like to go over every day just so I know I have the players prepared the proper way."

"As you know, I'm writing this book as much about the baseball intellect and down-and-dirty grittiness of the '86 Mets as I am about what they are doing today," I said. "With that in mind, what are some of the traits from that team that you have put to use in your managing here in Las Vegas?"

"Maybe some of the aggressiveness, the style of play we had," Wally began. "We were fortunate because we had some speed. We also had some power on that team. And it's always nice to be able to have that because you're not always fortunate enough to have that in the minor leagues.

"But if I take parts of the game, then I have to talk about the managers I played for—Lou Piniella, Joe Torre, Davey Johnson, and Jim Leyland [all world championship managers, by the way]," Backman continued. "I learned a lot from each one of them, but probably more so from Davey, Leyland, and Piniella because it was later in my career when I played for those guys. The success that Joe's had is almost second to none, so if I had been a little bit older I might have learned a little bit more from him, too. But you take the pieces and parts of the way they handled their personnel and how they ran the game, because the communication part of baseball with your players is so valuable. As long as I played and even here, managing in Triple-A, I want to *earn* the players' respect. And I want them to know that I respect them. Respect isn't something that's just given to you."

"You made a couple of points there that really stick out," I said. "You named a list of prestigious managers you've played for and you also talked about respect. It's been well documented how, by and large, you've earned both the love *and* respect of your players—two things that don't normally go hand in hand. Dan Uggla even wore number six in your honor earlier in his career. So here's a two-part question: Which of those managers you played for are you most like, and how do you earn the love *and* respect of your players?"

"Well, the latter part of your question is that my players know I have their back," Wally said. "They know if anything is to happen to one of them on the field or off the field, they know I'll have their back. And I think the players have my back as well.

"The first part to that question is tougher," Backman continued, "because I think a lot about Lou Piniella because I also get fired up once in a while. And I know it only works a couple of times a year when you blow the clubhouse up and you have to say something. And usually in those cases you're only really talking to one or two individuals to get more out of them. But of *all* those managers I mentioned, I would probably have to go to a guy I only played one year for as being the most I'm like—Jimmy Leyland. The way I saw him handle his players, especially the ones who didn't play every day—to have them ready—that's what I try to do. You have twenty-five guys and they all can't play at the same time. So to keep them sharp, the way that Leyland did, ensured that when there was an injury, we never missed a beat that year in '90 when we won the division. And, so, I take a lot from Jimmy Leyland."

"You have some rising stars on this team," I said. "And that presents a different kind of challenge for you. What is it like to manage a ball club when you know at some point during the season your best players are going to get called up to the major leagues?"

"You just deal with it," Backman said matter-of-factly. "Last year, I think at one point in time we had like twelve guys up in the major leagues at the same time. And that's *tough*. The clubhouse is constantly changing. And it's my job and it's my coaching staff's job to try to rebuild chemistry all the time. And I think chemistry is a *huge* part of success. But the turnover is just a door that never stops turning at this level. It's tough, but it's interesting and keeps us on our toes."

"After the Arizona Diamondbacks fiasco," I began, "where you were fired four days after accepting the manager's position, you went back to managing in the low minor leagues and even some Independent Ball with the South Georgia Peanuts of the South Coast League. You used those opportunities to get back on track to one day get another shot at the big leagues. I realize you had to do what you had to do, but did you ever feel like you were, for a lack of a better phrase, 'above it all,' and your skills weren't being used at the level they should have been?"

"Yeah, I *still* think that," Backman replied, his steely blue eyes revealing his unabashed belief in his statement. "But it's a daily process—to come to the ballpark and set really high goals for the guys that I'm with. I know I would be a good big-league manager, but I don't like thinking about that stuff, because if it happens, it's going to happen, and I'll be prepared for it. But again, these players know I care. And I would at any level. That's the best way I can put it. Players know I care about them."

"Along those lines," I said, "of all the '86 Mets I've spoken with, most have told me that if the Mets want to inject some intensity into the club and be winners again [Author's note: The interview was done prior to the Mets' championship run], one of the things they should do is make you the manager. Some have also alluded to how you would light a fire under the fan base, resulting in a badly needed boost in attendance for the cash-strapped Mets. What would you say to your old Mets teammates that have expressed such over-whelming support for you in this regard?"

"I would say 'thanks,'" Backman said with a laugh. "I appreciate it. You know, I believe in what they're saying. And when that oppor-tunity comes or if it comes, *wherever* it comes, I know one thing and it's that my players will be prepared."

The "*wherever*" part of Wally's answer was somewhat ironic. Unbeknownst to the two of us, at roughly the same *hour* of our interview, several baseball sources would later report that Florida Marlins owner Jeffery Loria was at Citi Field quizzing people who knew Backman about whether they thought he would make a good big-league manager. Loria was in attendance watching Florida get swept in a four-game series to the Mets that weekend, which only added to the misery of an already abysmal start of the 2015 season for the Marlins.

But just several days later, respected baseball reporter Ken Rosenthal reported that Wally would not be the next pilot of the Marlins in the event the team decided to fire manager Mike Red-mond. [Author's note: Rosenthal would be proven correct, as the

Marlins fired Redmond weeks later, inexplicably giving the job to their general manager, Dan Jennings, who had never managed a game above high school ball—and not since 1984!] No reason was given by Rosenthal, though while Backman is employed by the Mets, any club interested in interviewing him would first need the permission of Mets general manager Sandy Alderson.

A similar scenario played out prior to the 2015 season when a managerial opening arose with the Tampa Bay Rays after their skipper Joe Maddon bolted for the Chicago Cubs. Wally explained to me that he was originally on the short list of candidates considered for the Rays job, but ultimately an interview never took place and he was notified by the Rays that he was no longer being considered for the post.

Perhaps hypothesizing that Alderson isn't giving other teams permission to talk to Wally, Backman said to me, "If Sandy doesn't want me to manage the Mets, why keep me?"

I had an immediate theory for Wally.

"They have to keep you in the organization," I said, "because if they let you go to another club—and then especially if you are successful—there would be outrage from the fan base. You're one of their own."

Still, realizing that Backman's ultimate dream job is managing the team he grew up with, I stayed with that line of questioning.

"Didn't you first talk about becoming the Mets' manager with Jeff Wilpon years ago?" I asked.

"Actually, Jeff and I had a long conversation when I first signed back with the Mets in 2009," Backman said. "Jeff's words were 'Be patient.'"

With the Mets posting losing seasons ever since that discussion, patience could be added to the list of Backman's many attributes. And it would be remiss not to note that the Mets are in a practically identical situation to the one they were in in the years that led up to the team's halcyon days of the mid-eighties. I brought this up to Wally.

"In a way, in New York, if feels a little bit like 1984 again," I said. "The Mets have some strong veteran leadership with a lot of young, highly talented players that you helped nurture and develop here at the Triple-A level—just like Davey did in the early eighties. With that being said, it would seem like, with the tremendous job you've done here in Las Vegas, that, should the Mets struggle again this season [Author's note: The Mets would, in fact, make it to the World Series], you would be first in line to become the next manager of the Mets, like Davey became in '84. Do you agree and can you also see the similarities between now and back then?"

"I do see the similarities between '84 and now," Backman said without hesitation. "But the other part of the question is not up to me. But if I was given the opportunity, I know I would be prepared. I have had most of these young kids, and *I hope* that they have success. As much as I would want an opening for me, I don't want to see those kids struggle. But to see these kids I've had, I know I've sent them up to Terry [Collins] and they've been prepared. And that's the respect between me and Terry. I'm going to tell him what I think they can do and what they can't do. We've got a good, strong relationship that way."

"I want you to know that in asking you about the Mets job, it's in no way disrespectful to Terry," I emphasized. "It's just that the similarities with what Davey did and what you're doing are mirror images of each other."

"Well, that's how it happened with Davey," Backman replied. "He had all of us young guys together, and he was able to move up with us [to the majors], and the rest is history. We won a world championship doing that."

"There was a strong rumor right after the 2014 regular season ended that you were going to take over as third base coach for the Mets, and Teufel would move from the position to become the new hitting coach," I said. "But then they went out and hired Kevin Long as hitting coach and left Timmy at third. Nobody's really heard much about it since last fall. What happened?"

Backman started to laugh, and then jokingly told me to shut off my recorder and he'd tell me.

But then after a pregnant pause, Wally said, "It has been talked about more than once in different years about me being in New York as one of the coaches. And I've been told that I was going to be there and it didn't happen. Who's to blame for that, I don't know. But that's about all I can say. I've been asked twice to be one of the coaches there."

"And then it doesn't happen," I said.

Backman paused, and then with some resignation, in a lowered voice, said, "Yep. I was told it was going to happen and then it didn't happen. Twice. In two different years."

Feeling his strong disappointment on this topic, I moved on.

| | | | | | |

"Okay, this might be a difficult question for you to answer," I started out. "Perhaps no general manager in baseball plays a bigger role in the day-to-day operations than Alderson does with the Mets. Being the take-charge manager that you are, would it be a challenge for you to work under a general manager like him?"

His voice rising, Wally didn't hesitate, feeling that despite some of their differences, they share a common philosophy of today's game.

"I don't think it would be hard," Backman said. "Because I know that Sandy is a very hands-on person and the game has gone to the sabermetrics type of stuff that he likes to do. But I've been using the sabermetrics ever since I've been managing."

"Is that right?" I asked.

"Yeah," Wally said. "So it's nothing new to me. You know, I think general managers today are more hands-on than maybe they were in the past. I think that's part of the things that have changed. You've got to change with time.

"Would we bump heads?" Backman asked rhetorically. "I think every manager and general manager probably bump heads at some point in time, you know? But I think it's better to get all that stuff out in the open. Of course, the general manager is your boss and he has expectations just like as a manager you have expectations of your players. But I really don't think it would be hard as long as you're able to do the baseball stuff you're supposed to be able to do like making out the lineup and those types of things, because you're running the game. The general manager is not in the dugout with you. And the most important thing as a game-time manager is knowing how to run your bullpen, and that's what I take the most pride in doing."

Backman and I talked some more about sabermetrics and how he said he is always trying to outthink other managers with his fresh ideas.

"C'mon, Erik, I want to show you something that I've come up with," Backman said, and he led me onto the outfield grass just beyond the perimeter of the infield dirt.

Backman had twenty numbered divots inserted into the ground exactly ten feet apart, from the first base line around to the third base line, to better position his infielders against the scouted hitting tendencies of opposing hitters.

"Nobody else is doing this in baseball," Backman said proudly.

We went back inside the dugout and continued our conversation.

"When the Alderson regime came to the Mets, he brought along Harvard-educated Paul DePodesta to act in the role of the Mets' vice president of player development and scouting," I said. "He caught flak from some of your old teammates when, at an organizational meeting, he allegedly said he was tired of hearing about the '86 Mets, to put it in mild terms. Do you believe his statement may have been a part of the new regime's perceived alienation of the '86 team or more just a way of saying, *We need to make our own history?*"

"I think that they just want to make their own history," Backman replied. "That's what I think. I'll leave it at that."

I took Wally's answer at face value, though I was left to wonder if he was giving full disclosure of his true feelings on the matter. Still, if he did have more to say, I could hardly blame him for answering the question as he did. He is, after all, employed by the organization— one step away from the major leagues. So why rock the boat?

I changed gears and thought I would get straight from Backman what really happened one early autumn evening in 2001—an unfortunate incident which likely is the leading reason why he has never managed a big-league game.

"I've read about what's been reported regarding your domestic violence issue and how it led to the Diamondbacks letting you go just a few days after hiring you," I began. "But I can't help but think you were already in their organization for a full year, and it seemed that, first of all, they got the story wrong—"

Backman jumped right in before I could finish, calmly confirming, "They *did* get the story wrong."

"So what happened, Wally?"

"There was a domestic issue with a woman that was at my house," Backman tells me. "I came home from a fishing trip with my son, and this woman was saying things like how she was going to take half of her husband's money in a divorce. Her husband was a good friend of mine and I began defending him. That woman never worked a day the whole time they were married."

Then, pointing to his left arm, Backman said, "See that scar right there?"

"Yeah, on your arm. A long one," I said.

"There was a ten-inch plate in my arm where she hit me with a baseball bat," Wally explained. "And I was the one that got arrested for it. And that's the fucking truth."

"That's ridiculous," I said.

Wally expounded on his point for emphasis.

"I got hit with my own *World Series* bat," he began. "In my arm. And *that's* why the Diamondbacks let me go. And it happened years before the Diamondbacks hired me. It was a shitty deal what the Diamondbacks did. Shitty deal that they said they paid me, too, and they never did. But that's history now."

"Did you have a contract with them?" I asked.

"Not yet," Backman said. "We agreed on a $1.8 million contract and we shook on it. A handshake is legal in the state of Arizona. I was knocked over by lawyers who promised me a positive verdict."

But Backman told me that he was concerned it would hurt his chances of getting hired again if he brought a suit against a team, so he let it go.

"Ah, it was a long time ago. I don't hold grudges," Backman said, his voice trailing off.

Wally lighted up another Marlboro and looked out toward the

field where three members of the grounds crew were readying the infield for that night's game.

"What happened in Arizona, I believe, is unprecedented," I said. "I don't believe there has ever been another instance in baseball history when a manager was named and then a few days later, he loses his job because of legal issues uncovered from a belated background check. You had worked years to get your dream job of managing in the big leagues. What was going through your head at the press conference on the day you were named skipper of the Diamondbacks?"

Again looking back out at the field, Wally reflected for a moment, and said, "I was excited, of course. It was just like a player getting to the big leagues. You've worked hard to get where you want to go, and there was the light at the end of the tunnel right there. It was a very exciting time, and then it was a very bad time as well with what happened."

"When you accepted the Diamondbacks job, you took yourself out of the running for the managerial opening with the Mets that would ultimately go to Willie Randolph," I said. "Did you contact the Mets again after the Diamondbacks opportunity fell through?"

With some sadness and clear regret in his eyes, Wally said, "No, I didn't. The biggest mistake that I've made was not going and interviewing with the Mets when they called me after I had interviewed with the Diamondbacks. They wanted me to meet them in St. Louis after the World Series with [then GM] Omar Minaya. The plane I was scheduled to be on broke down, so I had to stay in Phoenix, Arizona, one more day, and I was told if I interviewed for that job with the Mets that I wasn't going to be guaranteed the job in Arizona. So the Diamondbacks basically tied my hands. And that's a mistake I should not have made. I should have said, 'Well, if that's going to be the case, then I should interview with New York.'"

"After what happened in Arizona, you took two years off from managing," I said. "What was that like for you and was there bitterness?"

"You know, I did that Bryant Gumbel show—it was tough," Backman said. "The first year, of course, I wasn't going to get a job anywhere. But the toughest part about it was the way I saw it affect my family. But I still felt that I had big shoulders. I went to the winter meetings the next year so I would be seen, but nothing happened. But I wasn't that guy that was going to crawl in a hole and not come out of it. That's because I still had goals I wanted to make. So I figured, well, I've done Independent [with Catskill of the Northern League in the late nineties] before and I love the game, so I went back in '07 to manage in South Georgia."

"When you hear about how Hall of Fame managers like Bobby Cox had his own domestic issue and Tony La Russa had a DUI, it's mystifying that you've had all this success in the minor leagues but haven't had that second chance at a big-league job," I said. "Do you feel you'll ever get that chance?"

"You know, I sure hope I get that chance," Wally said. "The knowledge that I think I have, the way I know how to run a game, I think it's second to nobody. And I really do believe that. My players are prepared, know what their roles are. I know how to get the most out of my players and know how to use the bullpen. And I would hope somebody would . . ."

Backman stops mid-sentence, trying to understand the logic of it all.

"They're not even taking a chance," Backman continued, somewhat dumbfounded. "As you said, Erik, other people have been in trouble. When is enough, enough? You know, this country is supposed to be about having a second chance. And it may happen, it may not happen. I'm the one that's going to have to live with it. But there are going to be people that are going to lose out."

"What a lot of people don't realize is that, when the opportunity arises, you do some managing in winter ball," I said. "Like this past winter, you spent some time managing in the Dominican Republic for the Licey Tigers. What drives you to work yourself this hard in baseball instead of taking some time off for a breather at your home in Pineville, Oregon?"

Wally laughed at my portrayal of him as a year-round manager.

"I love the game," he said. "You know, that's the reality of it. In that case [with Licey], I was home this past winter for a month and did my hunting [Author's note: Backman is an avid elk hunter and fly fisherman], when Manny Acta called me and said they had fired José Offerman and asked me if I wanted to come down to the Dominican and manage and I said sure. So I enjoy it. And I like the National League style they play because it's more of a chess match and I just think you get more into the game. Of course, the best is when it's the seventh inning of a one-run game. That's the type of game I thrive on because I really believe the manager can have an effect on the outcome."

"So how many more years do you see yourself managing?" I asked.

"In the minor leagues?" Wally asked.

"Yes, assuming you don't get a big-league job soon," I said.

"Not many more," Backman was quick to answer in a prideful manner. "If I don't get my opportunity, then it's shame on somebody else this time."

Backman is, of course, best known in baseball circles as one of the catalysts atop the Mets' order during their glory days in the eighties. I felt that no discussion with Wally would be complete without touching on that part of his life.

"It will soon be thirty years since the Mets won their last world championship, a championship that you were a big part of," I said. "In fact, '86 was decisively your best season personally over your fourteen-year major-league career. When you look back at that season, what are some of the things, above all others, that you cherish the most?"

"Well, personally and not just for me, but for Lenny and Mookie, as well, being one of the table-setters, so to speak," Wally said. "And we really did work good in pairs. And I think that's what hitting is all about. The first- and second-place hitters are really trying to set your three-four-five guys up. I took a lot of pride in getting on base however I had to. And while it was probably my best year average-wise, you know what? I took the most pride in winning. And the one thing that I've tried to instill in players today is that you've got to take it personal. You take the wins personal and you take the losses personal. And in our sport, there's only one winner in the end, and that's what you strive to become."

"I'm sure that's a philosophy that you shared with your son, Wally Jr.," I said. "I know he played for a while in the Texas Rangers' farm system. How did you help develop him into the ballplayer he was?"

"He was a good shortstop," Backman replied, "but I have to honestly say I probably didn't help him enough because I wasn't around because of my managing. I always felt that what happened to me in Arizona affected his opportunity [with the Rangers]. I mean, you can look up his numbers and they're not real good in the minor leagues. But he continued to play Independent Ball all the way into this season. He had a big dream—he's a good athlete, a big strong kid, not small like me. But he was in a tough spot because he never really got the chance to play like he should have."

"But how would what happened to you in Arizona affect him?" I asked.

"I think the questions [about Wally] that he had to answer, having been signed out of high school that year in 2004, affected him mentally at a young age," Wally said. "It was a tough burden for him to probably accept, and I really feel that Texas didn't give him the opportunity that he deserved. I really believe that.

"I took him in on the Independent team I was managing in 2008 [at Joliet], and despite being my youngest player," Backman continued, "he made the all-star team. I mean, he was playing in a league that had a lot of guys that were Double-A and Triple-A type of players. I even had some guys that played in the major leagues, so for him to accomplish what he did, it showed me that he was good enough to play."

"You have three other children from your first marriage," I said. "How are they doing?"

"They're great," Wally said. "My older daughter, Jennifer, is married with two children. The next one, Natasha, is actually here in Vegas, and she's going to be proposed to tonight on the video scoreboard and knows nothing about it."

Wally and I have a good laugh about that.

"And then there's Tiffany, who will be finishing college in November, at the same time as Natasha."

"So are you happy with Natasha's fiancé?" I asked with a smile.

"Oh yeah, he's a good guy, he's a good guy," Wally said happily.

With the interview about over, we walked out into the parking lot, to Wally's truck, so he could retrieve a pack of cigarettes. While there, he pulled out a letter from the mayor of Las Vegas and let me read it. The letter congratulated him on being named the Pacific

Coast League Manager of the Year, as well as thanking him for the excitement and civic pride that "Wally Ball" had brought to the city of Las Vegas.

"You should be really proud of this," I said.

"Thanks," Wally said. "Isn't that a nice letter?"

By the time we arrived back to the dugout, though it was still more than two hours before game time, most of his players were beginning to loosen up.

Wally went out to the mound dirt and, a few moments later, began throwing batting practice.

Still getting loose himself, he threw one low, near a hitter's ankles and, in a brief show of frustration, let out a "God dammit" under his breath.

But then the next pitch was right down the middle, and the hitter crushed a line drive hard off the protective screen in front of Wally, startling him for a brief moment before he and "his guys" broke into laughter.

For all Wally has had to endure, for all the dreams that to this point have been unrealized, I couldn't help but smile as I watched the pure joy Backman had at that very moment with his players. The way he says he cares for each and every one of them, it shows.

Wally, sweating profusely after throwing BP for twenty minutes or so in the desert heat, came back into the dugout and grabbed a water bottle.

I thanked him for his time, but told him I had one more thing I had to ask.

"Sure, go ahead," he said.

"If you do become Mets manager before my manuscript is due, would you grant me a few minutes to talk about it at Citi Field?"

Wally broke out his biggest grin of the day and said emphatically, *"Absolutely!"*

| | | | | | |

I would speak with Wally again prior to Game Four of the 2015 World Series. A lot had transpired since our meeting in Las Vegas. The Mets had stunningly won the National League pennant and were about to host the Kansas City Royals at Citi Field. With his mark all over this Mets team with no fewer than twelve of the twenty-five-man roster having played for Wally in the minor leagues, he sounded like a proud father who was very bullish on the team's future.

"It's exciting. It's such a big time, you know," Wally said. "I've had them, I've seen them, and it's just a matter of them being themselves. All of these guys, as long as they stay healthy, can have real, real big careers."

As for Backman himself, he remains hopeful the stellar job he's done in developing so many of the young Mets' stars will act as a stepping stone to his long-awaited dream of managing a major league team.

FOREVER KID

That "Kid" was always in him, and so much of it was the love of the game, the love of life, the love of his family, and the love of the Lord—it was just in him. Obviously, he wasn't joyous every minute—he was human. But he absolutely kept that spark, that spirit. "Kid" was the most perfect nickname he could have had because that really was Gary.

—SANDY CARTER
GARY'S WIDOW
(GARY CARTER, METS CATCHER 1985–89)

It was still only April, but the mercury had already registered ninety-three degrees on this sunny, cloudless, and quite lazy Sunday morning in Jupiter, Florida.

Jupiter, located in Palm Beach County, is one of the northern-most towns of the Miami metropolitan area. *Coastal Living* magazine recently ranked Jupiter the ninth "happiest" seaside town in America, which made it a most appropriate place to meet with Sandy Carter and her daughters Christy and Kimmy, who, like the late family patriarch, are three of the most happy, upbeat, and exuberant people you could ever meet.

Christy had been kind enough to email me back several times in the weeks leading up to this day, and was at last able to carve out some time when I could meet with her mother to discuss the legacy and impact that her husband's life had for so many.

We had settled on Autism Awareness Day at Roger Dean Stadium for our meeting, and would get together many hours before a scheduled game between the hometown Hammerheads and the Bradenton Marauders. The Gary Carter Foundation, which Christy is deeply involved with, would auction off baseball memorabilia, T-shirts, hats, and books inside the stadium to help raise money in the fight against autism. Gary and Sandy's oldest grandson, Carter James, was diagnosed with the developmental disorder as a young boy and was the inspiration behind the family's support of the cause.

I positioned myself outside the ballpark, by the press gate, and sat on a park bench under the shade of a palm tree while I waited for them to arrive. It was a serene spot, with a light breeze blowing and the chirping sounds of birds filling the air.

Christy and Sandy soon got there, along with some friends to help them unload boxes and set up tables for the event.

Christy greeted me warmly and introduced me to her mother.

"It's a pleasure to meet you, Erik," said Sandy, a California-raised blonde now in her early sixties, who is still in fabulous shape, looking like she just walked off a tennis court. "Thank you for coming down."

With the stadium still not open to the public, Sandy and I found another park bench to sit down on outside the stadium. It wasn't long before I realized that talking with Sandy was going to be an experience similar to speaking with Gary—lots of smiling, laughter, and not a foul word over what would turn out to be a nearly three-hour conversation that seemed more like twenty minutes.

"So, you've had a busy weekend so far," I started out. "Yesterday, you were at Palm Beach Atlantic University when they inducted Gary into their Sports Hall of Fame and retired his number 8 jersey."

"You know, it was so special because Gary always loved Palm Beach Atlantic," Sandy said with deep gratitude resonating from her voice. "Even before he coached and managed with them, he would do golf tournaments and fund-raisers there. It's a wonderful Christian school, so we were always really involved with it. But when he became the manager—and he did that for two years—it just filled his heart. I mean, it really was special because he was with our daughter [Kimmy], who was the head coach of their softball team, and that meant a lot to him. They retired his number, which I guess they had never done before there, and framed it beautifully for me. And they had a beautiful plaque of Gary, too."

"I can tell by listening to you that the honor Gary received meant a lot to you personally," I said. "It seems like you and Gary lived a fairy tale, especially when so many major-league marriages fail."

"February eighth would have been our fortieth anniversary," Sandy said slowly and with a hint of sadness.

"We were high school sweethearts. He was sixteen and a junior. I was a senior. I was the *older* woman," she added with a snicker.

"Gary's first full year in the majors was the year you married him," I said. "It was way back then that some of the Montreal Expos players gave him the nickname 'Kid.' But back then, it wasn't given exactly for his youthful exuberance, was it?"

"No," Sandy was quick to say. "It was more like, *Kid, go get me an ice cream!* or *Kid, go get me this!* Steve Renko and Steve Rogers and those other oldtime guys would bark out orders, but Gary would think, *No problem. I'm at the major-league camp and I'm going to run around and do whatever you want me to do.*

"So that's how it started and then 'Kid' just stuck," Sandy continued. "And then I think it became more about his personality because it just filled that nickname perfectly."

"You know, Sandy, it's funny," I began. "Because of the World Series Gary won with the Mets, fans could be forgiven if they forget that he actually spent *most* of his career in Montreal. And he had a real love affair with fans up there and helped put baseball on the map in Canada. But, please be honest with me, did he really learn French as has been so widely reported?"

Sandy laughed.

"He did *really* good," she said with a big smile. "He took a Berlitz class. We had a wonderful agent who was like a best friend—Jerry Petrie—who told Gary, 'You learn French and we'll get you involved in commercials here.'

"So Gary would do an English version and then a French one. And I guess Gary had perfect pronunciation, because people thought he could speak fluently—but he couldn't. At a banquet, he knew six lines perfectly, so he would rattle them off and roll his tongue in French and they'd go, '*Oh! Wow!*' But then someone would come up and start talking to him in French and, you know, he could do a little bit, but I was really proud of him. It was great."

Sandy continued about how much they enjoyed their Montreal experience.

"We really *loved* Montreal. Granted, it was the only place he had played major-league baseball those first ten years, so there was nothing else to compare it to, but we were so grateful and thrilled to be there. Other players might go there and think, *Ahh, the double taxes, the funny money, and the customs.* But we were like, *What's the big deal? We're in the major leagues!* It was heaven."

"I assume you saw the tribute the Montreal Canadiens paid to Gary," I said, alluding to a video montage of Gary's days with the Expos played to the Eagles' hit "New Kid in Town."

"I know," Sandy replied slowly, sounding and looking so touched by it.

"Yes, it was wonderful," she continued. "I got a message saying,

'You *have* to watch this video.' It actually got to my son first, and he came to me filled with tears and goes, 'Mom . . . ,' and he could barely get out the words. And, of course, we all watched it and cried. It was so beautiful the way they all had '8s' on and shot the photos of Gary across the ice. And then the Montreal team mascot Youppi—we loved Youppi—had the old Expos hat on and, oh, I get chills thinking about it. It was *so* special."

[Author's note: The video tribute can be seen on the Montreal Canadiens' website. If you haven't seen it, prepare yourself—it's a tearjerker.]

"Gary returned to the Expos to play the final season of his career," I said. "And in his last at bat, in a storybook kind of ending, rips a double over the head of—"

Sandy jumps in.

"*Andre Dawson!*" she exclaimed. "I thought that was *so* appropriate. Dawson was in right field. I later asked him if he let it drop in, but he said, 'No, I didn't. If Gary would have had good knees, he would have hit it out. And if I would have had good knees, I might have caught it.' They were both the same age and, of course, played for years together in Montreal. I said to him, 'Well, I'm glad you didn't catch it. Thank you, Andre!'

"But, yes, it was a storybook ending," she continued. "It was amazing because Gary was oh-for-three and he came up to bat the last time. Everybody was standing, knowing it was his last at bat in Montreal at Olympic Stadium. With tears in his eyes, he turned around and blew me a kiss, and then went to bat and popped that double—*a game-winner*—so it was really exciting."

"He did the same thing in his last at bat at Shea Stadium as a Met," I said. "He missed a home run by two feet and settled for a double. Do you recall that special moment as well?"

Sandy gave me a quizzical look, trying to recollect the moment.

"Oh my gosh!" Sandy exclaimed. "How did I forget that one? Really? I remember his first game as a Met—the game-winning home run—*that* was amazing. But the last at bat as a Met? I'm glad to hear that. I was there, but I just don't remember everything I guess."

"He was standing on second after his double," I started out, "and, very rare for Gary, he was grimacing and seemed truly upset that it didn't go out. It looked like he was thinking, *Geez, I just missed it.* Now, *that* would have really been amazing."

Sandy began laughing so hard at the visual of Gary being peeved at not hitting the home run that she began coughing.

"Oh, I can see him saying, *I wanted to start it and end it with the Mets with a home run,*" she said. "He was very hard on himself."

Sandy took a moment to reflect.

"Gary's expectations were always up here," she said, putting her hands well above her head. "But that was one of the reasons he was such a great ballplayer, too. He expected a lot of himself. He wanted to do things bigger and better. I used to have to talk him off a bridge and say something like, *It's okay. Maybe you went oh-for-four, but you threw two guys out.* I was his head cheerleader."

"Well, in the big spots, he had a flair for the dramatic," I said.

"Oh yes!" Sandy agreed. "The all-star games and the two MVPs. And then the World Series in Boston—he hit those two home runs over the Green Monster. He *definitely* had a flair for the dramatic."

| | | | | | | |

"Sandy, it's well known that Gary was a family man and didn't go out carousing with the other guys," I said. "He much preferred being with you and the kids, instead. Did he come home on off-days and then have you and the kids travel with him on the road a lot?"

Sandy was quick to answer.

"No. Back then, we were not allowed to go on team planes. It was like the big no-no."

And then Sandy brought up the one, infamous exception.

"Well, there was the one time, when we made the playoffs in '86," she began. "We couldn't go to Houston with the team, so we had to find our own way of getting there. But we could come back from Houston with them. So I was on that *crazy* flight."

"All right, Sandy," I said with a grin. "Now as a good Christian woman, tell me your thoughts about that trip."

"Well, the funny thing about that thing was I never saw seats getting broken and liquor being thrown around," Sandy began. "Of course, we were all completely ecstatic that we were going to the World Series after sixteen innings and the exhaustion and the whole thing. But I was with Gary, the [Howard] Johnsons, the Wilsons, and the Teufels—we were in the center of the plane. The bigwigs, the coaches, and the manager were all in the very front. It was in the back where it got crazy. I was quite surprised, going, '*Oh my gosh!*' I was just so happy we were in our own little groups. I might have seen something when I went back to the bathroom—that's where all the wildness was happening. I won't put names on anybody, but it was definitely crazy. But we weren't the wild ones—nobody could blame *us*!"

"Well, I'm glad you survived," I said to laughs. "What about at Shea? Where would you sit during games?"

"Right behind home plate," Sandy said. "They always put us behind the screen. The seats were phenomenal—five to ten rows off the field. And I always had my kids with me. And Gary was never content until he would see us back there. Then he would take his glove and give us a couple of signs that meant, *Hey guys!* And the kids would shout, *'Hey Dad!'*"

"Did your son DJ play ball like so many of the other Mets players' sons?" I asked.

"He played ball in high school, but baseball wasn't his passion, his forte," Sandy said. "And really it was quite unfortunate—well, it wasn't unfortunate to be the son of Gary Carter—but when you're the *only* son of Gary Carter, and you are following a sister, Kimmy, who was like a 'miniature Gary,' who was nicknamed 'Garietta,' a Florida State catcher and phenomenal athlete, it's tough. And his oldest sister, Christy, was an athlete, too—receiving a tennis scholarship.

"Kids can be mean," Sandy continued. "So baseball wasn't his passion. But what was beautiful was that DJ became president of his school his junior and senior years, got leads in musicals, sang, and acted. That was his forte and he shined at it. I'll never forget Gary going to his three main musicals at the King's Academy, where if you get a lead in one of the musicals it's as big as being the star of the football team—it's on the same level. It's a Christian school and they did six performances for each play.

"I would ask Gary, 'Honey, what night do you want to go to see him'—like when he did *Titanic* and *Carousel*—and he would always say, 'I'm going to *all* of them.' And he did—he went to every one of them. He would have tears, you know, because he was just so proud of him and knew that this was DJ's passion—just like Gary had the passion for sports."

"It sounds like they shared a love for the stage—just different ones," I said.

"Yeah, just not the same path," Sandy concurred. "At first, you thought, *Oh, my son's going to play baseball.* And he played—he was a good player—but wasn't phenomenal. He usually played first base because he's real tall, like six-three, and much leaner than Gary was."

"So moving on to the '86 Mets," I said, "there is some irony there with Gary. While most of his teammates kind of walked on the wild side . . ."

"*Kind of?*" Sandy asked incredulously, letting out a burst of laughter, as if I had just made the ultimate of understatements.

"Well, yes," I said sheepishly. "Gary, however, lived this clean life, and yet he's the only one—"

Before I could finish my sentence, Sandy jumped in, knowing full well where I was going with the fact that Carter is the only '86 Met who has passed away.

"I know," Sandy said. "Out of everybody on that list, he would have been the *last* person we would say would go first. Somebody else would be a drug overdose. Another would be in like a car accident because they were drunk—whatever. I don't know. God just chose to take him and, you know, we miss him terribly. I'd want him back in a second. It's just awful—I'll never replace my husband.

"There were very few on that team—Mookie was one, Teufel another—that lived clean lives," Sandy continued, "but they'd all go out to dinner together. But then afterwards, the rest would go to strip bars or whatever."

At this point, Sandy paused, likely wondering if she wanted to go down a certain road with me, but then she did.

"Gary wasn't a favorite on the team," Sandy confided. "As a teammate, they kind of alienated him. He'd say to me, 'Well, I went to a movie.' And I'd say, 'Oh, who did you go with?' And he'd say, 'My three friends.' And I'd go, 'Who?' And he'd say, 'Me, myself, and I.'

"But seriously," Sandy continued, "he did a lot of that, and not that he was *boo-hooing*. I mean, he could have taken somebody, but generally that's not what happened."

"I'm a little surprised he didn't ask Teufel or Mookie to tag along," I said.

"Well, Mookie was really close with some of the other guys," Sandy said. "They had a fine relationship, though. And Teufel and HoJo, I don't know if you want to call it cliques, but, you know, there were cliques, like based on where you were from, what color you were . . . There were cliques and that's okay. And the pitchers had their own, too. But when you're a catcher, there's not a lot in a group. So what he would do sometimes is take the rookies or the trainers with him. It wasn't like he didn't have *any* friends, but generally speaking, he did a lot of things alone."

"But I know they truly valued Gary as a player that could help them become a championship team," I said. "But you know how competitive baseball can be. They saw Gary out there doing commercials all the time and he just always seemed so happy."

Sandy started laughing.

"He probably irritated the heck out of them I'm sure!" she exclaimed.

"Well, he did," I said with a smirk.

"He did, but he didn't mean to," Sandy said, eager to convince me. "That's the thing. People would come up to him and say, *Hey, got a commercial for you. Why don't you do* Newsday? And he'd go, *Okay, that sounds cool.*

"What can you say?" Sandy continued. "He did it not because he was trying to be a showboat at all. He was a team player. But when somebody comes up to you and says that they want to do a commercial or they want to do a book, he'd say yes."

"He was just made-to-order for Madison Avenue," I said. "A star player who was well spoken with the perfect smile."

"*Exactly*," Sandy agreed.

"I've been told that things became easier for Gary after a few seasons with the club," I said. "But how hard was it for him to fit in with the other players when he first joined the team?"

"I don't know if it was hard," Sandy said. "It was a team of superstars. So where Gary was probably the main superstar with the Expos—and I'm not trying to put him up on a level, but he was the cleanup hitter and leader in some key offensive categories—with the Mets, he was *one* of them. They had Strawberry, Gooden, Dykstra, and Hernandez. So I think he realized soon enough that he was definitely more of an outsider there as far as off-the-field. But he was okay with that, too, I think. It wasn't like he was crying a river or anything, but there was a difference there."

"Did the nicknames 'Kid' and 'Camera Carter' bother him?" I asked.

"Yeah, Camera Carter did," Sandy said. "He probably wouldn't even tell me everything because he knew it would hurt my feelings, but there's a lot of teasing that goes on in the locker room. Obviously, I don't need to know what goes on in there, but there was a lot of teasing and he was an easy target to tease because of things like, *Oh, another commercial!* That kind of thing. I don't think anybody was mean or horrible to him."

Upon brief reflection, Sandy did remember one incident that Gary shared with her.

"He kept a perfect locker," she said. "I can't remember if it was the Expos or Mets, but one time they got back at him by just destroying his locker and that just set him over the edge completely.

I know that happened because he said to me [Sandy imitates Gary's 'hurt' voice], 'My locker was *trashed.*' They were just being naughty.

"But I remember Keith Hernandez saying to him, 'I couldn't stand you as an opponent. You were so irritating and smiling all the time. But as soon as you got on the same team, I saw how you played hurt, how you played hard, how you're a team player, how you bust your butt, and how you're here early.'

"So [Keith] realized they didn't have to hang out together, but they respected each other."

"The two were very different people," I said.

"Yeah. They were different people," Sandy said with a knowing grin, apparently another understatement on my part. "That's a good way of saying it.

"Plus, Keith was a newly divorced bachelor and Gary was a family man," Sandy reasoned. "But you know, it meant a lot to Gary to be named captain with Keith [the year after Hernandez was given the title]. I don't know how Keith felt about it, but the two really complemented each other—Keith leading the players on the field and Gary with the pitchers.

"And I was really touched when Keith came to the memorial service and everything," Sandy added. "He actually asked permission to attend through [promotor and Carter friend] Mead Chasky, if I would mind if he came. There had been some dumb comments that came out earlier on and stuff. But I said, 'Of course not. Absolutely.' When something like that happens, I'd forgive anybody. I wasn't mad. Please. I was very touched that he came."

The "dumb comments" that Sandy was referring to came after it appeared that Carter had thrown his hat in the managerial ring when then Mets skipper Willie Randolph's job was on the ropes during the 2008 season. This led to Hernandez admonishing Carter about it during a Mets telecast.

Sandy explained what happened.

"Gary was simply asked by a reporter, 'Would you like to manager the Mets?' And he said, 'Yes, of course I would.'"

I brought up how Keith's reaction may have been over a culmination of this and a few other past comments that Gary had made as a player, like when he reportedly questioned whether he should have been MVP of the '86 World Series instead of Ray Knight and when he reportedly said that Hernandez shouldn't have been named Mets captain because of his involvement with drugs while a St. Louis Cardinal.

Sandy smiled and said, "You know, he probably did say those things. But Gary didn't have a bad bone in his body. He was interviewed every day and sometimes things can come out wrong."

Sandy then talked about a time that she felt perfectly distinguished the difference between Gary and Keith.

"The day after the Mets won the World Series, they had a parade, which, of course, was unbelievable," Sandy said. "It was just snowing ticker tape and confetti and people everywhere. It was so exciting. I remember Keith and Gary that day because they were the two captains holding the World Series trophy up. Keith *definitely* didn't sleep—it looked like he hadn't anyway. He was scruffy. And Gary was all in a suit and clean-shaven. It was just so typical the way the two of them were. It cracked me up! Gary might have gotten two hours' sleep, but he at least looked dressed to the nines."

"Reportedly, Keith and Bobby Ojeda were out all night," I said. "They were running so late that legend has it that some fans had to help lift them over a fence to a secured area at Battery Park where the parade began."

"Oh, no, I didn't know that," Sandy said. "I'm surprised they made it at all. They must have had the 'Hand of God' carry 'em. Him and Bobby O, huh? Okay. They were a twosome for sure. Surprised Dykstra wasn't there with them, too. And Backman. All of them."

| | | | | | | |

"But times have really changed with how the '86 Mets now admire the way Gary lived," I said.

I then took out a list to show Sandy of testimonials about Gary I had received from most of the '86 Mets I'd interviewed.

The following were some of their comments:

WALLY BACKMAN: "What sticks out the most to me about Gary is how he was as close to a perfect human being as you can be. He really was. If you could go back in time after you've been somewhere, you would want to be that type of individual. He was a great, great person."

DARRYL STRAWBERRY: "Gary was a person of joy and did a lot of smiling, which everybody thought was phony. But we realized when he passed that he was the real deal because we wanted what he had but we couldn't get what he had because we wouldn't do what he was doing, which was following God. He was free while most of the rest of us weren't free. There was a freedom and peace over his life because he had been following God his whole career. He never wavered and never gave in to the sinful nature of most of the rest of us, which was to go out and party and go to strip clubs. He would go to dinner with us, but afterwards would leave and go back to his hotel room. All the other extracurricular activities he wouldn't do. I admire him for that."

ED HEARN: "We named our kid's middle name after Gary—Cody Carter Hearn—out of respect for him. In 1994, when Cody was born, and still today, I tell people that Gary Carter was a good man. And if your son grows up to be like Gary Carter, you'll be a very proud parent."

KEVIN MITCHELL. "It was just an honor for me to play with Gary Carter. He was excited to come to the ballpark, with a smile on his face every day. When he and my brother both had brain cancer, I had him talk with my brother and he gave him a little motivation. They died about a month apart."

DANNY HEEP: "When Gary Carter came over, he had a lot of stuff talked about him. Everybody in Montreal, it seemed, didn't like him. He had an ego—this and that—they said. He came over to us and we were like going, *I don't know. What's wrong with him? He plays hard. He plays every game. He roots for his guys. He's got a great family. How bad can it be?* He was kind of like the Tom Brady of the Mets back then."

DOUG SISK: "I can recall back in the day when Gary was doing some commercials for Ivory Soap, *Newsday*, and others and a lot of players made fun of him. Five years ago, when we were all together, Gary said, 'Those guys can all laugh about those commercials, but those commercials put money in my kids' pockets so all their college tuitions were paid.' He did it for a reason. He liked the camera, don't get me wrong, but I think that he was a planner.

"And he never complained. I never saw him cuss. I never saw him say anything that was inappropriate. The only time I ever saw him do something was when he threw the spread in Pittsburgh. We had just played like thirteen innings with rain delays and the post-game spread was some generic Salisbury steak that was heated up in an older heater. The Kid still had his chest protector on and walked over there and said, 'We're not eating this slop!' He picked it up and threw it and said, 'I'm paying for dinner tonight!' A couple of vans came and picked up all the players and we ate at a restaurant for dinner that night. Kid picked up the check."

HOWARD JOHNSON: "It was a privilege to play with Gary because this guy was a bona fide superstar. As a player, there weren't many catchers better than him. What made him great were his leadership qualities, and they showed up every day. He had knees so bad he could hardly walk. He'd tape them up, get treatment every day—pregame and postgame.

"I go back to the last inning of Game Six of the World Series when we were losing. I know some of the guys were up in Davey's office, but I was in the dugout, and Carter was going up and down the bench saying, 'I'm not going to be the last out of this World Series.' He kept saying it to everybody. As things progressed, and he came up with two outs and nobody on, he kept batting, battling, and battling before he got his base hit to start the rally. And so the feeling was that we were not going to go down. It wasn't going to end. And so when Kid got that hit, it was like, *Okay, we can do this*."

LENNY DYKSTRA: "I respected Carter like no other. I lockered next to him and I watched this guy strap it on every night, man—no drugs, a gamer. A guy you want your kid to grow up to be like. This is a man, you know? It was just a privilege, an honor, to play with the guy."

DWIGHT GOODEN: "The thing I admired about Gary was that he never judged me about what was going on off the field. After dinner on the road, most of us would go out and hit the town. Gary and Mookie and a few of the other guys would go back to the hotel. But Gary always said if I needed him to call him in his room at *any time*.

"And he knew how to deal with different personalities as far as the pitching staff went. Some guys needed just a talk, some guys needed Gary getting in their face. He knew how to do both. We spent a lot of time away from the ballpark together, going out to eat, just hanging out. He would have team parties at his house and have all the guys over. Just a tremendous leader and a tremendous guy."

Sandy thanked me for putting the list together.

"It's so touching," she warmly added, while keeping her emotions in check.

"Well, the thing that struck me the most in talking to people about Gary was how, even when he was so sick, he still made the time and effort to speak with others in need," I said. "And I probably only know about a fraction of the calls he made. Was Gary on the phone a lot, still trying to help others at the very end of his own life?"

"Well, it was mostly when they would call him," Sandy said. "Or if he was told or made aware of someone, like when Mead called to tell him that Doc was struggling, then he would call right away. But there seriously was so much going on and he was either so sick or weak. We had appointments all the time, so it was hard for him to be thinking who he should reach out to when he was trying to survive and just get through the night. But as soon as he would be made aware of something like that, he would definitely call. He was a great encourager."

"Sandy, you read the list of glowing testimonials from Gary's old Mets teammates—some of the same ones that you said, at times, would make him feel alienated during his playing days," I said. "So it seems that, in hindsight, he's much more revered now than he ever was as a star player by his contemporaries who are now middle-aged or older. It's like he became a sort of role model to some of them."

"I would *definitely* agree, at least with his teammates," Sandy said. "I know the neighbors and the family loved him just as much before, during, and after his career, right from the time when we started dating and I was a waitress and he worked at a gas station—there's no question about that. I think a part of what impresses the players now is how his faith stayed so strong through his ordeal and how Gary never asked, *Why me?*

"Instead, he'd say, 'Hey, I'm fighting this, I know God's got a plan, we're doing everything we can, we know we're at the right place [Duke Medical Center], so whatever God chooses to do, I'm not going to give up.'

"So I think the players saw an inner strength in him," Sandy continued, "that they might have known he had, but everyone was too much into their own world and their own career—and that's normal. And I think they thought, like you've said, *How could this happen to Gary?* It wasn't like he was on drugs or ran into a brick wall or something. But God just chose to take him and he's in a much better place for sure, even though in my boat, it would be for him to come back down here—that's where I want him. But anyway, I definitely think he's more respected, loved, and revered now than he was before."

| | | | | | | |

"Some of Gary's teammates believe that Gary would have been perfectly suited to become a baseball commentator, because of his love of the spotlight," I said. "But others I've spoken to believe he would have made a really good big-league manager. What do you think his true calling would have been had he lived?"

Sandy didn't hesitate.

"His passion, which I'm sure everybody knows by now, after baseball, was to be a major-league manager," she said. "And I remember when he sent out letters to all the major-league teams basically saying, *I have this passion and would love to be a part of your organization*. He didn't need to introduce himself—they knew very well who he was, of course. But I think he got like six letters back. And he was always like, *Why won't they even give me an interview?* He wanted it so bad. I know he would have been phenomenal at it just because of what a good catcher and hitter he was and how well he worked with pitchers. And, you know, I think catchers make the best managers."

"They generally do, yes," I said.

"But, I think it would have been very hard on him if he had been given the job as a major-league manager with the Mets because he probably would have read every article of every paper!" Sandy said, laughing. "Gary wanted to please and didn't want anybody to ever be upset with him. He would have wanted to do so good, to be the best, and never make a mistake; it might have been really hard on him.

"But he was a phenomenal manager," Sandy continued. "When he managed at Port St. Lucie, they won the championship, and when he managed an Independent League team in California, they won the title, too. But I remember Kimmy saying, 'Mom, I don't think God kept him from becoming a major-league manager, I think He *spared* him!'

"But as it turned out, managing at Palm Beach Atlantic was the most perfect fit for him. He was fifteen minutes from home and was kind of coaching alongside Kimmy at a Christian university. It was just a wonderful experience. I mean, they had some crazy long bus trips and it was college, but it was a blessing. So I think he would have kept doing that."

"At what point did Gary sense that something was not right with him and needed to get checked out?" I asked.

"Well, he came home one night after he had just finished managing the regionals at PBA," she said, "and he goes to me, 'I kept losing track of the score and the pitch count. What is wrong with me?' The thing you have to understand, Erik, is that Gary was so OCD that he never lost track of the score, pitch count, or anything. He was very neat and tidy with everything, so when he started forgetting this and forgetting that, we knew something was wrong. But still, his were such subtle symptoms that we couldn't believe when they found the tumors. And the fact that they were inoperable, we wondered how he was able to do anything at all. At the time, he was driving and golfing and doing all kinds of stuff."

"That's amazing," I said. "How about his disposition? Did it change after he got sick?"

Sandy exhaled and, after a pregnant pause, said, "Well, I'm not going to pretend it wasn't hard. I mean, it was *very* hard. He had *so many* side effects. He had horrible sores in his mouth, had to give himself shots in the stomach every day because of the blood clots, and the steroids he took blew him up. It was awful. But he had a will to live, he fought it hard, and we believed with all our hearts that Duke was the right place to be. We believed we were with the best doctors in the best place. And we went up there at least once a month and then the hospital here, Good Samaritan, which was like the little sister hospital where he was treated with chemo. But it was a very tough nine months. And they never gave us a choice. It was like if you do nothing, he might have two months. If you do all these things, we really believed like he would have two more years. So it was kind of shocking to go just nine months, but I heard that Tug McGraw was just nine months, as well. That was quick, too, huh?"

"Yes, it was," I said. "I know everybody was so surprised up in New York with how quickly Gary passed away."

What happened to Gary was not unlike the fate encountered by his mother, who died quickly from another deadly disease, leukemia, when Carter was just twelve years old.

"Gary would talk about how he always wanted to succeed in life for his mother and how that drove him," I said. "Did you two talk about that often?"

"Well, I certainly was aware," Sandy began. "Unfortunately, I never got to meet her. When I met Gary, it was still raw for him. He would talk about her as being so supportive and loving—like a 'team mom.' The hardest part of it was that he never knew she was dying. He thought she was just sick. Back then, they didn't tell. His dad *never* said, *Son, this is what's happening. Mom is dying.*

"And the way he actually found out she died was when he was on his bike on his way to a Little League baseball practice and somebody goes, 'Hey, you've got to go home, Gary. Your mom died.'

"*That's* how he found out," Sandy said incredulously.

"He rode his bike back, crying the whole way, and nobody was there," she continued. "His dad and brother were at the hospital, as were his grandparents. It was a neighbor lady and a pastor who hugged him when he got home, but he never got to say goodbye to his mother. He had a hard time with his dad, asking him why he didn't tell him. They were close, but once in a while he would tell Gary, 'I was protecting you.' And I don't even think his dad thought she would die because she was only thirty-seven years old, but six months later she was gone. There was nothing they could do back then for leukemia."

Now understandably somber, Sandy talked about Gary's father.

"His dad passed away *right* before the Hall of Fame induction ceremony," she said. "Gary would have loved for him to have been there. But at least his dad knew that Gary got elected into the Hall of Fame. He knew when that call came in January, so that meant a lot to him, of course."

Gary's medical updates and a diary of what he and his family were going through were logged by his daughter Kimmy on the website CaringBridge.org, right up until Carter's death on February 16, 2012. The memorial service was held eight days later at Christ Fellowship Church in Palm Beach Gardens.

"The service for Gary was covered by media outlets throughout North America," I said. "What do you remember the most about it?"

"Gary would have been so touched by how many came to the service," Sandy said with a smile. "Johnny Bench spoke and his speech was just beautiful. So was Tommy Hutton's. There were over a hundred ballplayers there. They just dropped everything and came. And so many others, Hall of Famers and other great people, called to say they would have come but couldn't, but it still meant a lot."

"Do you still feel connected to the baseball community?" I asked.

"I do," Sandy said. "I still get invited—which blows me away— and I don't know why it should shock me so much, but I get invited every year to the Hall of Fame. And they really welcome me. They pay for everything and tell me how happy they are to see me. You would think that Gary himself was coming through their doors. I'm always amazed because I think so often after the star is gone, things change. And it's great to go, because I have really dear friends that go there, too, like the wives of Carlton Fisk, Mike Schmidt, and Andre Dawson."

| | | | | | |

Sandy and I walked over toward the entrance of the stadium to check on Christy and how the setup of the auction items was going. But there was one nugget that the Carters owned that was not for sale—the ball from the final out of the 1986 World Series.

"Gary caught the final out in Game Six of the championship series against Houston and the final out of the 1986 World Series because they were both strikeouts," Sandy said, smiling. "He gave the Houston ball to Jesse Orosco, but kept the one from the World Series."

"You're kidding!" I said. "You know that Mookie's ball that won Game Six of the World Series sold at auction for over $418,000, don't you?"

"*What?!*" Sandy shouted incredulously. "No, I didn't know that."

"Well, your ball might be worth about that much because it's a perfect storm scenario—it's a one of a kind from the last World Series the Mets won. And it's from a New York team. So maybe some Wall Street hedge fund Mets fan would pay any price for it," I said, laughing.

"Well, I'm glad I put it away in a safe somewhere," Sandy said.

Sandy and Christy left the ballpark for a couple of hours and returned dressed more formally for the autism event. Kimmy, a dead ringer for her father in looks, mannerisms, and enthusiastic nature, appeared as well, and she graciously talked with me for a few minutes about her own memories of her father up in a much-welcomed, air-conditioned luxury box overlooking the playing field.

Following our discussion, I left the luxury box in somewhat of a rush to make an early evening flight back to New York, but made a point to give thanks and say my goodbyes first to Christy and then to Sandy, who was graciously greeting fans coming through the gate.

"Erik, there was one thing I wanted to ask your opinion on," she said with much sincerity. "You seem to know everything about the Mets. Do you think they'll ever retire Gary's number 8?"

I paused, wanting badly to tell her what she probably wanted to hear, but then offered my honest take on her query.

"Sandy, it just doesn't seem like something the Mets do anymore," I said. "They've only done it four times and only really once for one of their own players—Tom Seaver."

"But Gary was a part of their *last* championship," Sandy said with a smile, perhaps trying to convince me differently. "And that 1986 World Series was the greatest thrill of his life."

I didn't have any words to come back to Sandy with on her points. In fact, her words stuck with me on my flight all the way back home. While other organizations retire numbers seemingly like they're giving out candy, the 1986 Mets, one of the greatest and most beloved teams of all time, should have some of their outstanding players from that club celebrated with this honor.

And bestowing this distinction on a courageous man they called "Kid," their only Hall of Famer from that special team, would be an excellent place to start.

EPILOGUE

It's hard to fathom that any of the players from the 1986 World Series champion Mets team wouldn't have, to some degree, compelling stories to tell. Just to make it to the major leagues, and then to play for one of the most talented and charismatic teams ever, would practically make that a certainty.

Alas, by limiting this book to profiling just the fourteen players from that team whose lives I found to be the most compelling of all, I was forced to leave out the challenges and stories from the other ten Mets and their manager from the 1986 World Series roster.

Thus, in an attempt to do them all some justice, the following is what became of them after their days with the Mets were over:

RICK AGUILERA spent most of his five years with the Mets performing the relatively low-profile duties of either a fifth starter or

long reliever. Contrary to reports, he told me he never requested a
trade from the Mets, was surprised when it happened, and had
become comfortable with his niche roles on the ball club. Nevertheless, in part due to the emergence of pitcher David Cone, Rick was
dealt to the Minnesota Twins in 1989 as part of the deal that
brought the Mets Frank Viola.

The trade worked out extraordinarily well for "Aggie," who
would burst to stardom—making the AL all-star team three years
in a row—as Minnesota's closer and help them win the World Series
in 1991.

Aguilera would also pitch for the Boston Red Sox and the Chicago Cubs, though his best years were with the Twins, where he is a
member of their Hall of Fame. At the time of his retirement following the 2000 season, his 318 career saves ranked eighth all time.

Since retirement, he has devoted time to real estate investments,
while keeping a hand in baseball first as pitching coach and then as
head coach for the Santa Fe Christian High School baseball team.

He currently lives in San Diego with his wife Sherry. The couple have two children, Rachel, who enjoys water polo, and Austin, a
lacrosse player. Rick is contemplating a return to baseball in some
capacity now that his kids are grown.

RON DARLING was nicknamed "Mr. Perfect" by some of his Mets
teammates and with good reason. It's what happens when you're a
two-time all-American at Yale, appear on the cover of *GQ*, date
Madonna, and then go on to become a major-league all-star, Gold
Glove winner, and World Series hero.

Darling would be traded by the Mets to the Montreal Expos in
1991, after nine seasons in New York, leaving the club as their best
pitcher from their eighties glory days not named Dwight Gooden.

He has been a longtime color analyst on SNY and is, along with Gary Cohen and Keith Hernandez, part of a tremendous broadcasting team. He also does nationally televised baseball games, primarily during the postseason.

Darling lives in Brooklyn, New York, with his wife Joanna and has two children, Jordan and Tyler, from his first marriage, to model Antolnette O'Reilly.

KEVIN ELSTER was supposed to be the next Mets superstar and became the everyday shortstop in 1988. But he didn't come close to expectations and left the club via free agency after the '92 season. After limited action with the Yankees and the Phillies, he had a breakout season in 1996 with the Texas Rangers, hitting 24 home-runs with 99 RBIs, before resuming a somewhat pedestrian career.

Now living in Huntington Beach, California, the twice-divorced Elster has a happy, healthy, and tranquil life working out at the gym and spending time on the beach.

SID "EL SID" FERNANDEZ was practically unhittable at Shea Stadium throughout his ten seasons with the Mets and may very well be the most underrated starting pitcher in the history of the team. But it was his middle-relief work in Game Seven of the '86 World Series, which kept the Mets in the ball game before they rallied late to defeat the Red Sox, that will be the highlight of his career.

At the conclusion of his fifteen-year major-league career, the ever-quiet Sid returned to a peaceful existence in Hawaii, working for a time as an executive assistant for the mayor of Honolulu.

Today, he and his wife Noelani run the Sid Fernandez Foundation, which awards college scholarships to seniors from their alma mater, Kaiser High School. They have two children.

Fernandez, who wore number 50 throughout his career in honor of his home state, was named by *CNN Sports Illustrated* as one of the fifty greatest sports figures in Hawaii's history.

DAVEY JOHNSON came on the scene as manager of the Mets in 1984. With a winning pedigree as a member of four Baltimore Orioles pennant-winning clubs (which included two world championships), a knowledge of the young Mets prospects he managed at Tidewater, and an early adoption of sabermetrics, he immediately helped make the team relevant again.

Under Johnson's leadership, the Mets won at least ninety games in each of his first five seasons at the helm, including the world championship in 1986 and the NL Eastern Division title in 1988. However, after a slow start in 1990, he was fired by the club. Davey told me one of his biggest regrets was not having the opportunity to say goodbye to his players. Still, he is the winningest manager in Mets history and a member of their Hall of Fame.

Johnson went on to have further managerial success with other clubs, and is just one of two managers to have reached the postseason with four different teams. He also managed Team USA at the 2008 Summer Olympics.

Davey has experienced health issues—including a ruptured appendix and the need for five stomach surgeries—but is doing much better now. He has also experienced heartache, losing his daughter Andrea, a championship surfer, from septic shock after a bout with schizophrenia, as well as his stepson Jake, a special needs person, from pneumonia.

Now out of baseball, he works as a commercial real estate agent in Florida and enjoys fishing, travel, golf, and time with his grandchildren.

He currently lives with his wife Susan in Winter Park, Florida, and has not ruled out a return to managing.

RAY KNIGHT played in just barely over two seasons with the Mets, but during that time he was an invaluable clubhouse leader and enforcer on the field. He starred in the 1986 World Series and was named MVP, but after the Mets gave him a low-ball offer to return in '87—and with Howard Johnson ready to take over full-time at third base—he became a free agent and signed with the Baltimore Orioles. In practically every interview I did with the players I profiled for this book, they pointed to the hit the club took by not re-signing Knight as one of the reasons the team didn't win another championship.

After his career ended, he went into broadcasting and currently works as a cohost on the Washington Nationals' pregame and post-game shows. He was briefly manager of the Cincinnati Reds in the mid-nineties.

He currently lives in Albany, Georgia, with his three daughters, Ashley, Errin, and Torri, and has a son, Brooks, from his first marriage. He was married to his second wife, retired LPGA golfer Nancy Lopez, for twenty-seven years before they divorced in 2009.

LEE MAZZILLI returned to the Mets late in the 1986 season as a bench player after starting his career as the club's all-star center fielder and heartthrob matinee idol to the team's legion of female fans.

Mazzilli's post-career was just as fulfilling as his playing career. After taking up acting, he starred as Tony in an off-Broadway production of *Tony 'n Tina's Wedding*. After coaching with the Yankees, he was manager of the Baltimore Orioles for a brief period. He has also worked in broadcasting.

Today, "Maz" lives in Greenwich, Connecticut, with his long-time wife, television personality Danielle Folquet. They have three children together—Lacey, Jenna, and Lee Jr. Lee Jr. is currently a prospect in the Mets' minor-league system.

ROGER McDOWELL was the winning pitcher in Game Seven of the 1986 World Series and thrived as the Mets' long reliever for five seasons until he was traded to Philadelphia in 1989 along with Lenny Dykstra for Juan Samuel—one of the worst trades in Mets history. He finished a formidable career in 1996 after pitching with several teams, but his best days were with the Mets.

He made a brief guest appearance on one of the most popular *Seinfeld* episodes ever, "The Boyfriend," playing the role of the "Second Spitter." McDowell claims the nonspeaking part, in which he appeared on screen for less than ten seconds, earns him royalties of $13.52 every time it gets aired on television.

McDowell has been the pitching coach for the last ten years with the Atlanta Braves and currently lives in Marietta, Georgia, with his wife Gloria and their two daughters.

RANDY "NEMO" NIEMANN pitched in limited relief action for the Mets in 1985 and 1986 as a left-hander out of the bullpen. He left the Mets as a free agent and joined the Twins, where he closed out his eight-year career.

Ultimately, the mark he left on the Mets will go down in the annals of team history much more as a coach than a player. After retirement, he worked for twenty-four years in the Mets' organization as a minor-league instructor and major-league bullpen coach.

He currently lives in Port Saint Lucie, Florida, with his wife Mary Ann.

JESSE OROSCO's iconic pose when he dropped to his knees and raised his arms to the heavens after striking out Marty Barrett to end the 1986 World Series is etched into the collective memory of every Mets fan. He also closed out the final game of the 1986 NLCS against Houston.

Orosco enjoyed eight strong seasons with the Mets before being dealt to Los Angeles as part of a three-team deal following the 1987 season. He earned his second World Series ring with the Dodgers in 1988. Jesse would make a successful transition from closer to left-handed specialist and would go on to set a major-league record for career pitching appearances over his twenty-four-year career. He retired at age forty-six and is just one of twenty-nine players in baseball history to have played in four decades.

Orosco is a scratch golfer and currently works as the head pitching instructor for the Frozen Ropes Baseball Training Center in San Diego, where he resides with his wife Leticia. Their son, Jesse Jr., played four years of minor-league baseball.

TIM TEUFEL split time at second base with Wally Backman during much of his six years with the Mets. His most memorable moment as a Met occurred when he hit a game-ending pinch-hit grand slam in the eleventh inning of one of the more thrilling regular season games of 1986. He was traded to the San Diego Padres in 1991 after an early season slump.

Following retirement, Teufel spent many seasons coaching both at the minor- and major-league levels, and is now the third base coach for the Mets. He will most certainly be one of the candidates considered to succeed manager Terry Collins once his tenure with the Mets is over.

Off the field, Teufel was sued for $1.23 million in 2010 for profits he received from Bernard L. Madoff's multibillion-dollar Ponzi scheme.

He currently lives in Tequesta, Florida, with his wife Valerie. Their son, Shawn, is a pitching prospect in the Mets' organization.

ACKNOWLEDGMENTS

I would like to give special thanks to the following for their contributions to this book: Marc Falcone, Jim Gemma, Jay Goldberg, Ed Hearn, Kevin Kernan, Rachel Levitsky, Roy Markell, Tim Neverett, Jeff Pearlman, Michael Potenza, Heather Quinlan, Matthew Silverman, Doug Sisk, Mark Snyder, and Rosa Wilson.

Denise Silvestro is a wonderful editor who gave sound advice and guidance on how to approach this project. Her enthusiasm and professionalism is greatly valued and appreciated. Allison Janice's direction and feedback as assistant editor was always provided with a bright and positive demeanor.

Rob Wilson is a tireless literary agent who is always available to lend a supportive and critical ear to my ideas. He is a joy to work with and a treasured friend.

Mookie Wilson was instrumental in helping me set up meetings with his '86 Mets teammates and convincing them that I could be trusted to chronicle their fascinating lives. He has become like a brother to me and I cherish our friendship.

I would also like to give recognition to various publications that aided me in my research and helped me develop questions to the players profiled. They include *Doc: A Memoir* by Dwight Gooden, *The Bad Guys Won!* by Jeff Pearlman, *Winning in Both Leagues* by Frank Cashen, *Conquering Life's Curves* by Ed Hearn, *Nailed! The Improbable Rise and Spectacular Fall of Lenny Dykstra* by Christopher Frankie, *The Imperfect Marriage: Help for Those Who Think It's Over* by Darryl and Tracy Strawberry, *If At First: A Season with the Mets* by Keith Hernandez, the *New York Times*, the *Washington Post*, the *Los Angeles Times*, the *New Yorker*, the *Kansas City Star*, the *New York Post*, the *New York Daily News*, the *Baltimore Sun*, the *Palm Beach Post*, *USA Today*, and the websites Wikipedia, Fox News Latino, Philly.com, MySanAntonio.com, AmazinAvenue.com, UltimateMets.com, and BaseballReference.com.